Monographs in Social Theory

Editor: Arthur Brittan, *University of York*

Barry Barnes Scientific Knowledge and Sociological Theory
Zygmunt Bauman Culture as Praxis
Keith Dixon Sociological Theory
Keith Dixon The Sociology of Belief
Antony D. Smith The Concept of Social Change

A catalogue of the books in the other series of Social Science books published by Routledge and Kegan Paul will be found at the end of this volume

Tom W. Goff

Marx and Mead

Contributions to a sociology of knowledge

Routledge & Kegan Paul
London, Boston and Henley

First published in 1980
by Routledge & Kegan Paul Ltd
39 Store Street, London WC1E 7DD,
9 Park Street, Boston, Mass. 02108, USA and
Broadway House, Newtown Road,
Henley-on-Thames, Oxon RG9 1EN
Set in Linotron 202 Garamond 10 on 12pt by
Input Typesetting Ltd, London
and printed in Great Britain by
Redwood Burn Ltd
Trowbridge & Esher

ISBN 0 7100 0464 8

Contents

Preface vii

1 The critique of the sociology of knowledge 1

Elements of the critique
Critique and contradiction

2 Marx: elements of a sociology of knowledge 22

Reality and praxis: the presuppositions of a Marxian sociology of knowledge
Praxis and consciousness: the Marxian epistemology
Alienation and the social analysis of ideas
Summary and implications for a sociology of knowledge
Limitations within the Marxian framework

3 G. H. Mead: the perspective of social behaviourism and the sociology of knowledge 55

Mind, self and social process: the social theory of man
Qualitative or quantitative difference: the criticisms of social behaviourism
Basic presuppositions: an alternate image of social man
Implications for interpretation of the social theory of man
The social theory of mind and the sociology of knowledge

4 Marx and Mead: towards a critical sociology of knowledge 86

Interactionism and critical analysis: aspects of compatibility

Mead's social theory of man and the problem of alienation

Praxis and alienation: a Meadian contribution to the critical perspective

5 Conclusion: the critical perspective 110

Notes 118

Select bibliography 152

Index 165

Preface

The insight that has inspired the development of sociologies of knowledge, namely, the idea that thought and social context are integrally related, has become quite commonplace. It is present, if only implicitly in most of sociology, in the disciplines of psychology and linguistics and informs contemporary perspectives in the philosophy and history of science. Perhaps the clearest indication of the acceptance of this insight on at least a common-sense level is to be found in our editorial pages which increasingly speak of social and political conflicts less as matters of ignorance and power and more as matters involving cultural and sub-cultural difference.

But though the suspicion that ideas are fundamentally social in nature is becoming a virtual assumption in our approaches to a wide range of issues and topics, the effort to elaborate and clarify this assumption and to ground it in a cogent and acceptable theoretical framework has not yet been successful. Efforts to elaborate the insight and to achieve the necessary grounding are many and diverse. Indeed, few if any of the major figures in the development of sociology from Comte to Parsons or from Marx to Habermas have not attacked this question. The reason for this is obvious: sociology is rooted in the assumption that persons are social beings, and the elaboration of this general assumption forces one to attend to the nature of the relationship between man's thought and the social context of his consciousness. However, in response to these efforts, a highly unified and very definite critique has developed which ultimately denies the theoretical and empirical possibility of a sociology of knowledge in any but the most limited sense.

The reasons for this critique are equally obvious to anyone who has the slightest acquaintance with the debate. The belief that knowledge and social context are integrally related seems to carry an epistemological implication which is simply not acceptable in the mainstream of Western thought: the implication that all thought is relative, and thus that truth is an impossibility. In response to the critique, sociology has on the whole retreated from the radical implications of the insight. The sociology of knowledge remains a weak area within the discipline and generally accepts an extremely limited character.

This study concerns itself with this one-sided debate between critics and proponents of the sociology of knowledge. More specifically, it attempts to rekindle the debate and redress the balance by proposing the outlines of a possible solution to the issue of relativism, a solution which emerges through a synthesis of insights generated by Karl Marx and G. H. Mead. Many have proposed the potential of this synthesis for sociology and for the sociology of knowledge in particular; few have actually explored the possibility and none have done so in the necessary depth.

This work has of course benefited from a number of people, but from these in particular: from Roy Hornosty, a former teacher who has stimulated so many with an awareness of the pressing need to reconsider and reformulate traditional issues in the discipline; from Dick Brymer, another teacher whose interest in Mead was obviously infectious; from Terry Gillin, a friend and colleague whose concerns and arguments stimulated many of the ideas in this work; and lastly, from the students of the Tuesday night seminar at Mount Allison whose enthusiasm, constant questioning and insightful analogies stimulated many clarifications and revisions of the initial formulation of the argument.

I would like to dedicate this book to them and to my family.

chapter 1

The critique of the sociology of knowledge

It has been suggested by many writers, though often for very different reasons, that the problems facing the development of the sociology of knowledge might be resolved through a synthesis of the insights of Karl Marx and the American social pragmatist, George Herbert Mead.[1] This suggestion has never been pursued in anything approaching the necessary detail, yet its promise becomes increasingly important and for a number of reasons.

Of all the areas within sociology, the sociology of knowledge is of essential importance and yet seems to present the greatest number of difficulties and to have achieved the least. The elaboration of the guiding assumption underlying the discipline as a whole – that persons are fundamentally social in nature – demands a clear, precise and useable elaboration of the specific and important relationship between our sociality and our consciousness. Despite this fundamental importance, however, it must be admitted that much less agreement has been reached in this particular area than in any other branch of the discipline as a whole. Furthermore, though sociology itself has gradually gained credibility and acceptance despite its failure to achieve a single and generally agreed upon paradigm, the sociology of knowledge has remained highly suspect. Its various efforts continue to be subjected to the strongest and most persistent criticism from both within and without the sociological enterprise.

The basic, most damaging and persistent criticism is that none of the conceptual frameworks so far developed has managed to deal adequately with the apparent relativistic and self-contradictory implications of the insight that human consciousness, knowledge and social factors are somehow integrally related. Most, if not all of the major figures in the area, including Marx and Mead, have contributed to the elaboration of the basic insight and thus to the development of a social theory of knowledge. However, every attempt to take the insight beyond common-sense appreciation and unquestioned assumption is demonstrably deficient with respect to this and to other less basic problems.

Given the perennial impasse between proponents and critics of the sociology of knowledge, it may not be immediately apparent why one should seriously consider the particular suggestion that a Marx/Mead synthesis holds the key to advancement of the discipline. None the less, there are some very basic reasons to suppose that this particular suggestion has merit and is worth pursuing.[2] In the first place, most criticism of the discipline has been indirect if not direct criticism of what have been taken to be Marx's pronouncements on the subject. However, given the numerous and recent re-evaluations and re-interpretations of his work, it is no longer clear that the critique adequately comprehends the elements of a sociology of knowledge to be found in Marx's writing.[3] Specifically, it has become necessary to consider the implications for a social theory of knowledge of the distinction drawn between Marx as an a-critical, economic and historical determinist, and Marx as a critical, humanistic thinker.

Mead's work is also receiving long-overdue reconsideration. Broader analysis of his writing is generating new interpretations of the relevance of his ideas to sociology in general and, in all likelihood, this has implications for the sociology of knowledge in particular. In any case it is clear that the focus of Mead's interest and writing lies in areas that were undeveloped by Marx, and thus it is reasonable to pursue a determination of the degree of useful complementarity of their different insights.

Before proceeding with the analysis of their ideas, however, it is first essential to delineate the current impasse in more detail and to analyse the character, meaning and implications of the critique. Too often this step has been overlooked or ignored and the critique accepted too readily and quite uncritically by many of those who have worked and written within the discipline.[4] However, it is only on the basis of such analysis that certain historically repeated pitfalls can be avoided.

ELEMENTS OF THE CRITIQUE

Merton has argued that the most general statement describing the sociology of knowledge is that it is 'concerned with the relationships between knowledge and other *existential* factors in the society or culture'.[5] While there are severe reservations regarding the adequacy of this formulation,[6] it will suffice for the moment, if only because the majority of writers have perceived their task in these or in very similar terms – that is, as a task concerned with conceptualizing 'knowledge'; with conceptualizing the 'existential' factors of society or culture that affect knowledge; and with the question of the specific relationships between knowledge and these particular existential factors. A final question is that of the approach and method to be utilized in analysis. These questions have been provided with answers, indeed a variety of answers. However, none of the conceptual frameworks so far established has satisfied the critics.

The critics justifiably argue that individual writers and the area in general provide no clarity or agreement on the appropriate conceptualization of the terms of the relationship. Just what mental productions are related to social factors and which, if any, are free of such influence? What is the character of 'knowledge' that it can be so integrally influenced as claimed? Equally, it is seldom clear in the literature just what the social factors are that influence belief, or what the character of such factors is that they can have such influence or (reciprocally) be so influenced.[7]

Second, and of more central concern, critics argue that the relationship itself is poorly defined in the literature. This criticism concerns the problem of imputation– the problem of clarifying the relationship between knowledge and social factors such that particular ideas (or the perspective in which they are based) may be non-tautologically imputed to the appropriate social context. Is the relationship immediate or mediated, a one-way causal connection, a functional or reciprocal relation, or perhaps a dialectical relationship? What criteria allow one to demonstrate 'unequivocally' that the imputed relationship between specific ideas and a specific social context does indeed hold?[8]

In terms of these criticisms, the sociology of knowledge is, of course, not fundamentally impugned. To argue that no framework has been developed that is conceptually adequate, consistent and empirically testable, is insufficient ground to conclude that it could not be so developed. However, the third and central criticism is of this nature and is therefore of more fundamental importance to this study. Even should the problem of conceptual clarity be overcome, there remains the issue of the implications of the idea of social elements in thought: the closer a position or perspective is to adequate formulation and consistency with the insight, the more likely it is to be charged with committing the genetic fallacy and thus with relativism.[9]

This element of the critique argues that if it is held that the intellectual sphere is totally rooted in 'existential' factors and therefore that it can and must be 'extrinsically' interpreted or explained, then all statements of 'fact' must be regarded as but relative statements of opinion or simple rationalizations, statements which reflect the social biography, social location and social interests of an individual or group. If this is true, then clearly even those statements about social conditioning uttered by the sociologist of knowledge must themselves be reflections of a particular social biography. If the status of fact, of objectivity or of truth is claimed for such statements, then they are self-contradictory. Either such statements are true, thereby refuting their own claims about existential conditioning, or they are false and the position is obviously refuted.

Such a position is, in these terms, clearly nihilistic. It commits the apparent 'sin' of connecting validity and origin (the genetic fallacy) and, at worst, it represents thought as pure epiphenomenon or legitimation; the view devalues reason, destroys the concepts of responsibility, freedom, morality, creativity, etc. – all ideas that have historically been associated with our very capacity for reflection.[10]

Taken this far, if the sociology of knowledge is to serve any function at all, it apparently cannot be a scientific one; it becomes pure 'debunking' and an historical moment along the 'road to suspicion'[11] of all thought. Marx, for example, may have 'exposed' the bourgeoisie by demonstrating the apparently ideological, 'interest-supportive' character of their thought; but it would appear that his own mode of argument ultimately loses all credibility when it is turned against him via Mannheim's development of the concept of total ideology.[12]

To express this third and most important element of the critique in slightly different terms, it is basically the argument that a total acceptance of the insight underlying the discipline is, at the same time, a denial of all absolutes; a denial of all criteria in terms of which any statements could be judged as ultimately true or false. Criteria of truth or objectivity are themselves intellectual products, at least within the epistemological tradition of the West. If these criteria are socially relative then 'truth' loses its traditionally accepted meaning and the objectivity of particular statements would appear to become but a 'relative objectivity' tied to the specific socio-historical context in which these statements are made. In these terms it would appear that one must accept as many 'truths' as there are essentially different socio-cultural milieux, and this renders the adjudication of disputes not only over policy but also over fact, matters of force and violence, despite any 'gloss' of intellectual 'rationalization' or justification.

This third element of the critique leads immediately to the fourth: that the sociology of knowledge, understood as an empirical science, is theoretically impossible unless it accepts a very severely restricted meaning. The insight can and has been taken to mean that knowledge is radically social; that thought itself and all ideas are inextricably rooted in the social context or process. But since this implies the socially determined character, and thus the relativity of even the accepted criteria of validity and truth, the discipline is in essence self-contradictory, self-refuting and therefore theoretically impossible. In other words, the critics must ultimately argue that one cannot rationally adhere to the insight in its radical form for such complete adherence runs counter to or contradicts the possibility of attaining an a-temporal objectivity or truth. To be consistent the critique must render this verdict, although not all critics have done so.[13]

From this standpoint the only 'valid' sociological analysis of knowledge, if it can still be called that, appears to be the much less radical study of the 'functional' interrelationships of specific ideas and perspectives and the specific social group that factually holds and acts according to these ideas. However, such functional analysis bears little relation to traditional concerns of the discipline.

Furthermore, even such restricted versions of the insight do not ultimately escape the criticisms they were thought to resolve.[14]

If one briefly considers but a few of the range of major contributions to the sociology of knowledge, the sense and basis of these criticisms becomes more readily apparent. Durkheim, for example, was one of the first sociologists to address the question of the social rootedness of consciousness and knowledge in a direct and fairly detailed manner. However, though he appeared to appreciate the basic difficulties that would eventually be pointed out, he failed to develop a conceptual framework that would be acceptable to the critics.

In keeping with his basic belief that society could and must be treated as a 'reality *sui generis*'[15] and that actors were to be viewed as derivatives of their prior social and physical contexts,[16] Durkheim argued that the thought of individuals must also be viewed as a derivative phenomenon. Specific ideas were conceived of as reflecting particular conceptual frameworks or categorical structures consisting of basic 'collective representations'. These, in turn, were to be interpreted as rooted in and determined by the underlying 'social reality'.[17] Durkheim also argued that ideas both existed and found their 'truth' in relation to their functionality for society and its evolutionary change and development.[18]

The extent to which Durkheim adhered to the radical implications of the basic insight is most evident in his discussion of traditional epistemologies.[19] He rejected empiricism on the grounds that all thought proceeds in terms of basic and shared categories and concepts, and is therefore never purely inductive. However, despite this apparent agreement with the Kantian stance, he could not accept the idealist aspect of this view – that these basic categories existed a priori and universally in time and space. He held, in contrast, that the basic categories necessary to thought must themselves be explained, and that such explanation could and must be obtained through a demonstration of their emergence from the prior and evolving social context.[20]

Leaving aside for the moment the method by which Durkheim hoped to achieve this demonstration, it is obvious that the charges levelled by the critics are applicable to his position. Clearly, by arguing that all of our thought, including the basic categories in terms of which specific ideas have their meaning, are temporal and relative to specific historical social circumstances, Durkheim could not logically claim, as he did, that his own ideas about thought were themselves true. As the critics claim, the sociology of knowledge has a tendency to talk itself into this apparently obvious self-contradiction.

The same is true of Mannheim's work – a favourite target of the critics in their effort to demonstrate the inadequacies of the discipline. Like Durkheim, Mannheim adhered very largely to the radical implications of the insight. He accepted the common-sense appreciation that there are many different points of view, perspectives or, as he put it, stylistic structures which, as categorical frameworks, are responsible for the specific ideas we hold about ourselves and about aspects of reality.[21] In turn, he held that these perspectives are rooted in the differentiated, social situation of the persons sharing them, and that these differentiated groups therefore tend to develop characteristic and, in degree, unique modes of thought.[22]

Mannheim's proposed programme of analysis for the sociology of knowledge clearly reflects his view that ideas are socially determined. He argued that analysis must begin with an 'understanding', with a reconstruction of the basic thought-style or perspective underlying and unifying specific ideas expressed by a group. Analysis must then proceed to determine if that group of persons actually thinks as predicted by the reconstructed perspective. Finally, analysis must determine the causal connections that are presumed to exist between the perspective and the social aspects of the group's situation.[23]

Mannheim was very aware of the challenge to his and others' attempts to elaborate the insight. In response, he proposed a position that he labelled 'relationism' – the argument that the truth of an idea is a truth that holds strictly in relation to the socially determined perspective from which it is generated.[24] He also argued that it was or would become possible to investigate all partial perspectives and that through such analysis it would be possible to arrive at a synthesis of perspectives fully adequate to reality. This task would be accomplished by a 'free-floating intelligentsia', a group of individuals free of the limitations of specific and narrow social contexts.[25]

Of course the critics reject both these responses. As far as relationism is concerned, Mannheim simply deepened the problem by stressing the extent to which ideas are relative to specific perspectives and therefore to specific social contexts.[26] The second 'solution' is rejected simply because it clearly contradicts Mannheim's adherence to the belief in the social determination of ideas. It is difficult to see, given Mannheim's position, how the intelligentsia is to free itself from its own peculiar social bonds, and it is unclear on what grounds their synthesis could possibly be judged, let alone accepted, as a total and not just another partial, if broader, perspective.[27] In other words, the self-contradiction of claiming truth for the proposition that all thought is relative remains in Mannheim's work.

A third and final example is to be found in the more contemporary work of Berger and Luckmann, writers who very explicitly recognize and try to 'bracket' epistemological concerns within the sociology of knowledge. They describe their work as an effort to develop a position that will allow investigation of, and empirically based statements about, the social distribution, maintenance and change of ideas in relation to social factors – a position which does not, at the same time, become embroiled in relativistic implications and debates.[28] However, they fare no better than the various predecessors from whom they take their starting point.[29]

At first glance their framework appears unique and promising, for they initially take the stand that society is a collective human product in which patterns of interaction are based in reciprocally developed typifications or concepts about a group's needs and experience with its world.[30] They then argue that through objectification or institutionalization of these action patterns and ideas, established social forms take on an apparent facticity capable of acting back upon the original producers and especially on subsequent generations. This latter effect or 'determination' is said to be primarily constituted by internalization or the socialization process, and renders persons and their thought, to some extent, 'social products'.[31]

To this point, Berger and Luckmann present a very suggestive framework for the sociology of knowledge. In it ideas are viewed as performing a functional role for persons in their efforts to fulfil needs; ideas are collective products and are not viewed as products of 'society' in any simple, determinative sense. Had the writers pursued this notion they might well have avoided the usual impasse of relativism, but they failed to do so. Instead, they leave behind their initial emphasis on the social construction of knowledge[32] and shift to an emphasis on the total objectification of ideas and social form, and their subsequent, determinative influence on successive generations.[33] In fact, their ultimate view of knowledge is that it is primarily, if not completely, a means and matter of legitimation or rationalization which reflects and maintains existing social forms.[34] This understanding of the nature of knowledge and its function of legitimation is emphasized further through two additional contentions. First, they argue that man has a basic psychological fear of the unknown and different, and thus a primordial need to maintain and reinforce existing ideas and social patterns.[35] Second, they argue that social change is not at all a matter of the intentional reconstruction of knowledge followed by a reconstruction of social form. Rather, it is viewed as a matter of force and the relative power of competing groups and thus competing, socially determined ideologies and rationalizations.[36]

Thus the internal contradiction noted in the writing of Durkheim and Mannheim remains in that of Berger and Luckmann. In each case, the writers claim truth for a position which holds that what others take to be knowledge is socially determined and therefore relative in time and space. If this is true of all that we take to be knowledge, then the claim to truth presented by these sociologists cannot itself be accepted. It, too, must be a 'truth' relative to the social space and interests of these writers.

The answer to this difficulty has seemed absurdly simple to many. In the context of precisely defining the terms and nature of the relationship presumed to hold between knowledge and social context, one need only to exclude specific types or categories of knowledge from social penetration and influence. In particular, so the argument runs, one need only to exclude knowledge arrived at through the methods of science (and therefore these methods themselves). Or, as some have phrased the same point, one only need realize that the truth of ideas, or what can count as knowledge, is something independent of the social and temporal origin of these ideas. That is, while it might be accepted that ideas have a social origin and that at least some types of thought may remain socially influenced, true ideas are those which transcend such origin and influence. Thus, if the sociologist of knowledge avoided the genetic fallacy and utilized the appropriate intellectual method in research, a legitimate area of study might remain open to him.[37]

However, it has been quite impossible for major figures within the discipline to avoid committing this supposed fallacy completely, and it has remained a strong temptation to view all that passes for knowledge as socially determined in some sense. That is, it has always been a temptation to adhere to the radical implications of the insight. Thus Durkheim argued that even the basic categories of thought must not be accepted a priori as a-temporal and a-social givens. Scheler refused to exempt any basic mode of thought from continued social penetration.[38] Marx explicitly viewed scientific work itself as no more and no less a social activity. Mead viewed science in the same light and even more definitely raised questions regarding traditional notions of scientific truth.[39] Mannheim vascillated throughout his work in regard to the question concerning an exemption for the 'hard' sciences and mathematics from the general rule of social determination.[40] Berger and Luckmann bluntly state that all that passes as knowledge is the subject matter for the sociology of knowledge, and presumably this would include science or, more precisely, what is taken to be the method through which truth may be attained.[41]

CRITIQUE AND CONTRADICTION

In contrast to these positions, the critique remains adamant that the sociology of knowledge oversteps legitimate intellectual bounds whenever it results in such claims – thus the current impasse. However, there are two curious features of the debate that have not received the attention they deserve. Before acquiescing to the demands of the critique it is essential to consider these in some detail. First, considering the critique itself, a review of the relevant literature demonstrates that it has seldom been taken as at all necessary carefully to delineate and justify the basis on which the particular criticisms are levelled. In the majority of instances the particular critic writes as if the claims he is making are quite 'self-evident' and that the 'error' committed by the sociology of knowledge is 'obvious'. However, while an error repeated so often and for such a period of time may indicate the failure of sociologists, it may also reflect a stubborn and justifiable, if poorly understood refusal to reject an insight which remains valid in spite of its implications for traditional epistemological assumptions and logic. It is therefore essential to determine if indeed there are sufficient grounds in terms of which the critique must be accepted over the insight and its various implications.

The second curious feature of this debate is that the majority of sociologists of knowledge have themselves basically accepted and worked within the particular epistemological and methodological parameters demanded by the critique. For example, though both Durkheim and Mannheim may be criticized for their tendency to relativize all knowledge, including the 'knowledge about knowledge' expressed in the scientific tradition, they none the less proposed the utilization of traditional methods in particular analyses of the social determination of knowledge.[42] On the one hand this implies that though the sociology of knowledge and the critique are at odds, there would appear to be, rightly or wrongly, little or no quarrel between them in methodological terms. On the other hand, this attempted adherence to the parameters of the critique within a project which, according to the critics, ultimately runs counter to those very parameters, suggests a rather important possibility. It may well be the case that traditional efforts in the discipline have been self-defeating precisely because they have never totally and consistently rejected the critique in favour of a strict adherence to the basic insight they have attempted to elaborate. In other words, the sociology of knowledge may well be impossible as many critics claim, but impossible only within traditionally accepted epistemological terms. An adequate elaboration of the insight that our consciousness and knowledge are radically social in nature may require that particular epistemological and methodological implications of the insight itself be taken more seriously and pursued in much more depth than has been the case to date.

These unclear aspects of the debate demand answers to two if not three questions. First, it is appropriate and necessary to ask what specifically is presupposed and taken for granted in the critique and, second, whether or not there is adequate justification for granting priority to these presuppositions and thus the claims of the critique over the basic insight and its implications. Depending on the answers to these questions, it becomes relevant to ask what particular consequences an acceptance of the critique has for the sociology of knowledge.

In respect to the first question, one can do little better than to consider the work of Arthur Child. He has presented one of the most complete analyses of the insight in its many formulations and, typically, has drawn the conclusion that a sociology of knowledge in the more radical sense is theoretically impossible. In his view, any attempt to explain the development of ideas, especially in respect to their validity or objectivity, in terms of extrinsic or existential factors, commits the genetic fallacy and is therefore false. More specifically, he argues that the insight or belief that ideas are fundamentally social and historical – the central assumption of the discipline – is 'scientifically undemonstrable and is also, therefore scientifically irrefutable'.[43] It is impossible to establish the fact of the social relativity of thought scientifically or empirically precisely because to do so would be self-contradictory. To do so would be to refute the resulting statement as itself a factual, non-relative statement.

On the one hand, Child bases this argument on a very thorough analysis of the writing of several of the major figures in the discipline. However, like most critics, his conclusions are also arrived at on the basis of a particular and unexamined set of assumptions about what is intellectually appropriate. For example, in reference to the specific problem of attempting to impute a system of ideas to a particular set of social determinants such as a social class, Child bluntly disallows the possibility because, in his view, the issue

> is not the issue of what one does mean by imputation: it is the issue of what one *can mean*. And if one insists on meaning something *disallowed by knowledge of fact* then one's meaning is subjective and is, therefore, illegitimate.[44]

In other words, while the insight may mean or imply that ideas and systems of ideas are intimately related to particular social bases, this meaning must be illegitimate. It is illegitimate precisely because empirical knowledge of fact apparently disallows such meaning – at least it must if the self-contradiction of relativism is to be avoided.[45]

In similar vein, Plamenatz concludes that the notion that 'ideas and beliefs are "relative" to the social situation or points of view of the people who have them . . . is untenable'.[46] This is because it is 'necessary' that there exist at least some ideas free of social influence if rational discourse is to be at all possible, especially 'ideas about scientific method, about the functions of hypotheses and theories'.[47] Plamenatz points out, as was suggested above, that most sociologists of knowledge have themselves recognized this and retreated from the more radical implications of the insight.

Frank Hartung, whose particular target is Mannheim, is likewise quite content to state that the insight must be severely restricted in meaning because of the apparent self-contradiction involved in any effort to achieve its empirical verification. To Hartung, the very suggestion that the insight might compel revision of our traditional adherence to the empirical character of knowledge is simply a matter of asserting 'too much',[48] an obvious instance of the genetic fallacy.[49] Without carefully argued support for his own position, he immediately proceeds to differentiate the 'fruitful from the fallacious' in Mannheim's work. He does so according to the criteria of that which one 'may attempt to ascertain empirically', thereby avoiding the 'burden' of Mannheim's 'epistemological speculations'.[50]

Clearly, what is repeated in each of these and in other examples of the critique is a definite restriction of what one wants the insight to mean by what one can mean in terms of empirically ascertainable fact. This repeated demand for strict empirical verifiability, a demand which seems to require no justification in the critical literature, clearly reflects the positivistic or naturalistic conception of objectivity or knowledge. This position, so dominant in Western thought, is based on the assumption that validity or objectivity is confined to those ideas which are manifested or obliged by sensory experience, those which are free of the intrusion of value judgments and normative elements. Furthermore, it is a position which holds that true ideas are those attained, ideally, according to the experimental, controlled, observational method most clearly demonstrated in the physical sciences.[51]

> Defined in the most general terms, positivism is a collection of prohibitions concerning human knowledge, intended to confine the name of 'knowledge' (or 'science') to those operations that are observable in the evolution of the modern sciences of nature. More especially, throughout its history positivism has turned a polemical cutting edge to metaphysical speculation of every kind, and hence against all reflection that either cannot found its conclusions on empirical data or formulates its judgements in such a way that they can never be contradicted by empirical data.[52]

On the one hand, the critics are quite correct and consistent in their denial of the validity of the insight in its more radical form. At least they are correct if one accepts the positivistic framework in which the critique is based. Clearly, one cannot adhere at one and the same time to a notion of validity that precludes the intrusion of normative and evaluative elements and to the notion that all thought contains integral social and historical dimensions. However, on the other hand, it becomes appropriate and essential to raise the second question – whether or not there are sufficient and necessary grounds on which to argue that the demands of the positivistic framework must take priority over the insight and its various implications. In other words, are sociologists of knowledge obliged to accept the critique and to work within its parameters?

That there is a contradiction between positivistic prohibitions and insight does not alone provide sufficient support for the demand that the contradiction be resolved in the direction of the positivistic conception of validity. Nothing in the critics' actual statements of their rejection of the insight (except perhaps their pervasive self-assuredness) compels support for this demand in spite of the fact that so many sociologists of knowledge have felt themselves so compelled and have conceptualized their work within this methodological framework.[53] In contrast, there are a number of considerations that very clearly raise doubt that it is at all necessary to accept and to work within the positivistic parameters of the critique.

In the first place, it is not at all clear that the insight lacks sufficient empirical support for even its more extreme implications as is so often claimed. Positivists will themselves grant that historically there have existed very different world-views in respect to understanding of both social and physical reality.[54] The subsequent argument that such differences are only significant in that they reflect particular stages in a cumulative historical evolution of thought culminating in the supposedly correct positivistic mode is a position currently under debate even within the physical sciences and within the history and philosophy of these sciences.[55] At least one writer whose own stance is positivistic has recognized this point and has explicitly directed attention to the debate over the sociology of knowledge. Lavine takes both critics and proponents of the insight to task for what in her view is a very facile acceptance of positivistic canons of objectivity as themselves outside of the penetration of the social into consciousness.[56] Her work demonstrates that the methods of empirical science themselves presume certain axioms about the process of knowing which have no atemporal, empirically demonstrable basis.[57] Thus it is implied that the second half of Child's statement, that the insight is 'scientifically irrefutable', is just as relevant as the first half, that the insight is 'scientifically undemonstrable'.[58] In Lavine's view, this is precisely the status of the positivistic stance underlying the critique – it is neither refutable nor demonstrable in its own terms, and thus there is no basis for excluding it from the social penetration affecting other ideas.[59]

This consideration receives further and much more detailed support in the work of Stanley Taylor.[60] Taylor concurs with the observation that positivism is not self-validating, but he does so in the context of demonstrating that it is itself a particular approach to objective thought which has emerged from within the same historical struggle with the issue of relativism as characterizes the sociology of knowledge.[61]

He first points out that the positivistic presuppositions underlying the critique are, in turn, rooted in the classical, naturalistic theory of knowledge. Early forms of this theory stressed the purely perceptual, strictly inductive and empiricist aspect of knowing and reflected the nominalist promise that, 'things alone are real, and that abstract ideas or universals are valid only insofar as they correctly express, as symbols, the particulars to which they refer'.[62] This is a position which amounts to an attempt to root all ideas in a supposedly 'more real' or existential base through validation of statements strictly in terms of an individual's sense perception.[63]

However, this early epistemological stance, in its effort to state the nature of objective thought, failed to deal successfully with two problems.[64] First, in holding that 'man is the measure of all things', in terms specifically of individual sense perception, the position is quite unable to account for the existence and character of non-sensory, non-individual elements in thought, the basic concepts or categories. These basic organizing ideas appear essential to thought and to agreement, yet they do not appear to be inductive generalizations from sense experience.[65] Second, without the inclusion of the categorical element, which is the basis of relating disparate sensations by and between persons, the position remains hopelessly relativistic. Truth is no more than what each individual claims it to be according to his specific temporal and spatial standpoint.

Of course this extreme subjectivism is not the ultimate form that the classical theory of knowledge has been given.

> [The] fruitless consequences of this . . . perceptual theory of knowledge . . . has led many thinkers to feel that, in the nature of the case, objective thought must be conceptual thought . . . and . . . the problem of knowledge becomes that of introducing various modes of connection (categories) by which a manifold sense (perception) can be reduced to systematic order.[66]

Various reformulations have been developed historically in response to both the problem of including the categorical element and to the issue of relativism. Specifically, the basis of objectivity has been transferred from the possibility of pure individual sense perception to the thought that perception is mediated by a particular categorical framework. Attempts to introduce this categorical element have ranged from utilitarianism to the position developed by Kant. However, despite considerable historical reformulation, the problem of relativism has never been demonstrably resolved.

For example, Kant's 'solution' to the issue of the existence and basis of the categorical element in thought consisted basically of the delineation of what he considered the universal categories of reason. For Kant, the achievement of objective knowledge was a matter of obtaining 'necessary judgments', and he held that because perception alone could never yield such necessity, then the process of knowing implied the operation of such categories. Since these necessary categories were not arrived at through induction, he argued that they were simply 'innate to the understanding, that is, a priori'.[67] Furthermore, Kant argued that this transcendental element in thought was both a-historical and a-social; that it was an element shared by all men regardless of place and time.[68]

If one accepts his specific delineation of the twelve categories that appear to be operative in thought, then one has an apparently absolute basis on which to judge statements as objective and non-relative. 'For Kant, objectivity is obtained when the judgment expressing a relationship between objects is in accordance with his categorical framework.'[69] This basis of objectivity is still the individual cognitive act, but it is an act of the individual involving an 'interaction' between sense perception and the trans-individual categorical framework. The latter is responsible for order in perception, and therefore for intelligibility and communication. Thought is thus a synthesis of subject and object; of observation and the reason (categories) in which each individual mind participates.[70]

However, an important question remains in respect to this 'solution'. As Taylor suggests, 'beyond the question of what categories adequately perform this ordering function is that of discovering the source, ground or basis of the categories and accomplishing their derivation or deduction'.[71] Kant does not provide the requisite, non-relative ground or basis. He argues that the categories he enumerates are deducible from a consideration of how individuals think. However, in the context of historical variation in thought, this deduction does not justify an acceptance of his particular categories as trans-historical.

Furthermore, granting the categories an a priori, transcendental or ideal status, has a particular consequence. Even though the categories are considered to be 'necessary' elements in empirical investigation, they are not themselves amenable to such investigation.[72] That is, any empirical investigation of the categories would have to presuppose the very categories under investigation thus leaving one with a clearly circular argument.

To this point in the argument, it can at least be said that the critique of the sociology of knowledge is on somewhat weak ground when it chastises the discipline for its relativistic implications and its inability empirically to validate its basic insight that knowledge is essentially social in nature. The critique itself clearly rests on a particular epistemological stance which cannot be empirically validated and which has dealt with the common problem of relativism only through the introduction of a set of categories; a set of categories deduced from the 'way people think', but within a particular socio-historical context. Given this and that there is indeed considerable, if not conclusive empirical support for the view that knowledge is social in nature, it becomes quite questionable that such evidence and the implications of the insight must be denied in favour of the positivistic prohibitions of the critique.

There is one further characteristic of the debate between critics and proponents of the discipline which must be considered. This concerns the implications and consequences for the sociology of knowledge of the fact that most writers within the field have conceived their work basically within the methodological parameters of the critique. That the discipline should display this tendency is not of course unexpected, for it is true of much if not most of sociology in spite of a continuing debate over the appropriateness of the positivistic stance in the analysis of the social dimension.

To begin with, it is often said and perhaps generally accepted that sociology emerged as part of the conservative reaction to and rejection of the thought of the Enlightenment, and to what were perceived as the negative social consequences of such thought. In one respect this argument is quite meaningful; in contrast to the Enlightenment emphasis on the individual and his potentialities and on the institutional or social sphere as primarily negative and limiting, a basic element of sociological thought has been the interpretation of persons as fundamentally social beings. This assumption has of course been elaborated in numerous specific ways. However, despite variations, there remains a common and integrating factor: the assumption that there is a positive, integral and necessary relationship between persons and the institutional framework. In other words, in this respect at least, sociological thought contrasts fundamentally with the still-predominant individualistic image of man and society.[73]

On the other hand, it must be acknowledged that sociological thought is not a total rejection of, but, in part at least, a continuation of Enlightenment thought. As indicated, the predominant development, methodologically, has been within the positivistic framework. With hesitation in the nineteenth, but with commitment in the twentieth century, sociology has largely developed in the image of the natural sciences. It is generally understood as the 'science of society', as an empirical study of social 'reality' according to the canons and proscriptions of positivistic analysis. In this particular sense, sociology clearly reflects a basic continuation of the Enlightenment respect for, and elaboration of, the methodology and methods of natural science.[74]

In consequence, sociology, at least in its predominant, positivistic expression, is essentially contradictory. As both a reaction against and perpetuation of Enlightenment thought it clearly combines quite incompatible assumptions. On the one hand, sociology assumes an image of man as fundamentally social; on the other hand, it has adopted a methodological stance that is rooted in a fundamentally individualistic conception of man. As Taylor has argued, the classical theory of knowledge in which positivism is rooted is clearly individualistic in nature. In each of its forms the classical position has remained consistent in its basic reference to the individual subject and to his perceptual abilities, which are viewed as the essential and secular ground for objectivity and certainly in thought.[75] The methodological consequence of placing such faith in the individual has been to detach the subject both from any sacred basis or justification for ideas, and from the social, institutional framework as well.[76] As a result, the social context has been interpreted as bearing none but a negative, biasing relationship to thought. The determination of valid ideas, of truth, has therefore demanded that social influences be controlled and transcended.[77]

Positivism is one outcome of this historical effort to discover a rational method or procedure through which individual perception might be rendered pure and ideas freed from factors of distortion and bias, especially the influence of 'idols of the mind' or traditional institutions. The so-called 'faith' in human reason, so evident in the seventeenth and eighteenth centuries, was a faith already tempered by a respect, though a negative respect, for such social influences.[78] However, the very search for a method to control such influences presumes both that knowing is an individual undertaking and that a negative relationship exists between thought and social factors or processes.[79]

Furthermore, as Taylor also notes, classical, individualistic epistemology omits the category of value. However, as he goes on to argue,

> it is precisely this order of category – Value – that is embodied predominantly in institutions. Societies in which the conception of institutions is sacred find the validation of thought in institutional structure [e.g. in the performance of ritual] and hence, largely in value. . . . No society has been able to demonstrate with certainty that values have any objective existence or validity other than as ideas in the mind. It follows that the objectivity that obtains in sacred society rests entirely upon agreement concerning values and their possible hierarchical arrangement.[80]

The consequences of this omission are, on the one hand, positive in that a mode of knowing is developed that is basically directed to and permits a comprehension of physical objects and processes in detachment from values. On the other hand, this mode of knowing tends to overlook the fact that values, and therefore the institutional framework, remain relevant and operative – even, as Taylor suggests, within that mode of knowing itself. The positivistic conception of the grounds of objective thought may itself be interpreted as rooted in a specific value and in a specific historical social form – the central and often exclusive value placed on the individual over society as is expressed concretely or objectified socially in the contemporary contractual form of human relationships. In other words, 'Individualism itself may be viewed as an institution',[81] and thus is as socially relative and as contingent as its predecessors.

It is in these terms that sociology can be said to be contradictory in its predominant methodological expression, and this is perhaps most acutely apparent in the sociology of knowledge. To assume on the one hand that persons are fundamentally social beings would seem to imply the basic insight that the consciousness and ideas of persons are integrally intersubjective or social in nature. To then adopt the methodological stance of positivism is contradictory precisely because positivism constitutes a rejection of this conception of ideas, both in respect to its inherent individualism and in respect to its omission or rejection of the category of value. A positivistically conceived sociology of knowledge is therefore a contradiction in terms and the conflict between critics and proponents of the discipline must be seen less as a debate than as a conflict between divergent and radically incompatible perspectives. For its part, the sociology of knowledge has seldom displayed sufficient awareness of this depth of contradiction and, as a result, has repeated the same errors time and time again.

To summarize, the central implications of the argument to this point are, first, that in its own struggle with the historical issue of relativism, the classical theory of knowledge does not constitute a self-validating logic and, as a result, the critique is subject to the self-same criticisms that it levels at the sociology of knowledge. It therefore becomes quite unclear as to why positivism should be considered free of social penetration or why the insight should be rejected out of hand. If anything, this would appear to be the case simply because the insight, in its radical form, has such consequences for the basic presuppositions of the critique. Second, by virtue of the individualistic presuppositions of the critique, it does become clear that there is not simply a debate, but a fundamental and thorough-going contradiction separating critics and proponents of the sociology of knowledge. In consequence, it may indeed be theoretically impossible to develop a sociology of knowledge acceptable to the critics – but precisely because of this contradiction. However, in the absence of empirical validation for even the presuppositions of the critique, this is not to say that a sociology of knowledge could not be developed; just that its development must be pursued within an entirely different epistemological framework – a framework which, minimally, must be consistent with the implications of the insight that knowledge is social in nature.

This analysis and its conclusions are of fundamental importance to the analyses of Marx and Mead that follow, and to the effort to verify the suggestion that a synthesis of relevant elements of their perspectives will resolve basic issues in the sociology of knowledge. If it had been concluded that the critique and its basis must indeed take precedence over the insight and its implications, a particular and traditional path would have been indicated. In this instance, the analyses of Marx and Mead would have been directed to the possible discovery and elaboration of elements of a clearly expressed, yet severely limited and strictly empirical, sociology of knowledge. However, since it was found, to the contrary, that granting such precedence is indeed questionable and that, in any case, the attempt to develop a sociology of knowledge within the positivistic framework is contradictory, and can only perpetuate a hopeless socio-cultural relativism, an entirely different path is indicated. Instead of directing analysis to possible anticipations of and response to the immediate demands of the critique, analysis must seek anticipations and response which involve recognition of the contradiction between insight and critique. In other words, the proposed synthesis must involve a non-positivistic conception of objectivity if it is to be of relevance to traditional problems in the discipline. It is this path that is pursued in subsequent chapters.

chapter 2

Marx: elements of a sociology of knowledge

The results of the analysis of the debate between critics and proponents of the sociology of knowledge set very particular criteria in terms of which the suggested Marx/Mead synthesis can possibly contribute to a resolution of persistent difficulties faced by the discipline. Specifically, the proposed synthesis must include an epistemological framework different from the positivistic and consistent with the insight that knowledge is a social phenomenon; that is, it must involve a social theory of knowledge.

On the one hand this finding can be considered positive in that it proposes an entirely new direction in which to seek a resolution of the debate, a direction that is essential if traditional barriers are to be transcended. On the other hand, traditional interpretations of Marx and Mead, as well as the spirit in which the proposed synthesis is usually suggested, do not promise the same.

For example, Marx's elaboration of the insight, as most often interpreted, has been persistently rejected in the very definite terms of the critique. The basic criticism is of course that to argue that 'social being determines consciousness' or that the 'economic substructure' or 'real foundation' determines the superstructure including ideas is to render human consciousness epiphenomenal and thereby to relativize all thought. It is therefore claimed that Marx's perspective is fundamentally self-contradictory; if all thought is relative to a changing social base, then Marx's own statements claiming the ideological nature of the thought of others must themselves be socially rooted, ideological and thus invalid. Many critics as well as proponents of the sociology of knowledge conclude that Marx's work is, as a result, of little but historical and pre-paradigmatic interest.[1]

These claims are justified at least to some extent for one can easily find considerable evidence supporting the critics' views within Marxist literature.[2] Furthermore, even such sympathetic critics as Dupré[3] and Avineri[4] argue that the deterministic and thus relativistic developments of Marx's thought by various materialists (to which the criticisms are indeed applicable) can be justified by and are developments which are very largely consistent with at least some aspects of Marx's own writing.[5]

At the same time however, these particular analysts are clearly not willing to accept such difficulties as adequate grounds on which to dismiss Marx's work as of no contemporary relevance to issues in sociology. Though a very extensive literature has been developed that supports the critique in respect to Marx's formulation of the insight, it is also and repeatedly suggested that there is more to be found in his writing than these critics are able or willing to admit.[6]

In particular, relatively recent analyses of Marx's writing, which make extensive use of previously unpublished material, insist that the interpretation of his perspective as consistently deterministic with respect to human consciousness and knowledge is fundamentally in error. While acknowledging the presence of inconsistencies,[7] Avineri, Dupré, Ollman, Petrovic, Kolakowski and others argue that Marx's perspective, and thus his conception of the relation of thought and social context, can only be properly and fruitfully interpreted in relation to his attempt to achieve a synthesis of idealist and materialist philosophical frameworks. It is argued that 'historical materialism', 'dialectical materialism', 'naturalism – humanism' – call it what you will – constitutes a very definite alternative to the ontological and epistemological stance represented by the positivistic tradition.[8] If this can be demonstrated then it can perhaps be shown that the critique has incorrectly interpreted Marx's statements on the social nature of consciousness as necessarily implying a total relativization and reduction of thought. In other words, this interpretation holds out the possibility that at least the outlines of an alternative epistemological stance consistent with the insight informing the sociology of knowledge is indeed present in Marx's writing.

The following analysis is first of all directed to those aspects of Marx's writing that are relevant to a comprehension of his sociology of knowledge as well as to the relevance of those insights to contemporary issues faced by the discipline. In particular, the study focuses on his conceptualization of knowledge, of the social dimension and of the relationships implied by the insight. However, in light of the conclusions of the previous chapter, the analysis pays specific attention to the ontological and epistemological bases of Marx's ideas and to the extent to which these premises adequately anticipate the critique in their consistency with the idea of knowledge as an essentially social phenomenon.

REALITY AND PRAXIS: THE PRESUPPOSITIONS OF THE MARXIAN SOCIOLOGY OF KNOWLEDGE

An adequate comprehension of the presuppositions underlying Marx's perspective requires recognition of his early disenchantment with both Hegelian and Young–Hegelian idealism, and the materialism of Feuerbach and the political economists.[9] Marx was quite aware of the tension, and apparent incompatibility, between these modes of thought: the former reducing reality to the historical realization of spirit; the latter reducing reason or spirit to the status of an epiphenomenal product of the existential, material world; the positivistic stance. This is exemplified in the *Theses on Feuerbach* in which he argues that

> The chief defect of all hitherto existing materialism – that of Feuerbach included – is that the thing, reality, sensuousness, is conceived only in the form of the object or of contemplation, but not as human sensuous activity, practice, not subjectively. Hence it happened that the active side, in contradistinction to materialism, was developed by idealism – but only abstractly, since, of course, idealism does not know real, sensuous activity as such. Feuerbach wants sensuous objects, really distinct from thought objects, but he does not conceive *human activity itself as objective activity*. Hence, . . . he regards the theoretical attitude as the only genuinely human attitude, . . . he does not grasp the significance of 'revolutionary', or practical-critical, activity.[10]

To put this two-fold rejection in more contemporary sociological terms, Marx rejected an individualistic nominalism that conceptualized the social as but the sum of individual actions, as but a negative phenomenon in relation to the individual, and as amenable to change simply through the medium of a change of consciousness. On the other hand, he also rejected the reduction of individuals to prior social facts, or to a material reality *sui generis*; that is, the reduction of the explanation of human thought and action to sociologism. In these terms, Marx's basic problem involved the attempt to think the significance of human sociality, or the clearly social character of human existence, without, at the same time, thinking 'society' or social determinism in any positivistic sense. Phrased somewhat differently, the issue for Marx concerned how one could accept the experience of the predictability of action, conformity or apparent social determinism without, at the same time, denying the equally important historical experience of individuality, human freedom, responsibility and creativity.

To criticize both idealism and materialism is to attempt to place oneself outside both. This necessitates, or at least implies, an entirely different position; a third standpoint in which such dual criticism is rooted.[11] The standpoint that Marx achieved, although the degree of achievement is debatable, is, in his own words, 'materialist' and 'scientific'. However, it is a gross error to take the classical theory of knowledge as being his standpoint on grounds of his choice of words, and on the basis of an interpretation of these words within the positivistic framework.[12]

Perhaps the key to a comprehension of Marx's perspective, of his dialectical approach at the level of basic presuppositions, is the central notion of praxis as reality-for-man. Essentially, this conception denies, and yet unites, both a priorism and empiricism, and does so in a different way in comparison with the position developed by Kant. Reality, *for man*, is in this view neither the evolutionary unfolding of and participation in reason; nor is it the realm of matter-in-motion, perceived by the senses and reflected in thought. Furthermore, reality is not the interpenetration of timeless, a-historical categories inherent in mind, with empirical, physical reality, although this idea approaches the idea of praxis. Rather, reality, in the human sense, for the human species, is the active, dialectical relationship between persons as social beings and physical nature: a relationship that is at once mental and material, a unity of thought and action. Reality, interpreted as praxis, is an on-going, historical process, a 'humanizing of nature and a naturalizing of man'.[13] This idea of praxis and the critique of both idealism and materialism is captured in the following passage from the 1844 *Manuscripts*:

The natural sciences have developed a tremendous activity and

> have assembled an ever-growing mass of *data*. But philosophy has remained alien to these sciences *just as they have remained alien to philosophy*. Their momentary *rapprochement* was only a fantastic illusion. [Such *rapprochement* is essential and involves recognition that]. . . *Industry is the actual historical relationship of nature, and thus of natural science, to man.* If industry is conceived as the exoteric manifestation of the essential human faculties, the human essence of nature and the natural essence of man can also be understood. Natural science will then abandon its abstract materialist, or rather idealist, orientation, and will become the basis of a human science. . . . Nature, as it develops through industry . . . is truly anthropological nature.[14]

Although the term used here is industry, rather than praxis, the essential idea is clear; that reality involves the *relationship* between men with their given faculties, and a physical nature that is the object of these faculties in respect to the fulfilment of need.[15] This fundamental premise of Marx's perspective and analysis can be discerned in greater detail in the *German Ideology*. Though Marx speaks analytically here of several 'moments', or 'aspects', or 'elements' of reality, his overall emphasis is placed on the 'whole' of praxis; on the idea that each of these elements co-exists, interpenetrates with, and cannot be understood apart from the others and the whole at any point in time.

The first moment of praxis or human reality is

> that men must be in a position to live in order to be able to 'make history'. But life involves before all else eating and drinking, a habitation, clothing. . . . The first historical act is thus the production of the means to satisfy these needs, the production of material life itself. And indeed this is a historical act, a fundamental condition of all history, *which today, as thousands of years ago*, must daily and hourly be fulfilled merely in order to sustain human life. Even when the *sensuous* world is reduced to a minimum, to a stick as with St Bruno, *it presupposes the action of producing the stick*. Therefore, in any interpretation of history one has first of all to observe this fundamental fact in all its implications and to accord it its due importance.[16]

Earlier, in the same text, Marx made this point by arguing that

> The first premise of all human history is, of course, the existence of living human individuals. . . . Thus the writing of history must always set out from these natural bases and their modification in the course of history *through the action of men*. . . . Men can be distinguished from animals by consciousness, by religion or anything else you like. They themselves begin to distinguish themselves from animals as soon as they begin to produce the means of their own subsistence. . . . By producing their means of subsistence men are indirectly producing their actual material life.[17]

In other words, before all else, one must acknowledge the fact of life itself, the needs of life, and the necessity of their fulfilment – a fact that is fundamental and transcends time. Furthermore, Marx is arguing that human life is different from that of other animals not simply because men think or have consciousness, but because the fulfilment of human needs is accomplished only by the active intervention of men themselves. The implication is that our comprehension of reality cannot be divorced from our activity of transforming nature into means of subsistence. Reality is, therefore, reality-for-man, an interpenetration of nature and human activity.[18]

> The second point is that the satisfaction of the first need (*the action of satisfying and the instrument of satisfaction* which has been acquired) leads to new needs; and this production of new needs is [also] the *first* historical act.[19]

Here Marx is noting the necessity, in any analysis of the human situation, of recognizing that human life is more than the mere perpetuation of life; persons cannot be understood solely in terms of some given and static set of needs or instincts, and some process of adaptation. He is presupposing that the fulfilment of basic biological needs immediately, and 'at the same moment', opens up other possibilities, if only in the mode or form in which life is maintained.

> The third circumstance . . . is that men, who daily remake their own life, begin to make other men, to propagate their kind: the relation between man and woman, parents and children, the family. The production of life, both of one's own in labour and of fresh life in procreation, now appears as a double relationship: on the *one hand as a natural, on the other as a social relationship*.

> *By social we understand the co-operation of several individuals*. . . . It follows from this that a certain mode of production, or industrial stage, [form of praxis] is always combined with a certain mode of co-operation, or social stage, and this mode of co-operation *is itself a 'productive force'*. . . . Thus it is quite obvious from the start that there exists a materialistic connection of men with one another which is determined by their needs and their mode of production, and which is as old as men themselves.[20]

Men are therefore recognized as naturally and necessarily social in essence. Men actively produce their means of subsistence in relation to their historically developing needs; but this is accomplished always on some social, interdependent basis, which is given different forms through time. Marx therefore implies that reality is not simply 'there' for individuals, nor inextricably bound up with *individual* activity, but that this activity must be comprehended in terms of its social character. He implies, further, that this is the case despite appearances to the contrary; for example, despite the apparent competitive character of capitalist forms of praxis. This important point will be considered in more detail in the context of a discussion of alienation and reification.

Finally, to complete the whole of praxis, Marx argues that

> Only now . . . do we find that man also possesses 'consciousness'; but even so, not inherent, not 'pure' consciousness. From the start the 'spirit' is afflicted with the curse of being 'burdened with matter', which here makes its appearance in the form of agitated layers of sound, in short language. Language is as old as consciousness, language is practical consciousness *that exists also for other men, and for that reason alone it really exists for me as well*; language, like consciousness, only arises from the need, *the necessity*, of intercourse with other men.[21]

Consciousness is therefore viewed as but one interdependent element or moment in human being and becoming, in reality for man, or in praxis. It is neither the prime nor leading presupposition in understanding human existence as for the idealists; nor is it but a 'reflection' of matter as for the positivists. Rather, consciousness is interpreted as a *functional*[22] element in the maintenance of life *and* in the development of potentialities; in the fulfilment of present needs and the creation of new possibilities. Furthermore, as but an element in praxis, consciousness is necessarily bound up with the human sociality that is also involved in man's relation to nature.[23] In sum, reality is a process of interaction between conscious, social beings actively fulfilling and thereby creating potentialities, and physical nature or the environment necessary to this fulfilment.

The development of the idea of praxis as reality-for-man can be interpreted as an attempt to delineate an absolute ground for the development of a conceptual framework amenable to the study of human activity and its social-historical forms. Marx's perspective, as he indicates,

> is not without presuppositions, but it begins with the real presuppositions and does not abandon them for a moment. Its premises are men, not in some imaginary condition of fulfilment or stability, but in their actual, empirically observable process of development under determinate conditions. As soon as this active life-process is delineated, history ceases to be a collection of dead facts as it is with the empiricists (themselves still abstract), or an illusory activity of illusory subjects as it is with the idealists.[24]

Praxis therefore constitutes a 'phenomenological' description of reality-for-man, presumed to be stripped of all ideological presuppositions. Praxis is the essential basis, the *substratum* that underlies and is always present in, and in spite of, the more superficial and historically contingent or relative concerns of individuals and groups.[25] In simplified terms, Marx asks that one grant the initial and fundamental importance of the fact that individuals must be in a position to live before all else, and that, unlike other animals, though still a part of nature themselves, individuals survive as a species only by *producing* their means of subsistence. He presumes further that this production results in new possibilities and, therefore, in history, and that it is also a social process necessarily involving self-consciousness. Consciousness is interpreted as a functional moment in praxis that facilitates interaction and need fulfilment, and as necessary for the recognition of the potentialities that result.

The totality of these interdependent elements, praxis, is nowhere given any specific content beyond this; nor is it given any specific or timeless form. This absolute ground, or characterization of reality-for-man, is described precisely as a *process*, an active, intentional development in which each stage of fulfilment engenders new potentialities to be realized. With this idea of process, Marx thereby includes change as a fundamental presupposition, change as an essential aspect of praxis and, therefore, as an essential fact of reality-for-man.

> The same men who establish relations in conformity with their material power of production, also produce principles, laws, and categories in conformity with their social relations. Thus, these ideas and categories are no more eternal than the relations which they express. They are historical and transient products. There is a continuous movement of growth of the productive forces, of destruction of social relations, of formation of ideas; nothing is immutable but the abstract movement – *mors immortalis*[26]

Praxis, while itself a changeless, irreducible absolute, is essentially understood as a historical project that results in specific forms and specific contents which are contingent and constantly changing as new needs or potentialities are appreciated and pursued.

It should be noted, however, that while constant change is indeed presupposed and viewed as an essential characteristic of the perpetuation and development of the human species, praxis is not to be viewed as a mechanistic or necessarily 'inevitable' process. In the following passage the assumption of change or process is repeated but with an important qualification.

> The conditions under which individuals have intercourse with each other . . . are conditions appertaining to their individuality, in no way external to them; conditions under which these definite individuals, living under definite relationships, can alone produce their material life . . . are thus the conditions of their self-activity or are produced by this self-activity. . . . These various conditions, which appear first as conditions of self-activity, later as fetters upon it, form in the whole evolution of history a coherent series of forms of intercourse, the coherence of which consists of this: in the place of an earlier form of intercourse, which has become a fetter, a new one is put, corresponding to the more developed productive forces and, hence,

> to the advanced mode of the self-activity of individuals – a form which in turn becomes a fetter and is then replaced by another.[27]

The term 'fetter' in the passage suggests a specific problematic associated with praxis. This will be discussed later in relation to the concept of alienation.

It should be emphasized as well that this description of praxis obviously characterizes the individual and society in a highly specific manner. Basically, the individual is presented as an active, intentional and social being. No ontological distinction is made between the individual and society. Thus no 'artificial' or abstract idea of their relationship is developed, either in terms of a causal sociologism or in terms of a political-legal contractual union of individuals.[28] What distinguishes men from animals is, to repeat, the production of their own means of subsistence, a production that is seen as a necessarily social process intrinsic to which is the emergence of individual consciousness. Marx argues therefore that

> It is above all necessary to avoid postulating 'society' once again as an abstraction confronting the individual. The individual *is the social being*. The manifestation of his life – *even when it does not appear directly in the form of a communal manifestation* – is, therefore, a manifestation and affirmation of social life. Individual human life and species-life are not different things, even though the mode of existence of individual life is necessarily either a more specific or a more general mode of species-life. . . .[29]

For, as noted earlier, 'By the social is meant the *co-operation* of several individuals, no matter under what conditions, in what manner or to what end.'[30]

Praxis, therefore, entails the idea that individual action and thought are to be comprehended as social, but without an hypostatization of society; that is, without conferring ontological status on the social dimension as an entity. If nothing more, this elaboration of praxis as the fundamental presupposition of Marx's perspective, should introduce questions as to the adequacy of interpretations of that perspective as a socio-economic or historical determinism in relation to human thought and activity. However, these questions can only be clarified through an analysis of the implications of this idea of praxis for Marx's epistemology, for his conception of thought and objectivity.

PRAXIS AND CONSCIOUSNESS: THE MARXIAN EPISTEMOLOGY

The critique basically accuses Marx of reducing all thought to the level of a manifestation or product of a 'social-existential' substratum, which is other and more real than ideas. Marx's perspective is rejected in the strongest terms because his position apparently relativizes all thought – including that developed by himself, though claimed as objective.

However, as noted previously, a writer's position would not be self-contradictory if it recognized the necessity, and included the development of an alternative to the positivistic conception of objective thought; and if this was, at the same time, consistent with the basic insight of the sociology of knowledge. In terms of the fundamental idea of praxis, it is no longer clear that Marx shares the positivistic stance of his critics, which is often used to interpret his work in this regard. To argue that 'it is not the consciousness of men that determines their being, but, their social being determines their consciousness',[31] is obviously to hold that human thought is tied to and cannot be independent of the social dimension. However, the 'substratum' or reality to which consciousness is tied is that of praxis, and praxis clearly includes rather more and other than the term 'social-existential base', which the critics apply so freely.[32] Furthermore, the relationship between thought and praxis is not adequately comprehended in terms of the idea of determination understood positivistically.[33]

Material reality, for Marx, is that of living individuals whose life is praxis – an active, social and conscious relation with physical nature. Consciousness does not determine this life, but neither can this life be reduced to prior existential factors known in themselves. Consciousness is but a *part*, an aspect of the *whole* of praxis. This life, this social being, 'determines' consciousness; that is, it is the context, the whole, in terms of which consciousness makes sense as a process and product. However, equally, the whole depends on the parts, as Marx continuously points out with respect to consciousness:

> Nature constructs no machines. . . . They are products of human industry, natural materials transformed into instruments. . . . They are instruments of the human brain created by the human hand; they are the materialized power of knowledge.[34]

Avineri has argued that

> The identification of human consciousness with the practical process of reality as shaped by man is Marx's epistemological and historisophical achievement. To Marx reality is always human reality not in the sense that man exists with nature, but in the sense that man shapes nature. This act also shapes man and his relation to other human beings; it is a total process, implying a constant interaction between subject and object. . . . Classical Materialism, on the other hand, never considered that human activity had any such philosophical significance.[35]

If reality-for-man, or praxis, is the relationship of men in acts of need satisfaction with nature as the object of such satisfaction, then, clearly, human cognition must be understood as intimately bound up with needs and therefore with praxis and the forms it is given. To clarify the specific manner in which Marx includes the practical activity of need fulfilment in the process of knowing, it is helpful to consider Kolakowski's contrast of Marx's perspective with that of later Marxists and with that of the pragmatic school.[36]

For Engels, the truth of ideas was an empirical matter of determining their correspondence with an independent reality. Human activity was understood as analogous with experimentation; that is, as a method of verification, 'success proves the truth of our knowledge, failure forces us to reject or modify it'. This clearly positivist version of Marx's concern with practice not only misses his point, but, as indicated earlier, is often mistaken for Marx's own perspective by the critique.[37]

The pragmatist, on the other hand, gives practice a more central role; practice ceases to be a method of verification and becomes the creator of truth in itself; in pragmatism, as opposed to positivism,

> man's practical activity has been elevated to the rank of an epistemological category, so that its functions are not limited to verification of . . . correspondence . . . but are broadened to encompass the defining of the very concepts of truth, falseness, and nonsense . . . the truth of a judgment is defined as a practical function of the usefulness of its acceptance or rejection.[38]

Kolakowski goes on to suggest that this pragmatic position implies that 'cognition is a form of biological reaction that permits the best possible *adaptation* of individual organisms to their environment.'[39]

In contrast, Marx's epistemology stands between these poles in regard to the relevance of practical activity and needs. Against idealism, Marx maintained the distinction between consciousness and its objects. Physical reality, nature is ontologically independent of thought, action and need; indeed, man himself is recognized as fundamentally a part of nature:

> Man is directly a natural being. As a natural being and as a *living* natural being he is on the one hand furnished with natural powers of life – he is an *active* natural being. These forces exist in him as tendencies and abilities – as impulses. On the other hand, as a natural, corporeal, *sensuous* objective being he is a suffering [experiencing], conditioned and limited creature, like animals and plants. That is to say, *the objects of his impulses exist outside him, as objects independent of him*; yet these are objects of his need. . . .[40]

However, to hold that nature exists independently of consciousness does not require definition of consciousness as reflection or of truth as correspondence. As argued earlier, the only reality one can know is reality-for-man, and this implies that consciousness must be understood as an active process. It must be understood as one of man's 'natural powers' and as integrally *part of* reality-for-man. Thus, against 'abstract materialism', Marx argues that while human consciousness does not create objects, it does *establish*

> '*thinghood*' . . . an abstract thing, a thing created by abstraction and not a real thing . . . [which] is totally lacking in *independence*, in *being*, *vis-à-vis* self-consciousness; it is a mere construct established by self-consciousness.[41]

This establishment of 'thinkhood', this *act* of knowing,[42] *functions* within praxis, within reality-for-man, in relation to needs, and implies that objects are always objects-for-man; that is, *sensuous* objects as well as objects of sense. Therefore, any materialist discussion of 'nature . . . taken abstractly and rigidly separated from man, is nothing for man'.[43]

This is to argue, with Kant, that sense-experience is alone insufficient as a basis for the phenomenon of human consciousness. The infinity of stimuli from the natural substratum are but raw data, data, which, in turn, are rendered 'knowledge' in terms of a conceptual and ultimately categorical selection and organization. To use the phrase 'reality-for-man' is an attempt to capture this mediated character of knowing. However, unlike Kant, Marx refused to define, or give content to the basic categories; he refused to see them as a-temporal and inherent in mind, and demanded that one avoid the reification of what, for him, were historically and culturally variable bases of the cognitive organization of stimuli (sense experience).

In fact, Marx defines the categorical element in terms precisely of 'sensuous need', the fulfilment and development of which is praxis. This is to argue that the categories, as *forms* involved in the organization of perception and in reflection, emerge as but *functional* elements within the dialectic of persons actively pursuing need fulfilment against the 'opposition' of physical nature.[44] The categories are therefore understood as changing historical emergents within praxis.

It must be recalled at once, however, that praxis is integrally a social process; thus, the needs, in terms of which our sensuous activity interacts with sense activity, include social as well as biological needs. Furthermore, specific categories and concepts are human products, and thus are social in a dual sense: some (e.g. the category of value), are specifically rooted in social need;[45] others are products of human social activity.

In summary, Marx is arguing that 'knowing' is but a moment within, yet necessary to, the practical process of shaping reality; a process that allows fulfilment of need and the production of new need or possibility. It is an active process that is limited by human need on the one hand, and by the 'obduracy' of physical nature on the other. Therefore, he holds to the argument that 'Science [knowing] is only genuine science when it proceeds from sense experience, in *the two forms* of sense perception and sensuous need. . . . '[46]

While the use of the word 'genuine' implies the possibility of 'false science', this problematic, as will be discussed in the next section, is not the same as that which concerns positivism or idealism. In the perspective of praxis, the problem is not that of achieving a correspondence between ideas and an independent reality, nor is it the issue of constructing reality in conformity with an evolution of 'pure spirit'. Rather, at the root level of praxis, 'men set themselves only such problems as they can solve',[47] and the specific products of consciousness, as a capacity within, and functional to, praxis, constantly change with the fulfilment of need and the concomitant emergence of potentiality. Marx's epistemological stance can be considered neither positivist nor idealist; and therefore his ideas on the relationship between consciousness and the social cannot be properly interpreted in these terms.

Thus, Marx's conception of knowledge, of the social context and of the relationship between these terms, does indeed emerge in a rather different form from that traditionally assumed by the positivistic critique. If man is defined as ultimately a being of praxis, as an active, intentional, conscious and social being, then a *specific* form and content of consciousness, and a specific form of co-operation or social form, are *co-emergents* from or 'products' of praxis in relation to a specific level of need. And just as Marx makes no ontological distinction between persons and 'society', so the unity of praxis demands that no distinction be made between the process and products of consciousness, and the process and product of social interaction, of co-operation.[48] As argued earlier, the social context, institutions or modes of interaction, are specific forms given to the basic co-operative nature of persons. Thus they are, in a sense, solutions in terms of organization; solutions to basic needs which must be considered meaningful phenomena that are inextricably bound up with the conscious element of praxis and its products. In these terms, knowledge is clearly not an ideal phenomenon rooted in the social context viewed as an existential phenomenon; rather: 'Thought and being are indeed distinct but they also form a unity'.[49]

Thus, the interpretations of Marx's position as positivist, as mechanistic, and even as a narrow economism, are very narrow if not totally mistaken. The presentation of his ideas about the social context and knowledge in a deterministic, relativistic manner, stands in immediate contradiction to his intention in regard to idealism and materialism, and to important aspects of his writing. Rejecting the possibility of such contradiction, this analysis concludes that Marx's work proceeds on the basis of fundamentally different presuppositions than those underlying the critique. These different presuppositions form a basis that grants to practical activity and to human need a basic philosophical significance.

Thus, it must be concluded that Marx's writing does not, with any consistency, imply a sociology of knowledge that would consist simply of the empirical study of the relationship of ideas to social-existential factors. To the contrary, while for Marx there is a problematic to be dealt with in regard to knowledge and the social context, it is not a problematic whose meaning is captured in positivistic terms. At the root level of praxis as reality-for-man, there is fundamentally none but an analytical distinction between the ideational and the social. As Avineri suggests, the proposition that social being determines consciousness is fundamentally tautological, at least when interpreted from a positivistic perspective that ignores essential presuppositions underlying Marx's writing.[50]

Clearly, the interpretation developed to this point is quite general, if suggestive, in relation to the sociology of knowledge. The intention has been to clarify the presuppositions of Marx's work and this suggests a more consistent framework than was ever fully elaborated in any detail by Marx himself. Indeed, the very lack of full conceptual development, in addition to the fact that many works were not published until long after Marx's death, contributes to the ease with which his work can be interpreted positivistically.[51] Such misinterpretation severely distorts understanding of the Marxian sociology of knowledge, especially in regard to the central concept of alienation, in terms of which the social analysis of ideas acquires its character and meaning. The following section will consider this concept in relation to Marx's presuppositions as presented above. Only then can the Marxian sociology of knowledge and the issues associated with it be adequately delineated.

ALIENATION AND THE SOCIAL ANALYSIS OF IDEAS

Traditionally, the sociology of knowledge has been positivistically oriented to empirical analysis of the relationship between specific ideas, the perspectives or conceptual frameworks in which these ideas are rooted, and some social-existential base to which they can supposedly be imputed. At the most general level, such positivistic study is concerned ultimately to determine propositions or laws describing and explaining how ideas and social factors are related.

In contrast, this particular problem clearly disappears as an empirical issue in Marx's framework. In terms of his basic ontological and epistemological presuppositions, ideas and the social context constitute an integral unity in praxis. Marx, in other words, *presumes* the existence of a relationship and, further, presumes that this relationship is dialectical in character. That which is an empirical question from the positivistic perspective becomes, within the dialectical perspective, a conceptual question *prior to* any sort of empirical analysis.

If the unity of praxis implies the integral unity of consciousness and the social, what then is the problematic and how is this problematic to be analysed? In other words, within Marx's perspective, what specific problematic is a social analysis of knowledge concerned with, and what must be the specific character of such analysis? Clearly, the problematic is not that of the nature of the relationship itself, for this is presumed, but this does not mean that a sociology of knowledge of a particular genre is absent from Marx's writing.

Essentially, the answers to these questions involve a comprehension of Marx's concern with 'false science', or with the common problematic expressed in slightly different ways by such terms as false consciousness, fetishization, reification, deification – in general the problematic of alienation:

> This crystallization of social activity, this consolidation of what we ourselves produce into an objective power over us, growing out of our control, thwarting our expectations, bringing to naught our calculations, . . . is one of the chief factors in historical development up to the present.[52]

Though continuously present in the texts referred to so far in the analysis, the concept has been intentionally avoided up to this point in order to clarify the presuppositional base from which Marx writes, and in terms of which the concept acquires its meaning. This phenomenon, which concerns an apparent reversal in the basic process of practical objectification or need fulfilment and production, can now be elaborated and used to clarify the specific character of the Marxian sociology of knowledge.

It must be noted that the nature of the problematic denoted by these terms has been considerably abused in the literature since Marx's first conceptualization. In most studies, alienation has acquired a meaning quite the opposite of the meaning intended by Marx. Once again, this is a result and one of the best examples of a positivistic interpretation and use of his work.[53] For Marx, alienation was precisely that concept which captured the problematic character of man's social-natural existence. Alienation describes and explains the apparent lack of correspondence, not between belief on the one hand, and an independent reality on the other; but between the historical *forms* of being generated and the fundamental and dynamic praxical character of authentic human existence.

In *function*, the concept is little different from Durkheim's idea of anomie or Weber's concept of rationalization. However, the concept of alienation is rooted in Marx's own and rather different attempt to resolve the apparent contradiction between the individual and 'society'.[54] To perhaps oversimplify, Marx argued that capitalism was a particular and historically specific mode or form of praxis. It was a system of social relationships, ideas and techniques through which men produced their means of subsistence. However, it was also a system or order that had become a 'system of alienation'.[55] It was a historical situation in which men fetishized their products and reified the ideas objectified in these products; whether they be material goods, forms of social relationship, philosophical systems, religions, etc.[56] More simply, capitalism was a system in which certain needs were (or had been) fulfilled, but in which new needs or potentialities were ignored. The system was therefore self-contradictory in that the human social element, which was its basis, was ultimately lost sight of, as concretely evidenced in hardening class distinctions and exploitation, persistent or growing poverty, the business cycle, and so forth.

Unlike Durkheim, Marx did not comprehend the situation as anomic or normless; in fact, capitalism was viewed as a system that had rather clear-cut norms.[57] If, for Durkheim, the negative, unjust character of nineteenth-century society lay in a lack of consistent social constraint by society over men, for Marx the negative arose precisely from 'too much' constraint of a particular kind. This particular constraint, captured in the idea of alienation, involved the apparent denial of the basic reality and process of praxis.

Centrally, alienation denotes an historical situation, or social form, in terms of which specific interaction, thought and production seem to deny, rather than to fulfil or develop, the human species. To refer to a previous section: as beings of praxis, men produce their means of subsistence; that is, they must actively appropriate and modify nature to fulfil their needs, and this to a degree evidenced by no other species. Such production is always a social production that is mediated and augmented by consciousness, and which results not only in the fulfilment of present need but in the creation of new need or potential. However, the history of the human species, in regard to its self-production through the realization of potentialities, has not been an automatic or smooth process. Rather, the process has been continuously distorted and fettered by alienation; by situations in which specific forms given praxis (specific modes of thought developed, specific structures given social interaction, specific material products relevant to existing needs) are not transcended, thus hampering the realization of potentialities.

Marx argues, for example, that under capitalism in the mid-nineteenth century

> The worker becomes poorer the more wealth he produces and the more his production increases in power and extent. The worker becomes an even cheaper commodity the more goods he creates. The devaluation of the human world increases in direct relation with the increase in the value of the world of things.[58]

Though this statement refers specifically to the actual results of capitalist production, or to the specific character of alienated being at this time for the mass of men,[59] it also captures the general, historical character of the problematic. At this general level the 'economic substructure' or level of praxis seems to result in its own denial. In other words, the worker, man himself as producer of the means of subsistence and therefore of himself, becomes devalued and poorer, rather than richer in human value within particular forms of praxis. This occurs despite the fact that the realm of 'products', which includes not only material goods, but also institutions, ideas and values, continues to become richer in the sense of possibilities to be realized. The existing form of praxis is no longer but a means to the fulfilment of needs which must be transformed in any realization of potentialities. Rather, the existing form of praxis, a specific structure, becomes identified as praxis, and identified with the nature of the species, thereby denying in some manner the dynamic character of reality-for-man.[60]

> This fact implies that the object produced by labour [by praxis], its product [the historical form given praxis], now stands opposed to it [to praxis] as an alien being, as a power independent of the producer. It is just the same as in religion. The more of himself man attributes to God the less he has left in himself. The worker puts his life into the object, and his life [under the circumstances of alienation] then belongs no longer to himself

> but to the object. . . . The life *which he has given to the object* sets itself against him as an alien, hostile force.[61]

Of course, as beings of praxis, men must by definition 'objectify' themselves, or create objects ranging from material products to ideas and forms of interaction, in order to survive and develop as a species. This is no more than a restatement of 'man is the producer of the means of his own subsistence'. But this objectification, though necessary to life and development, tends to be alienated from us; tends to develop into a situation in which we literally forget the true character of objects (even objects of nature in terms of how they are comprehended) as human, social constructions; as contingent and changeable; and as powerless, save through the medium of human action.[62]

As Marx maintains throughout his work, it is precisely the goal of his conceptual and empirical analyses, including the analysis of ideas in relation to social form, to comprehend this apparent contradiction between alienation and praxis, and to explain it as a prologue to its transcendence.[63] The clearest and most detailed development of this problematic, on a conceptual level, is presented in the *Manuscripts*. Here Marx outlines four basic and interdependent aspects of alienation which parallel the aspects of praxis already discussed.

First and centrally, men become alienated from the process of production itself, a process that Marx also calls the alienation of men from themselves, from their species-nature as producers of the means of subsistence:

> This is the relationship of the worker to his own activity as something alien and not belonging to him . . . as an activity which is directed against himself, independent of him and not belonging to him.[64]

To be thus alienated from the process of production or from one's self is to be in a situation wherein

> labour is external to the worker, i.e. it does not belong to his essential being; . . . in his work, therefore, he does not affirm himself but denies himself. . . . He is at home when he is not working, and when he is working he is not at home. His labour is therefore not voluntary, but coerced; it is forced labour. It is

> therefore *not the satisfaction of a need; it is merely a means to satisfy needs external to it.*[65]

In other words, in terms of the idea of praxis, it is man's fundamental nature to work; that is, to produce means of subsistence and to be self-developing. Thus, one is alienated from one's basic nature in so far as one works, not to fulfil this nature, but simply to obtain the means to the fulfilment of other needs – the essential need or end becomes but a means to survival. Such a condition most clearly holds in capitalist society wherein the majority of men do not control but sell their labour-power to others, others who control and direct the process of production.

A second aspect of the problematic involves the estrangement of the specific products or objectifications which result from the productive process. And it is an aspect of alienation quite inseparable from the first, for

> the product is . . . but the summary of the activity of production. . . . In the estrangement of the object is merely summarized the estrangement, the alienation, in the activity of labour itself.[66]

In praxis, objectifications, or objects and forms produced, are understood as a fulfilment of needs on the one hand, and on the other, as making possible the appearance and realization of new needs; they are but contingent means in this dual sense. Furthermore, they are expressions of man, expressions of his essential powers. However, in a condition of alienation, the relationship is apparently the reverse:

> The alienation of the worker in his product means not only that his labour becomes an object, an external existence, but that it exists outside him, independently as something alien to him, and that it becomes a power on its own confronting him.[67]

In other words, to be alienated in this sense is to be 'subject to', instead of being a subject in control of the objects produced by one's labour. What a man produces in praxis is his 'capital'; is that which he creates to fulfil his needs, and which he 're-invests', as it were, in his own further development. In alienated production, the product no longer belongs to the worker, it is no longer an expression of himself or in his control:

> It is no longer the labourer that employs the means of production but the means of production that employs the labourer. Instead of being consumed by him as material elements of this productive activity, they consume him as the ferment necessary to their own life-process.[68]

This condition is most fully developed under capitalism, wherein the worker himself becomes an object, and no longer a subject; that is, wherein individuals themselves become but 'factors' in production.

It should be noted that the 'objects' referred to are not simply material objects, or what we normally think of as commodities produced by men. Recalling that reality in praxis is always reality-for-man, it is significant that Marx includes, in this aspect of alienation, man's very comprehension of natural objects; this alienation, 'is at the same time [an alienation of] the relationship to the sensuous external world, to natural objects. . . .'[69] This becomes clearer in relation to a third, interdependent aspect of alienation, the alienation of man's very species-being or self-conscious being, which is also an essential aspect of praxis.

Within praxis, consciousness is a functional moment in need fulfilment, in interaction, and is essential to the awareness of potentialities or new needs. However, with alienation this relation appears to be reversed:

> Consciousness, which man has from his species, is transformed . . . so that species-life becomes only a means for him. Thus alienated labour turns the species-life of man, and also nature as his mental species-property, into an alien being and into a means for his individual existence.[70]

Once again the idea is expressed that under alienation, the fundamental, dynamic nature of human life as praxis is apparently denied. Consciousness specifically in this instance ceases to be an advantage over other animals and instead becomes a disadvantage.[71] Ideas become reified; they are no longer understood as expressing contingent and fluid meanings within praxis, and instead are reduced to reflections of the existing form of praxis. Thought ceases to be concerned with the possible, or with development, and instead is rendered 'but a means for existence':

> For labour, life activity, productive life now *appear* to man only

> as a means for the satisfaction of a need, the need to maintain physical existence. Productive life is, however, species-life. It is life creating life. In the type of life activity resides the whole character of a species, its species-character; and, free, conscious activity is the species-character of human beings. Life appears only as a means of life.[72]

Finally, whereas the reality of praxis involves the essential sociality of man, alienation involves the apparent destruction of the social character of human life:

> Every self-alienation of man, from himself and from nature, appears in the relation which he postulates between other men and himself and nature. Thus religious self-alienation is necessarily exemplified in the relation between laity and priest. . . .[73]

This aspect of alienation is expressed in the a-social or a-cooperative, class/exploitation relationships between men within the system of capitalism. It involves an emphasis on relations of competition and domination rather than on co-operation; and it involves a division of labour in which men tend to identify each other in terms of what they have and what they do; that is, relationships in which men become objects and means for one another, rather than a completion of each other's social nature.[74]

Together, these interdependent aspects of alienation directly parallel and are, in a particular sense, the opposite of the reality presumed by Marx; the reality of praxis as man's essential and dynamic nature. To repeat: the description of what an alienated existence entails is a description of the problematic of human social existence that Marx is concerned to understand and transcend. In general, it may be argued that his studies amount to: (*a*) an attempt to expose the alienated character of especially the capitalist system – a description of the discrepancy between existing forms of life and praxis; and (*b*) an attempt to account for the historical emergence of such a situation but, precisely as a part in, and preview to its intentional negation.

SUMMARY AND IMPLICATIONS FOR A SOCIOLOGY OF KNOWLEDGE

Within this general orientation, the analysis of ideas in relation to the social can only be one particular, though essential aspect of the overall concern of dialectical social analysis. As well, the specific character of a social analysis of ideas within this perspective can only be a critique of 'knowledge'; that is, an attempt to expose the reified or alienated aspects of consciousness as themselves an aspect of the overall 'system of alienation', and in relation to a criterion rooted in the conception of human life as praxis.

To elaborate, it has been argued that the assumed nature of human life for Marx is that of praxis. This idea presents man as an essentially social being who must intentionally and consciously modify nature in order to fulfil needs. Praxis is, however, a dynamic process in which the fulfilment of present needs constantly opens up new possibilities whose realization requires the transformation and transcendence of these products including the forms of social relationship and specific ideas that are, or have been adequate in the present. Man's specific species-being, or self-conscious being, is considered an essential moment in relation to fulfilment of present need, and in relation to the recognition and realization of possibility. In other words, consciousness is an interdependent and essential aspect of praxis and it therefore forms an integral unity with man's social being.

However, men can be falsely conscious; to be alienated involves, along with other aspects, the reification or crystallization of a specific content of consciousness. When this occurs, consciousness, as indeed the form of activity, no longer contributes to the dynamic process of praxis; rather, it becomes a limitation or fetter on the realization of possibilities. Men then act for the most part in terms of crystallized definitions or intellectual formulae about their world, their relationships and themselves; the dynamic aspect of knowing within praxis appears to have been negated.

Thus, it is concluded that within the perspective of praxis, a social analysis of knowledge is primarily an attempt to point out the reified character of ideas. It is a *critical* analysis of existing ideas that are generally and uncritically accepted as true in every-day life.[75] It is presumed that ideas are dynamic (and thus contingent) at the level of praxis. Thus, the central and specific question concerns why ideas do not always and readily change in relation to the problematics faced by men. The answer to this question involves the problematic of alienation, and entails the critical investigation of existing ideas. Specifically, such critical investigation of what is taken to be knowledge must involve the demonstration of: (*a*) its reified character in relation to persistent human problems; (*b*) its role within the persistence of the total system of alienation; and (*c*) its reciprocal 'determination' or reinforcement by other factors within this totality.

In other words, given that the essence of human life and reality is praxis, and thus that the activity of the analyst himself can only be meaningful as a part of praxis, then the sociological study of 'knowledge' becomes a critique rooted in, and validated in relation to, the actuality of praxis. An important qualification is, of course, that such analysis is only partial—it must be supplemented by, and is interdependent with, the critical analysis of other social forms, and both, for Marx, must entail practical activity. In general,

> It is the task of history, . . . once the other-world of truth has vanished, to establish the truth of this world. The immediate task of philosophy, which is in the service of history [praxis], is to unmask human self-alienation in its secular form now that it has been unmasked in its sacred form. Thus the criticism of heaven is transformed into the criticism of earth, the criticism of religion into the criticism of law, and the criticism of theology into the criticism of politics.[76]

This 'programme' is clearly different from that of the sociology of knowledge, or, for that matter, of sociology in general, when positivistically conceived. A positivistic sociology of knowledge attempts to construct empirically verifiable, universal and a-historical 'knowledge' in the form of general laws which are presumed to govern the hypothesized relationship between ideas and social-existential factors. It thus cannot help but carry the self-contradiction of relativism as discussed earlier. Marx, in contrast, does accept the premise of an integral, and in fact, necessary relationship between ideas and social relationships, but he presumes the nature of this relationship as a dialectical, interpenetrating unity within praxis.

Thus the object of analysis for the positivistic sociologist of knowledge disappears in the Marxian perspective. Instead, the problematic of alienation is introduced in terms of which the concern of the analyst, himself a being of praxis, shifts to the apparent dysjunction that develops within the presumed dynamic unity. From this point of view, what is 'discovered' as law, and considered knowledge by the positivist, becomes but the description of existing relations within alienation, and indeed, becomes a part of the very reification of existing consciousness that it is essential to transcend.[77]

The main conclusion to be drawn from this analysis is that Marx's work does contain the elements of a sociology of knowledge in which there is no contradiction between his epistemological stance and the insight that knowledge and the social context are integrally and positively interpenetrating. However, the type of analysis that is implied has a character quite divergent from the mode of analysis demanded by the positivistic perspective. The Marxian perspective does not view knowledge as something existing separate from activity, or something which is to be validated according to particular intellectual canons of objectivity. Rather, consciousness and its content is understood as an interpenetrating and functional moment within praxis, which is, in fact, constantly validated in relation to the developing process of practical activity itself. The task of a sociology of knowledge does not end with a description of how specific ideas and perspectives are related to social divisions within praxis. In contrast, it constitutes a critical evaluation of such ideas to discover the extent to which they are reified; and thus the extent to which they constitute a limitation on the dynamic character of praxis within an intention of transcending such limitations.

This is not to say that the Marxian perspective in this regard is complete or fully developed. Specific questions remain and these must be considered before proceeding with the analysis of Mead.

LIMITATIONS WITHIN THE MARXIAN FRAMEWORK

It was noted earlier that even Marx's most sympathetic critics agree that his position is not as unambiguous as is perhaps suggested above, and that there are grounds within his own work to support a positivistic interpretation of his perspective. This study is not so much concerned with this question *per se*, as it intends to draw out of the framework those elements that appear fruitful in the development of an adequate sociology of knowledge according to the parameters laid out in the first chapter. However, there is a specific formulation of this ambiguity in Marx's work that bears on the adequacy and completeness of the critical orientation which has been derived so far. Centrally, this concerns the absence of any clear elaboration of the relationship between praxis as reality and alienation as an apparent denial of this reality. The issue can best be discussed by way of a brief review of the major elements so far considered.

In the first place, Marx has characterized the authentic existence and essence of man in terms of the idea of praxis. The natural and authentic problematic of human life is therefore social man's interaction with and humanizing of nature; his historical transformation of nature (and therefore of himself as a part of nature) which is both a sustainment of life and its constant development. This situation is, *in itself*, not theoretically problematic for Marx; rather, it is the essence of historical being. Man is basically a problem-solver in this sense. Furthermore, consciousness is assumed to be an integral part of this process, as is its constant change, as 'tested' continuously in relation to human need, to nature as the object of need satisfaction, and to potentiality.

What *is* problematic concerns man's propensity for alienation, his propensity for losing sight of his essence and for submerging himself in, and subjugating himself to, the momentary and historically contingent product of praxis, or the form that praxis is given. Within this problematic of alienation, the reification of consciousness is an integral component, and the specific subject-matter of a social analysis of knowledge. Social analysis, in general, is therefore understood as valid when it is an effort to comprehend and to change or transcend this alienated existence; when it is an integral part of praxis itself. Marx's work amounts to such a study in regard to his analysis of capitalism as a 'system of alienation'.

However, Marx tends simply to *state* the position on alienation, and then moves directly to specific critiques. He fails to conceptualize, at least not with any clarity, the process and appearance of alienation itself.[78] Without such clarification, it would appear that there is a basic contradiction or at least an incompleteness in the critical perspective. On the one hand, Marx presumes the nature of human reality as an on-going, continuous process of change in respect to dialectically related material products, social forms, ideas and values. On the other hand, this process is apparently *not* continuous; the problematic of alienation intervenes. But why does this occur? What is the connection between praxis and alienation that would explain the latter, and to what degree does alienation deny praxis? If praxis is a continuous process in which 'men set themselves only such problems as they can solve', then what is the basis in praxis itself, for the emergence of this problematic?

In so far as these questions are not answered in Marx's own work, it could be argued that the concept of alienation, as a problematic specific to human life, is simply an *ad hoc* or residual category, tacked on to, yet logically inconsistent with, the theory of praxis. Alienation could be considered an idea that is inconsistent with the 'utopian' flavour of the idea of continuous development, yet none the less an idea that is necessary in order to account for the historical experience of discontinuity and tension in human history. The idea of praxis presumes the integral unity of thought and the social aspects of human life, as well as the more general assumption of the unity of individual and society contained in the notion of man as a social being. Alienation, on the other hand, concerns the historical experience of the apparent absence of this unity; for example, the recurrent tension between the individual, his thought and the demands of social form. The logical link between such seemingly disparate conceptions of situations is essential to any adequate critical theory, yet it is not clearly developed within Marx's own writing.[79]

This issue is compounded in so far as Marx himself is not consistent in regard to the efficacy and necessity of critical analysis and, therefore, is not consistent in regard to the centrality of the presuppositions captured in the notion of praxis. On the one hand, he remains within the presuppositions elaborated in the previous sections in so far as he demands critical reflection both on the form of production that has been developed to any point in time, and on the ideas supporting that form, as a prelude to and essential element of negation and change. On the other hand, however, passages can be found in his work which involve or imply a suggestion that action must necessarily be predicated on 'material' or mechanistic developments in situations.[80] In other words, he tends to reduce the dialectical character of praxis to its 'material' side, and thereby to de-emphasize the importance of the understanding and intentional activity which are integral elements of praxis.

In relation to a social-critical analysis of ideas, this problem involves an apparent reduction of consciousness to epiphenomenal status; from a mechanistic point of view, consciousness ceases to have any integral role in change: change in ideas simply follows from or is determined by changes in 'material factors'. It follows immediately that a concern with the critical analysis of reified ideas within alienation is rendered meaningless, or at least inessential. This, in turn, raises a question as to how seriously one should take the idea of praxis and the presuppositions it entails.

It is precisely these aspects of Marx's work that allow, and support, the traditional positivistic interpretation of his stance, and thus its reduction to some form of economic or historical determinism. In regard to the specific question of the explanation of alienation, this interpretation is reflected in the positivistic conclusion that alienation must be 'caused by' material factors, and is therefore only overcome as these factors themselves change according to historical, impersonal laws of economic development.[81] However, as an answer to the question of the existence of alienation, this formulation is inadequate, if only because it implicitly rejects the presupposed nature of human life as praxis. Such a causal interpretation of the phenomenon does not demonstrate any consistency with or integral connection between the notions of praxis and alienation which at the same time does not deny the basic character of praxis.

Some writers have argued that this problem would have been resolved if Marx had developed a conceptualization of the basis on which men – who are alienated – none the less contain a 'need to rebel' against inauthenticity *despite* the denial of praxis supposedly entailed by alienation. On the assumption that it is this particular question that is not answered in Marx's work, various answers have been proposed, answers which range from Marcuse's use of Freud's notion of repression, to Engel's and Lenin's use of material forces in a positivistic sense.[82]

The common element in these efforts involves the acceptance of the idea, supposedly consistent with Marx's thought, that alienation can conceivably be a 'total' phenomenon, and thus a total denial of praxis. However, it is clearly contradictory to hold that alienation could develop to a point wherein praxis itself, the very nature of human being, could be totally negated; to the point wherein 'inauthenticity' replaces 'authenticity'. In terms of the moment in praxis of self-consciousness, this is to raise the question as to whether or not consciousness can be totally reified and inadequate. If this were a possibility, the supposed inauthentic becomes the authentic, and the question of realizing one's alienated condition becomes impossible, except perhaps in mechanistic terms, and this implies the necessity of a theoretical appeal to factors outside of praxis.

If consciousness in particular can be totally reified or negated at the fundamental level of praxis, then the essential if partial role it has in the dynamics of praxis, in rendering sub- and super-structure contradictory, disappears. Marx would thereby have contradicted the presuppositions of his work, as many critics claim he does, and it would have to be agreed that his 'youthful' solution to the man/society duality is superfluous to, and inconsistent with, his 'mature' and apparently mechanistic doctrine.[83] Specifically, his own concern to produce a recognition of alienation (and thereby of the need to rebel) through analysis, and his various attempts to organize opposition to capitalism, would have to be viewed as superfluous to the mechanistically conceived, inevitable clash of forces and relations of production.

However, there is an alternative to this view that a situation of alienation implies a total dysjunction in, or denial of praxis. In contrast, it is possible to argue that alienation, as the problematic, can be conceived as a condition *co-existing with* but never totally negating praxis. There are several considerations that lend support to this interpretation. First, to argue that alienation and praxis co-exist allows one to remain consistent with Marx's basic presuppositions as to the nature of reality-for-man. Second, this interpretation reflects the continual usage of the term 'appearance' in Marx's discussion of the various aspects of alienation,[84] a characterization that is supported by numerous passages which imply the persistence of the moments of praxis, despite such appearances to the contrary. For example, Marx argues that

> Social activity and social mind by no means exist only in the *form* of activity or mind which is directly communal. *Nevertheless*, communal activity and mind, i.e. activity and mind which express and confirm themselves directly in a real association with other men, occur everywhere this direct expression of sociability arises from the content of activity or corresponds to the nature of mind.
>
> Even when I carry out scientific work, etc., an activity which I can seldom conduct in direct association with other men, I perform a social, because human, act.[85]

Third, in any consideration of the character and basis of change, or transcendence of alienation, it must be kept in mind that this is conceptualized by Marx as involving the development of contradictions between 'the *three* moments; the forms of production; the state of society *and* consciousness'.[86] In other words, the transcendence, or negation of alienation, is precisely a matter of praxis itself; and praxis can only be comprehended in terms of each of its elements and in terms of their reciprocal relationships. The forces of production do not develop independently of human consciousness, and the relations of production, as a particular form or state, are themselves a productive force.[87]

Thus, in this possible formulation, while the products or objectifications of praxis may become problematic, their alienation or 'loss' cannot totally negate any of the interrelated moments of praxis itself – the products become 'fetters' to be comprehended and removed, not the 'authentic' reality. In terms of Marx's idea of praxis, the 'need to rebel', or the need to change, is itself an integral and presumed part of the basic human reality. Therefore, the central question that is not adequately answered in Marx's own work is not a question of the location, nature and basis of a 'need to rebel', but is a question of how men come to realize the *discrepancy* between the *on-going* level of praxis and the level of products or objectifications that have been and are continuously alienated; for example, the discrepancy between consciousness integral to on-going praxis and reified ideas or false-consciousness.

Stated in this form, however, a prior question is implied – the precise question that Marx himself posed but did not fully or adequately answer: 'How does it happen . . . that man alienates his labour, his essential being? *How is this alienation founded in the nature of human development*?'[88] The usual answer given this question involves some reference to 'society' or to various economic forces which supposedly alienate man. However, this type of response falls prey, as indicated above, to the deterministic and positivistic interpretation of Marx's work. Such a formulation reintroduces the contradiction with the presuppositions of Marx's position precisely by granting the concept of society, or technology, an ontological status and a power that it cannot have independently of the activity of men.

Clearly, Marx himself does not ask only or simply *what* alienates man, but, rather, *why* man alienates himself as a being of praxis. For example, he argues that

> although private property [a social factor] *appears* to be the basis and cause of alienated labour, it is rather a *consequence* of the latter; just as the gods are fundamentally not the cause but the product of confusions of human reason. *At a later stage* however, there is a reciprocal influence.[89]

This comment does not of course explain nor describe why human labour or praxis is alienated in the first place; however, it does suggest the inadequacy of the more standard answers. And, though the necessary elaboration of the relationship between praxis and alienation as a limitation is not readily apparent in Marx's writing, at least it is suggested that this has something to do with 'the nature of human development'.[90]

In summary, the argument to this point has explicated the basic presuppositions of Marx's position. Second, it has demonstrated that the position demands that appropriate social analysis be critical analysis, referred to and rooted in the reality of praxis. For example, since, at the level of praxis, there is an integral unity between consciousness and social being, the analysis of what is taken to be knowledge in relation to the social context can only be a critique of consciousness in terms of its adequacy or inadequacy in relation to praxis. Such analysis follows not only from Marx's presuppositions, but from his conception of the essential problematic of human existence, which is captured in the term 'alienation'.

But, as indicated, it is precisely at this point that the incomplete and unclear aspects of Marx's work most clearly emerge and render it susceptible to the positivistic critique. Marx posits praxis, he posits alienation, and then his work shifts immediately to a critique of capitalism as a system of alienation. Too many questions about the nature of the problematic, and about its persistent occurrence, are left unanswered in relation to the dynamic, on-going character of praxis. This results in a tendency to concentrate on the apparently deterministic, 'reciprocal influence' of alienated products, with insufficient emphasis on the process itself; the emphasis is on certain factors important in the maintenance of alienation, and foremost among these are the alienated products themselves. As a result, too little attention is paid to the element of consciousness in these products, and this results in the inconsistent denigration of the integral and necessary role of consciousness in praxis. In turn, this gives the analysis a mechanistic tone; a tone that emerges, for Marx himself, as a hesitancy in regard to the possibility of intentional efforts in change.

Clearly, if one is to hold that critique is the essence of social analysis (because such study is of contingent products in terms of their relevance to the producers), and that the critical study of what is taken to be knowledge is legitimate and essential (as Marx obviously did in terms of his constant critique of the ideas of the political economists), then one must have a clear conceptualization of the process of alienation, which is the basis of the meaningfulness of the approach.

It is in these terms that Mead's work becomes important and it is to his ideas that the study now turns.

chapter 3

G. H. Mead: the perspective of social behaviourism and the sociology of knowledge

If traditional, materialist interpretations of Marx's writing do not promise a great deal with respect to problems in the sociology of knowledge, this is even more the case in terms of traditional interpretation of Mead's work.[1] Both critics and proponents of Mead's 'symbolic interactionist' perspective have tended to interpret his insights in clearly positivistic terms, in terms that reduce man and thought to the status of derivations of a prior, 'more real', existential social reality.[2] This is to argue that Mead presents an 'oversocialized conception of man',[3] a sociologistic perspective that disregards non-social determining factors on the one hand, and, on the other, tends to devalue reason and exclude the human experience of freedom, volition, responsibility and creativity.[4] In these terms, Mead's writing can be accused of the self-contradiction of relativism since it ties knowledge to the social context.

To complicate matters, Mead and subsequent interactionists have been attacked from the opposite direction as well. Critical theorists who trace their ideas to Marx interpret Mead's perspective as idealistic; they argue that his position contains no appreciation of the socio-structural constraints on activity and reflexion.[5] In particular, they point out that in respect to social change, Mead ignored the conflictual, intentional and active side of the process in favour of an overriding emphasis on continuous, largely unproblematic social evolution.[6] In these terms it is often argued that Mead's writing is 'untouched by a concern with alienation' and thus contains no problematic in which to base a critical sociology of knowledge.

Despite these interpretations and criticisms, various writers continue to propose a basic compatibility between the work of Marx and Mead as well as the suggestion that a synthesis of their ideas will be fruitful in relation to issues in the sociology of knowledge. If these proposals are meaningful then a third interpretation of

Mead's perspective must be possible and it is the task of the present chapter to explore this possibility.

Furthermore, it is the task of this chapter to carry out this exploration within the constraints that have emerged in the previous discussions of the critique and of Marx's perspective. First, if Mead's insights are to display relevance to issues in the sociology of knowledge, they must be compatible with a conception of objectivity which reflects an underlying social theory of knowledge or epistemological stance. Second, and in terms of the hypothesis of compatibility, Mead's ideas must prove consistent with Marx's critical orientation and with the related concepts of man, social context and thought expressed in Marx's framework.[7]

Mead's work does present more difficulty in these respects than did that of Marx. On the one hand, Mead's ideas, and especially the larger corpus of his work, have not received the same attention from sociologists. On the other hand, his work contains very definite elements which clearly contradict the critical, non-positivistic orientation essential to the sociology of knowledge. None the less, it can be demonstrated that Mead's perspective is of considerable value.

MIND, SELF AND SOCIAL PROCESS: THE SOCIAL THEORY OF MAN

Mead's posthumously published lectures, *Mind, Self and Society*, along with selected articles,[8] are the most well known to sociologists and the most immediate source of ideas that have been considered relevant to the development of sociology. However, while it is fair to say that little of the remaining work is of the same immediate importance, this writing is also the most susceptible to misinterpretation if not read in the context of the total corpus of Mead's work. Almost all of Mead's ideas are present in *Mind, Self and Society*, least implicitly, but they are only fully and less ambiguously developed in his other writings.[9]

Mind, Self and Society begins with a particular question: how can one comprehend specifically human life 'behaviouristically', and yet, at the same time, not deny the existence and essential importance of mind, of reflexivity, of human self-consciousness?[10] Mead is extremely critical of Watsonian behaviourism which, in his opinion, reduces the specifically human to the level of conditioned reactions in terms of biological and physiological mechanisms.[11]

On the other hand, Mead is equally critical of the idealist perspective that would place mind and self totally outside and apart from behaviour, and yet offer no explanation for these phenomena.[12] Mead, like Marx, intended to develop a synthesis of deterministic and idealistic perspectives.

To be more specific, Mead holds that man, like all other species, is himself a part of nature, a part of an assumed 'world that is there'.[13] However, the totality of quantitative distinctions which differentiate him from other living organisms constitutes an essential qualitative difference that must not be lost sight of in the theoretical comprehension of human thought and activity.[14] All organisms, as parts of nature, depend on nature and have a particular, selective relationship[15] with the environment; indeed, some are recognized as having a conscious relationship with nature.[16] The human species, in contrast, is qualitatively different in so far as man's relationship to nature is a *self*-conscious, reflexive relationship.

For men, in Mead's view, the human environment is not simply specific to the physical characteristics and biological needs of the species; it is also an environment that includes man's own responses to it.[17] That is, men are the only beings that can be 'objects for themselves',[18] self-conscious beings who thereby become capable of reflexion. Other animals react to stimuli; men can, in addition, react to themselves as stimuli. This emergent fact in nature, as Mead terms it,[19] is understood as the basis of the ability to inhibit overt and immediate reaction to stimuli, to think or act implicitly, or in mind, before responding overtly and intentionally to the environment. In his view, men thereby acquire a control over their own activity and their environment which is denied to other species.[20]

Clearly, Mead wishes to develop a perspective on human activity that recognizes that the human species is, like other beings, a part of nature, and yet is qualitatively distinct from other beings in acquiring a self-conscious and controlling relationship to nature. However, despite this intention of avoiding the pitfalls of both positivistic reductionism and idealism, it is the opinion of his critics that the resulting perspective is not successful. As noted, Mead is accused by some of developing a sociologistic stance, and by others of constructing a basically idealist image of man and society.[21]

These criticisms can best be understood after first delineating the concepts to which they are directed; the concepts of man, thought, the social and their development that Mead outlines in *Mind, Self and Society*. The critics' concerns can then be clearly elaborated and utilized to identify specific elements of the perspective which are basically problematic, or require further elaboration. These problems can, in turn, be pursued through consideration of the broader context of Mead's thought, as developed in his other works.

As indicated, Mead began with the assumption that the human species is qualitatively distinct from other beings. Men are self-conscious beings; they have selves and minds that are emergent characteristics based in the quantitative differences between themselves and other living species. This emergence of mind and self is understood both as an historical event, in the initial evolution of the species, and as an event which must repeat itself in the biography of each individual.[22] Self and mind are, then, absent at birth; both have a development, which presupposes the prior presence of particular factors.[23]

First, mind and self are rooted in the biological evolution of a highly complex central nervous system, which, in terms of its complexity, is potentially a 'mechanism of implicit response'.[24] The human animal also has greater physical complexity than other species; for example, Mead emphasizes the importance of the hand as mediating our experiences with the 'world that is there'.[25] In addition, he points to the importance of the biologically evolved physical ability to emit and distinguish between a tremendous variation in 'vocal gesture'.[26]

Second, Mead holds that, by nature, the human animal is a 'herd' or social animal like others – a factor that does not necessarily involve greater quantitative development than is the case with other species except that it involves the appearance of a more complex gestural communication.[27] One essential factor that is noted even involves less development than is the case with other animals. This concerns the 'early' birth of the human infant, the consequent lack of 'instinctual patterning' at birth and the long period of dependency on adults.[28] Mead argues that the child is born with relatively undefined 'impulses', as opposed to the highly specific instincts of other animals. This fact, associated with dependency and social context, leaves a broad scope for the 'shaping' of behaviour within human existence.[29]

However, it is the unique combination[30] of these factors in the evolutionary history of the species that results in the emergent capacity, or at least the potential for self-consciousness and, therefore, for minded behaviour or minded and reflexive activity. It is important to phrase it in this manner because for Mead, and as implied by Marx, this capacity not only emerged in the past; it is also a capacity that each person in each generation must realize for himself – mind and self cannot be presupposed historically nor in the biography of any particular individual.

The emergence or realization of this potential depends on the organism occupying 'two or more systems at once': in the broadest sense, the emergence of reflexivity depends on the 'sociality' of the human organism[31] Specifically, the emergence of mind and self depends on the interaction of the 'biologic' being (with the characteristics noted above) with 'others' in an organized or patterned social environment that is characterized by symbolic communication or interaction. Mead argues that it is in this 'observable' interaction that the potentialities of the organism are realized through a process of internalization, a process which, only if broadly understood, can be called 'taking the role of the other'.[32]

The essential moment in this process (and the initial moment in the appearance of mind and self) arises with the ability to 'stimulate one's self as others stimulate one'. To use a simplistic example: the newborn infant, 'driven' by undefined impulses, yet helpless, emits rather undifferentiated cries. The adult responds intentionally to the cry in terms of existing cultural patterns and, in time, establishes specific patterns of response to these 'biologic' gestures of the child[33] – the presentation of the bottle, changing, cuddling, etc. In each case, these patterns are meaningful for the adult and established primarily by the adult.[34] However, at some point in the relationship, the child ceases to be passive in regard to these patterns and begins to cry intentionally for different responses from the adult – a mother is quickly aware of the differences in the crying that subsequently develop. What Mead suggests 'happens' is that at some point the child becomes imaginatively aware of the meaning of his cry; his own cry, as a gesture that he himself can hear, comes to 'stand for' the adult's response, which has become habitual. At the same time, the response comes to 'mean' the biologic discomfort or impulse of which the cry is initially an integral part.

What is required for this 'internalization' to occur involves the combination of factors discussed above: the social aspect, the relational pattern established by the adult, and the biological and physical characteristics outlined, especially the organic complexity allowing such implicit response. Mead also emphasizes the necessity, for the appearance and functioning of mind, of a 'problematic situation' – a break in the habitual pattern established by the adult. He argues that the internalization of what is there externally, of the response of the other to one's gesture as its meaning, occurs when the pattern does not occur normally.[35] At such a point, what is not completed factually, is completed, or potentially completed, imaginatively.

> Here *in the field of behavior* we reach a situation in which the individual may affect itself as its affects other individuals, and may therefore respond to this stimulation as it would respond to the stimulation of other individuals; in other words, a situation arises here in which the individual may become an object in its own field of behavior.[36]

To summarize, the child automatically cries as an outcome of undifferentiated and undefined impulses. This piece of behaviour initially implies only a 'biologic' self which cries – the cry must be seen as part and parcel of the organism and of the organic response. The adult establishes patterned responses to these 'gestures', and through some instance of a break in the routine established, the child is able, given its potentialities, to 'complete' the pattern in 'imagination'. This is, at the same time, the development of 'awareness' of the cry, awareness of self in this minimal respect, and an ability to respond (at least in imagination at this stage) to itself as an object. The 'meaning' of the gesture is clearly external and prior (established by the adult and inherent in the form of the response relationship), and only subsequently becomes internalized.[37] Furthermore, this internalization not only defines the cry as a gesture (renders the gesture significant),[38] it defines the impulse which set free the gesture in the first instance; what one is 'doing', what one 'is', and the possiblity of awareness of either, emerge concurrently through this internalization of the social patterns into which one is born.[39] From this point on, the child is capable, albeit minimally, of gesturing intentionally, of crying for something (the completion of the act established by the parent), and has the primitive rudiments of mind and self. From this point on, the child is qualitatively different from other animal species in terms of how he relates to the 'world that is there'.

Put somewhat differently, Mead suggests that once internalization begins, the child is enabled to take an 'attitude'[40] towards his situation (which now includes himself) and begins, thereby, to be self-consciously 'attentive'[41] to stimuli in the environment – he can begin to 'act' and is not simply reacting to stimuli in terms of some well-defined instinctual or drive structure 'there' at birth. That is, one can act (gesture significantly or meaningfully) 'in order to' elicit a response that one desires from another. Mead argues that a 'conversation of gestures' also occurs between other animals, but that these gestures remain strictly stimuli which call out an instinctual reaction from the other, and which are themselves emitted strictly on an instinctually patterned and reactive basis.[42]

The central point of his argument is that mind is not conceptualized as an entity, but as an emergent and functional ability or process; an ability to 'indicate those things in the environment which answer to responses so that control of responses is possible'.[43] Through mind, through the internalization and organization of responses as attitudes, the individual is able to be attentive to particular characteristics of his situation in terms of possible responses which, for the moment, are carried out 'imaginatively' – the attitude stands for the completed act; it is an idea.[44] Thought or reflexion (human intelligence)[45] is defined, in these terms, as an 'internalized conversation of gestures'.[46] It is a process through which the individual is enabled to choose between alternative responses (in terms of attitudes), in a problematic situation, those particular responses that hypothetically will achieve the end or need desired. The so-called trial-and-error behaviour of animals can therefore take place implicitly or in mind; one can respond with a degree of choice to one's situation.[47] One can, through attitudes, indicate to oneself (be attentive to) those elements (stimuli) in a situation which answer to certain responses that one wants to make before actually responding.[48]

Clearly, the self in the term self-consciousness, emerges concomitantly with mind. As indicated, the response of the other defines not only the gesture but also, and at the same time, the being, the self, which emits the gesture. Mead defines the self as that object which becomes a part of its own environment.[49] He argues that knowing one's self, as a specific object among objects, is only possible by internalizing the responses of others to this object; thereby coming to know what we are as others know us and as they express this knowing in their responses to us. Just as the meaning of things and others is 'there' as an objective, prior relationship between gesture and response, so the meaning of one's self is equally 'there' prior to signification, prior to mindedness.

So far the chapter has outlined the social process of internalization, the emergence of attitudes 'within' the individual, and the implications that this process has for comprehension of meaning, thought and the character of human action as intentional. Clearly, Mead is not arguing that mind and self emerge as a whole or all in a piece, but that these human qualities have a development, a growth, which implies some notion of constant change through interaction. Specifically, he breaks this development down into two basic stages, but it is clearer for the sake of exposition to break these stages down into four.[50]

The first stage was implied in the example of the infant – the internalization, through breaks in patterns of relationship, of specific meanings (responses) as the meaning of the child's own gestures and impulses. At this rudimentary level, the child's self and mind and his world are constituted by specific meanings on a rather simplistic level; specific cries, as significant symbols, stand for specific responses demanded. This stage merges into what Mead termed the 'play stage', a stage during which meanings are organized into specific others, objects or 'rôles'. At this stage the child can 'play at' being another to himself – words like mother, brother, pink rabbit, etc., are understood as meaning or standing for the whole complex of responses that can be called out from, or originate with, or be expected of, those specific others or objects.[51]

The 'game stage' refers basically to further internalization of attitudes and their further organization along broader situational lines. Words such as family or team or game are symbols understood as meaning the whole complex of responses others make in relation to one another and to one's self. Through internalization, the child has built up, within himself, and in a structured manner, the attitudes of all others with whom he is directly implicated.[52] This stage spills over into a fourth stage which Mead designates the 'generalized other' – an internalization and organization of attitudes of the larger social circles or communities in which one is implicated. At this stage of the broadest development of self and mind, the individual knows himself, or is an object to himself, in relation to his class, political party, national group, religious affiliation, particular languages, and so forth.[53]

Mead does not suggest that there is any necessary end point to this process for any particular individual. What one is, what one thinks and how one acts, can constantly change, develop and vary depending on the social situations one is in and, therefore, on the responses of others to one's actions in these situations. The self and mind do not emerge and then become static; they retain their tie to the responses of others in different situations.[54]

As is generally recognized, the social situation or on-going social process within which mind and self emerge and change, is not understood by Mead as a reality '*sui generis*'. Society is not conceptualized as an 'object in itself' which can be studied in formal terms, separate from the interaction of persons.[55] Rather, Mead comprehends man as, biologically, a social being, and this sociality as essential to the emergence of mind and self. The survival of the individual and the species depends on the success of social acts, on the fulfilment of needs in co-operation with others.[56] Indeed, Mead argues that institutions or specific forms of interaction depend upon the organization of attitudes for their 'existence', their continuity *and* their change.[57] It is the social, interactional *process* that is important to Mead, and specific forms of this process are understood as realized solutions to species' problems which require social action for their fulfilment.[58]

Furthermore, Mead attempts to deny this social context any totally determinative character through an explicit differentiation of the self into two separate aspects or dimensions. Though the self is not present at birth and depends for its emergence on the process of internalization, it 'does not consist simply in the bare organization of social attitudes'.[59] Rather, the self has two analytically distinct parts, the 'I' and the 'me':

> The 'I' is the response of the organism to the attitudes of the others; the 'me' is the organized set of attitudes of others which one himself assumes. The attitudes of the others constitute the organized 'me', and then one reacts toward that as an 'I'.[60]

Mead introduces this distinction in terms of its 'significance . . . from the point of view of conduct itself',[61] and then implies that this significance basically refers to the fact that 'we are never fully aware of what we are' and that we often 'surprise ourselves by our own action';[62] that 'this response of the "I" is something more or less uncertain'.[63] Men reflect or think about their situation in terms of internalized attitudes or the 'me' of the self. This alone, of course, implies that what one is and what one can decide to do is rooted in and limited by the *given* meanings one has internalized from the social situations one has experienced, or been a part of. However, the further significance of the 'I' aspect is that it accounts for 'the sense of freedom, of initiative'[64] that man experiences.

In these terms, the freedom of mind is conceptualized as involving the fact that men do not act precisely as they or others think they will act, given reflexion and action strictly in terms of the 'me'.

> The self is essentially a social process going on with these two distinguishable phases. *If it did not have these two phases there could not be conscious responsibility, and there would be nothing novel in experience.*[65]

Mead also argues that the 'I' is always consciously present to an individual himself only as a part of the 'me', as an 'historical figure'.[66] In other words, since the 'I' is the more or less unpredicted actual response of one's self to a situation, it is always known to one's self, as to others, after the fact; 'I cannot turn around quick enough to catch myself.'[67] In this sense, novelty, freedom, initiative, and even responsibility are unpredictable and uncontrolled aspects of life even to the person performing a particular act that can be so labelled. None the less, with this distinction between the 'I' and the 'me', along with the conceptualization of society as process rather than entity, Mead at least attempts to capture the notion that persons are, or can be, more or less, more and other than the on-going social situation which lies at the basis of self and mind.

QUALITATIVE OR QUANTITATIVE DIFFERENCE: THE CRITICISMS OF SOCIAL BEHAVIOURISM

It was suggested earlier that Mead's work contains contradictory elements and that opposing criticisms are directed at his perspective. In this section, Mead's conception of man, thought and the social, will be elaborated further through a discussion of these criticisms.

This will allow the identification of specific problems, which may then be dealt with in relation to the broader context of his writing. The two predominant criticisms appear quite divergent: that Mead presents an 'oversocialized', determinist position, and that he is an idealist, especially in his conception of the nature of social factors and of social change. Interestingly, these criticisms are not totally divergent for they are rooted in the same factors interpreted from different standpoints. Furthermore, these specific factors are those which contradict the overall thrust of Mead's perspective.

It was noted that Mead intended to develop a perspective that captured the qualitative differences between man and other species; a perspective that was neither idealist nor determinist, but which recognized that man was both a part of nature and yet capable of a reflexive and controlling relationship to his environment. However, the degree to which his position can be accepted as non-deterministic, or non-reductionistic, is apparently the degree to which the conception of the self, as involving an 'I' aspect, is convincing.

The 'me' aspect of the self is admittedly and clearly presented as a reflection of the on-going social situation. Mead's justification for introducing the 'I' aspect, at least in *Mind, Self and Society*, is precisely that, without it, the theory could not account for human creativity, responsibility, freedom, intentionality; the qualities that transcend the determinant base. But it is this type of justification that is unacceptable to some critics. In their view, the 'I' is a fictitious element; it is a 'residual' category introduced to account for those experiences for which the 'me' cannot account.[68] The 'I' appears to have no basis in the socialization process itself, which, as Mead argues, is the very basis for the development of self.[69]

Furthermore, the 'I' is almost identical to the notion of chance. It exists as the unintended and unexpected actual action as over and against that which is demanded by the 'me'. It is only known after the fact, in memory, when it has become a part of the 'me'. It is not at all clear how such a concept captures the notions especially of intentionality and responsibility as they have been traditionally understood, and which are involved in man's qualitatively different being.[70]

If the concept of the self as both 'I' and 'me' cannot be maintained, at least in this form, then Mead's perspective does indeed fail to achieve its intended goal. Self and mind, and thus the individual, become reducible to the prior social process. Thought may remain essential to human activity but only as something quantitatively and not qualitatively different from the consciousness of other animal species.[71]

A second and related concern involves the conceptualization of social change as presented in *Mind, Self and Society*; the notion of change as a specific and determinative evolutionary process. Mead argues that man is basically a creature of non-reflexive habit in the absence of any problematics within the social process, and in relation to nature.[72] Social action, based on internalized attitudes, does not require reflexive thought, except in those instances of unexpected response from others or from objects. Thought, or the internalized conversation of gestures, comes into play when the habitual response or action one wishes to carry out is inhibited by contrary stimuli present in a situation, or by failure to achieve the result expected.[73] Under such conditions, reflexion may lead to another response than that habitually expected in that situation, and thus to change in the typical pattern of response. Furthermore, the unpredictability of the 'I' aspect of the self may involve novel elements, and therefore, as well, contribute to change in the typical response, in so far as these new response patterns are internalized by others.[74] As Mead maintains, the social is a process and not an entity.

However, Mead places definite limitations on just what change can occur, and with what success. He does not argue, idealistically, that it is open to men to construct freely whatever socially patterned response he chooses in relation to desired goals. To the contrary, he is quite aware that, as a being dependent on a natural environment, or 'world that is there', the construction of response patterns is limited, if broadly, by the 'patience of nature'.[75]

This limitation is, in itself, not necessarily reductionistic, as will be shown. However, Mead goes further; he argues that the form of social life, or the sum of typical response patterns or of institutions, changes within the limits of a specific evolutionary process.[76] The role of the individual in such change is thereby limited, both to the 'unexpected' contribution of the 'I', as discussed above, and to those novel elements that are eventually accepted by others – his social audience[77] – within the further limitation of 'social progress'. For example, Mead argues that

> it is their possession of minds or powers of thinking which enable individuals to turn back critically, as it were, upon the organized structure of the society to which they belong . . . and to reorganize and reconstruct or modify that social structure to a greater or lesser extent *as the exigencies of social evolution from time to time require.*[78]

The role of mind is, of course, already delineated in terms of the unexpected, novel contribution of the 'I'. But, in addition, the novel contributions must conform to the 'requirements' of a social evolution to which Mead attributes a specific content and form in the future:

> Ultimately and fundamentally societies develop in *complexity of organization* only by means of the *progressive achievement of greater and greater degrees of functional, behavioristic differentiation* . . . or . . . *mere specializations of socially functional individual behavior.*
>
> The human social ideal – the ideal or ultimate goal of human social progress – is the attainment of a universal human society in which all human individuals would possess a perfected social intelligence.[79]

Thus, the reduction to social process that Mead is charged with, while not precisely a sociologistic reduction to 'society' as such, is a reduction, none the less, to the demands of an evolutionary process in nature which is reflected in social form. Furthermore, within the discussion of this process, Mead clearly reduces the future of individuality to an equivalence with the differentiated social function performed by each individual. He suggests that there is, in each of us 'a demand . . . to realize one's self in some sort of superiority over those about us',[80] but this impulse [81] is only 'genuine' and 'legitimate'[82] when, in the course of evolution, it becomes (as it is becoming in his view) formalized as an expression of specialization of interdependent function in the community.[83]

In general, Mead discusses social evolution as a process that has a predictable direction and outcome, at least in terms of functional differentiation and socially functional, individual behaviour. Mead himself argues that this outcome or future follows precisely from 'the basis of the [social behaviourist] theory of the self that we have been discussing'.[84] This would appear to reinforce the opinion that the human capacity for reflexion not only emerges out of the ongoing social process, but that it is also totally subsumed by that process and its predictable future.

The contrary charge, that Mead's position is idealist, is concerned with precisely the same points, though from a slightly different angle. Most specifically, it is argued that the perspective represents a rather naïve appreciation of social structure and of human history; that the perspective has no adequate appreciation of the conflictual nature of human social development.[85]

Mead does of course speak of conflict, but it is conflict understood in terms of unexpected responses from objects and others in relation to the initial attitudes internalized.[86] Such conflict constitutes a problematic for persons that calls forth reflection, reformulation of attitudes and modification of response such that the conflict is removed and action can proceed.[87] Of central importance are those conflicts that arise between persons and groups, especially those resulting from the meeting of persons whose internalized conceptual frameworks differ significantly.

Mead argues that in such social situations the immediate reaction of each group concerns a desire for the preservation of self—not in the physical sense necessarily, but in the sense of a desire to impose one's own content of mind and, therefore, one's own expectations, on the other.[88] Whereas, in the past, such conflicts may have led to the annihilation or subjugation of one group by another,[89] under the impress of social evolution such conflict is supposedly resolved, both by the gradual functionalization of difference and, within this, by the reorganization of the selves involved in the conflict.[90] In other words, Mead argues that, in light of his theory of self, conflict is automatically resolved through an eventual and reciprocal internalization of responses of others in the conflictual situation.

> The reflexive character of self-consciousness enables the individual to contemplate himself as a whole; his ability to take the social attitudes of other individuals and also of the generalized other toward himself within the given organized society of which he is a member, makes possible his bringing himself, as an objective whole, within his own experiential purview; and thus he can consciously integrate and unify the various aspects of his self, to form a single consistent and coherent and organized personality. *Moreover, by the same means, he can undertake*

> *and effect intelligent reconstruction of self or personality in terms of its relations to the given social order whenever the exigencies of adaptation* [e.g. social conflicts] *to his social environment demand such reconstructions.*[91]

Such reformulation of selves, in relation to social conflicts, is more likely under the conditions of functional interdependence which, in Mead's view, apparently constitutes an inevitable historical realization.

One example of such conflicts that Mead alludes to are those

> involving interactions between capital and labour, that is, those in which some of the individuals are acting in their socially functional capacity as members of the capitalist class, which is one economic aspect of modern social organization; whereas the other individuals are acting in their socially functional capacity as members of the laboring class, which is another (and in social interests directly opposed) aspect of that organization.[92]

In his view, this conflict is gradually overcome through the reorganization of selves, a process which is supported by the growing functional interdependence between these classes. In other words, what is required, and what supposedly does occur precisely because of the nature of the development of self and mind of individuals, is the emergence of a common set of attitudes. It is Mead's understanding that the modern labour movement is achieving this; it has broken down caste barriers, has 'brought the situation actually involved before the community', and has enabled others 'to enter into the attitude of the laborer in his function'.[93]

Mead nods to the fact that there 'is not this development of communication so that individuals can put themselves into the attitudes of those whom they affect' to any complete extent.[94] He also notes that existing institutions, or internalized response patterns can be 'oppressive, stereotyped and ultra-conservative'.[95] However, he fails to elaborate these 'insights', and leaves the impression that it is quite simply a matter of time before the general process of social evolution, and, within it, the nature of self development and change, will culminate in the 'ideal society'; the universal society of a common global consciousness and functional interdependence.[96]

In general, these criticisms all point towards the idea that while

Mead attempts to find a place in his theory for the human characteristics and capacities of self and mind, he does not succeed in doing so in any manner which captures the qualitative distinctions between men and other organisms. Though human life is understood as involving reflexive intelligence, such intelligence is apparently only a more elaborate tool involved in the effort to achieve adaptation, both to the physical and to the social environment; environments that change according to evolutionary laws, and which therefore have predictable and determined futures.

BASIC PRESUPPOSITIONS: AN ALTERNATE IMAGE OF SOCIAL MAN

If the criticisms discussed above can be maintained in respect to essential aspects of the theory, then the hypothesis that the Meadian and Marxian frameworks are compatible is, in any major sense, refuted. A position that reduces man and limits the expression of his capacities to reflections of a prior, on-going and determining evolutionary social process, is not compatible with a perspective rooted in the ideas of praxis and alienation.

However, of more immediate importance is the fact that if the criticisms hold, then a fundamental contradiction is introduced into Mead's own work. The adequacy of the criticisms would imply that he lost sight of the fundamental, emergent character of men which he himself maintained and which he accused others of denying. Mead objects to any total reduction of man to psychological and biological processes but, while he sets out to avoid such reductionism, he apparently concludes with a reduction of man to a predictable social evolutionary process. It is important to determine why this is the case and, further, if it is a necessary and consistent part of his perspective.

In *Mind, Self and Society* Mead seems to anticipate his critics. His persistent emphasis on the social as process rather than as a set of absolute determinants, and the division of the self into conservative 'me' and creative 'I' aspects, reflects an attempt to deny any total sociologism. The inadequacy of both these ideas has been considered; on the one hand, the 'I' is not clearly integral to his theory of the social basis of self and mind, and, as well, it reflects the existence of chance more than the existence of what could properly be called freedom, responsibility, creativity, etc. On the other hand, the social process, while itself dependent on a common attitudinal content of minds for its specific form, is in turn characterized as reflective of a specific evolutionary movement of predictable structural outcome.

However, a consideration of the broader context of Mead's writing introduces at least two further, basic and essential considerations that must be taken into account before adequate appraisal of the criticisms of his perspective can be undertaken. First, the 'I'/'me' distinction, as presented in *Mind, Self and Society*, is *not* the sole manner in which Mead attempts to account for the qualitative difference between men and other species. In that work, but only elaborated in his other writing, Mead develops the concept of emergence, and especially the emergence of self and mind, as a fact of nature. Second, and related to this idea, Mead develops an epistemological position that implies that all human thought, including science, is indeed quite distinct from its positivistic/materialist or idealist conceptualizations. It is in this context that Mead clarifies his synthesis of these positions with much less ambiguity. In contrast with this work, the actual contradiction in *Mind, Self and Society* can be more clearly specified and its basis uncovered.

The notion of emergence contains the presupposition that a whole or compound is always greater than the sum of its constituent elements; that a particular emergent whole has unique characteristics that are not inherent in its pre-existent parts, and that the relationship of whole to part is reciprocal, or is a relationship of interdependence.[97]

> When things get together, *there arises something that was not there before*, and that character is something that cannot be stated in terms of the elements which go to make up the combination. . . . In any compound, say water, if we take the elements hydrogen and oxygen separately, we cannot get the character that belongs to the compound in them. There is something that has happened, fluidity and the capacity for satisfying thirst. . . . *When combinations arise, we are in a new world, but that new world has not any mechanical causal relationship to the world out of which it arose.*[98]

Not just physical compounds, however, but life itself is considered by Mead as an emergent reality in nature. The quality of being alive, or of having 'a tendency to be self-maintaining',[99] cannot be understood fully in terms of the non-living elements that are its basis (the questions of the biologist are necessarily different from those of the physicist).[100] Furthermore, in Mead's view, the emergence of life confers on the world a whole new set of characteristics that are only potentially there prior to this emergence; for example, physical objects become food only in the presence of the digestive system of living organisms.[101] Thus, part and emergent whole, the physio-chemical and the living, form and environment, constitute an interdependent unity.

The notion of the 'I' appears to be a rudimentary and inadequate reference to the emergence in nature of human reflexive self-consciousness through the interaction of the living animal form and physical nature, and the interaction of these living forms themselves. Self-conscious or reflexive intelligence is indeed rooted in certain basic elements; physio-chemical elements such as the complex central nervous system, the complexity of the hand, the animal consciousness of men, man's existence as a herd animal and gestural communication. However, self-consciousness is also an emergent reality in itself, which cannot be fully comprehended by analytical reduction to the characteristics of these elements; it is something more and other than its components.[102] The most essential emergent characteristic that renders the human animal qualitatively different from other species is that his own being becomes a part of his environment; that he becomes an object to himself and therefore a subject, both aware of, and in self-conscious control of, his responses.[103]

One essential element in the emergence of self and mind is, of course, the internalization of meanings, the internalization of responses of others, and of things eventually, as the meanings of one's gestures and, in turn, of one's self. This element is that which is initially labelled the 'me' of the self, the *content* of attitudes, in terms of which the *capacity* to be reflexive and to reason before acting emerges. Furthermore, in terms of the idea of emergence, this capacity to reflect is not understood as reducible to a given content, and is therefore not reducible to the on-going social process. The social process is but one element out of which a complete self and mind arise. Thus, Mead is arguing that while the capacity for reflexive intelligence depends upon the internalization process, it is more and other than that process.

As Miller argues, one of Mead's major tasks

> is to show how it is possible for individuals to create or give rise to new ways of acting, to new ideas, new perspectives, and indeed to new universals. To some readers, no doubt, Mead's social behaviorism suggests that his theory not only leads to a reduction of mind and thinking . . . to a social determinism in which whatever the individual thinks, says, or does is determined by society or culture, or the mores, and so forth. Nothing is farther from the truth. *Mead does not have the problem of explaining why it is that individuals are creative despite the fact that every self has a social component and that thinking involves the other. Rather, he shows that it is only because the individual is social that he can be creative.*[104]

The essential point brought out here is that it is precisely a *presupposition* on Mead's part that man is an intelligent, creative being, and that this emergent fact must be the beginning point of any analysis. Mead's specific problem is the conceptual, pre-empirical problem of delineating how this capacity could have arisen, and how it functions within nature. His solution concentrates, in part, on the sociality of human species and on the process of internalization, but within the general presupposition of emergence. Thus, to argue that reflexive intelligence, that self and mind, are rooted in, or presuppose a social, interactional process among other elements is not to argue that the former is reducible to the latter.[105]

Not only is reflexive intelligence not reducible to its social and physical components; consistent with the general idea of emergence, it is also a 'whole' that reciprocally affects its constituent elements. For example, both physical nature and, perhaps more so, the social basis, become interdependent with and, in part, dependent on the reflexive intelligence of men. Simply put, the social context, which is presupposed by mind, becomes interdependent with that mind once it emerges as a part of nature.[106]

This idea is reflected, in turn, in the epistemological position that Mead constructs, a position that is centred on the notion of knowing as an active and interdependent *relationship* between knower and known. To begin with, it must be emphasized that knowing, or specifically human reflexive awareness, is something that emerges historically with self and mind, which is to say that it also is integrally connected with the prior, 'self-maintaining' activity of man as a living organism.[107] Indeed, Mead clearly views thought as a higher-order, or qualitatively different capacity of the human animal to deal with his environment in the fulfilment of both physical and social needs.[108] Human reflexive intelligence is a capacity that is brought into play in the face of problematic situations, or in situations in which desired, habitual or unreflexive action is inhibited in some manner. Thought enables persons to reconstruct their situation imaginatively, or 'in mind', before responding overtly; the so-called trial and error reactions of other species are carried out implicity or in mind.

> Knowing is an *undertaking* that always takes place within a situation that is not itself involved in the ignorance or uncertainty that knowledge seeks to dissipate. Knowledge is *not then to be identified with the presence of a content in experience. . . . Knowledge is a process in conduct that so organizes the field of action* that delayed and inhibited responses may take place. The test of the success of the *process of knowledge*, that is, the test of truth, is found in the *discovery or construction* of such objects as will allow conduct to proceed. . . . Reflection is the operation of inference in the field of ideation, i.e. the functioning as symbols of contents and characters of things, by means of which construction of objects sought can be carried out.[109]

Mead explicitly rejects the positivistic, 'copy' or 'correspondence' theory of knowledge in this passage.[110] Nature is a 'world that is there' apart from mind, but it cannot be known, in itself, as a reflection in mind. Reality is always reality-for-man in that knowing is an active, selective 'process' and 'undertaking'. Furthermore, what is understood as reality is not solely determined by what can possibly be known, but as well and fundamentally, by the needs of men whose fulfilment has become problematic.

Perception is never a raw reflection of data, nor a simple effect in the organism.[111] Rather it contains, at once,

> all the elements of the act – the stimulation [or impulse], the response represented by the attitude and the ultimate experience which follows upon the reaction, represented by the imagery arising out of past reactions. It is a *process* of sensing . . . *itself an activity.*[112]

What is seen is therefore always

> a *hypothetical*, hence future, *accomplishment* of an *initiated* process to be tested by contact experience. . . . *The environment around an individual is a set of such hypotheses* . . ., objects which then [have] . . . a *provisional* assurance which may be shaken at any moment.[113]

Reality-for-man is, in these terms, a reality of perspectives of the individuals involved – perspectives that contain more or less common elements or attitudes or 'hypotheses'.[114] Furthermore, such realities are understood as 'means' – means to achieve the ends of persons that have this capacity for reflexive perception.[115] Thus, in general terms, knowing is a *relationship* between the 'world that is there' and the need to organize perception so that 'delayed and inhibited responses may take place', or so that problematic situations (from the point of view of species' needs), may be overcome and ends achieved.

It is essential to note, as well, that Mead further and carefully distinguishes between 'knowledge' and 'information':

> *Information* is the experience arising from the direction of attention through the gestures of others to objects and their characters [the 'me' aspect of self] and cannot be called 'knowledge' if that term is denied to perception as immediate experience under the direction of the attention springing from the organic interest of the individual. Perception is not itself to be distinguished from information in so far as one uses a social mechanism in pointing out objects and characters to himself as another. The perception of a self may be already in the form of information. . . . Knowledge, on the other hand, *deliberately fashions* objects whose reality it tests by observation and experiment. The justification for this is found in the actual disappearance of objects and their characters in the problems that arise in conduct.[116]

Mead understands the scientist in these latter terms, as a person responding to problematic situations by an active construction of hypothetical objects, which are then tested in experience. He does not picture the scientist as cumulatively building an accurate and final picture in correspondence with the 'world that is there'.[117] Though he is in high praise of the efforts of 'science', it is precisely the essential character of it as a critical, probing *activity* in response to problematics of life that he is attached to[118] – not any specific causal, positivistic framework that is often involved in the self-understanding of science.

> The experimental scientist, apart from some philosophic bias, is not a positivist. He has no inclination to build up a universe out of such scientific data. . . . The reference of his data is always to the solution of problems in the world that is there about him. . . . Nothing would more completely squeeze the interest out of his world than the resolution of it into the data of observation.[119]

Further, the activity of even the physical scientist is a social activity:

> The analysis of experimental science, including experimental psychology, never operates in a mind or experience that is not social, and by the term 'social' I imply that in the thought of the scientist the supposition of his mind and his self always involves other minds and selves as presuppositions and as standing upon the same level of existence and evidence.[120]

One further aspect of the human conscious relationship to nature must be considered before proceeding to a discussion of the implications of these ideas for Mead's social theory of man. This concerns the notion, mentioned above, that *knowing changes* or is a process of changing the world for men in which it, as an emergent capacity or activity, takes place.

> A world within which an essential scientific problem has arisen is a *different* world from that within which this problem does not exist, that is, different from the world that is there when this problem has been solved.[121]

Mead adheres to the assumption 'that the *world that is there* is a *temporal* world; i.e. that it is continuously *passing*, or is a world of events'.[122] Thus, reality-for-man is always, and necessarily, 'contingent' in this sense; as well as in the sense that perception and the construction of objects is always a hypothetical relationship to the world that is there. Man's emergent consciousness, his ability to indicate things to himself as attitudes, enables him to stretch out the immediate and passing 'knife-edge' present by means of 'memory and anticipation'.[123] However, this ability to extend the 'specious present' of the organism does not rule out the contingency of the future (nor of the past, for that matter').[124] 'Knowing' something may be functional for man at the moment and adequate for some time in the future, but it is always uncertain, hypothetical. Problematics arise in the passage of events and are or can be solved only through active reconstruction of the content of mind, and therefore through a change in the pre-problematic perspective to a greater or lesser extent.

Thus Mead argues that the truth or objectivity of a perspective, and of particular ideas, is relative to the capacity it affords man to satisfy his needs actively, and to the period of time during which this is unproblematic.[125] With passage in nature, perspectives lose their 'objectivity', and the world must be constructed anew, at least in respect to those aspects that have become problematic.[126] Thus, the prediction of future events is also fundamentally contingent and always hypothetical:

> Things emerge; and emerge in the mechanical order of things, which could not have been predicted from what has happened before.[127]

For Mead, the 'world that is there' both is and is not, our world. Reality is always reality-for-man, a reflexive construction that answers both selectively to the world that is there and to the needs of the species, or to the perpetuation of action essential to the fulfilment of needs. Furthermore, given passage and emergence in nature, what is understood as reality must constantly change as the inadequacies of present perspectives are indicated by the appearance of problematics. The human species is qualitatively different from other species in that problematics may be defined and solved through reflexive intelligence; through the reflexive reconstruction of perspectives. Particular reconstructions are 'proven' by virtue of the maintenance of the life of the species that results from action based in the reconstruction.

At the same time, reflexive reconstruction of perspectives is the constitution of a new reality-for-man that is not totally reducible to the prior reality or past, and could not have been predicted on the basis of past 'information' or internalized attitudes.[128] Obviously Mead does not view knowledge in positivistic terms and does not view science, whatever its self-understanding, as a cumulative approach to a mental reflection of the 'world that is there' which allows anything like certain prediction of the future. As argued in *The Philosophy of the Present*, he holds in contrast that men live always in a present. This present can be 'stretched out' and given a temporal, if contingent, span through the reflexive capacity rooted in internalization. Still, the past and the future must change through reconstruction in the face of problematics. Thus, Mead views science as but the highest form or expression of man's reflexive capacity to reconstruct his world so that it is amenable to his needs.[129] He comprehends the truth of the results of scientific work as precisely the functional relationship of reconstructions to the needs of man as a social being. The predictive aspect of science is always temporally limited and contingent.

IMPLICATIONS FOR INTERPRETATION OF THE SOCIAL THEORY OF MAN

The criticisms of Mead's theory of the development of mind and self, as that theory is presented in *Mind, Self and Society*, can be viewed as a refutation of the adequacy of his attempt to develop a synthesis of positivistic and idealist theories of human life. These criticisms concentrate on two specific issues. Briefly, it was shown that Mead's introduction of the 'I' aspect of the self is not consistent with, nor logically integral to, his theory of self and mind as arising through an internalization of the prior, on-going social process in the form of conscious attitudes. The 'I' is considered as a residual category that is not explained within the theory of socialization, and is largely spoken of in terms of 'chance'; the unexpected aspect of the actual response of the organism to the situation. Without the necessary elaboration, the individual is reducible, without contradiction, to the 'me' aspect of the self, to the internalized meanings present in his situation. Mead is quite clear in arguing that the self is continually undergoing change, but this is predicated strictly on changing responses of others and things to the specific individual.

Second, it was demonstrated that the social process, out of which self and mind emerge is, in turn, reducible to a specific and predictable idea of an evolutionary process in nature. Mead clearly expresses the view, especially in the chapter entitled 'Society', that human history is an almost automatic expansion of universality; the gradual realization of a global community of common and shared attitudes, characterized by democratic government and a high development of functional social differentiation and interdependence. In fact, he argues that this predicted future follows precisely from the social-behaviouristic theory of mind and self that he develops, and that this future is indeed being realized.

It cannot be denied that the charge that Mead develops an 'oversocialized' conception of man has considerable warrant. However, the preceding discussion of the ideas of emergence, and of knowledge as an active, creative process, cannot be ignored. At minimum, to the extent that the criticisms are warranted, then a contradiction exists between the social theory of man found in *Mind, Self and Society*, and both Mead's desire to achieve a synthesis of idealism and positivism which recognizes the qualitative differences between men and other animals, and his development of these particular ideas in other works. However, having outlined the ideas of emergence and Mead's epistemological stance, it can be demonstrated that the criticisms rest, in part, on incomplete elaboration of his ideas and, in part, on the existence of quite gratuitous elements.

In the first instance, it was suggested that the 'I' is but an inadequate and awkward reference to the presupposition that self and mind are emergent aspects of the 'world that is there'. That is to say, self and mind emerge as specific processes in nature, rooted, in part, in the prior social interaction and gestural communication that goes on between persons. In these terms, the 'me' aspect, spoken of in *Mind, Self and Society*, must not be identified with the emergent self; rather, it is but an integral part of the emergent whole that is more and other than the combination of elements. Thus, the 'I'/'me' distinction must be understood as an analytical distinction between an emergent capacity for mental reflexion, and the attitudinal content of mind that is internalized through socialization. Furthermore, the 'me' aspect is but one of the necessary elements at the basis of this capacity of the human species. It is through the internalization process that individuals become aware of themselves, become objects to themselves, or become parts of their own environment. It is on this basis, *in turn*, that they can then gain reflexive control of their own responses. Given internalization, the *potential* for a reflexively conscious self is present, but is not identical with, or reducible to, the content internalized.

Thus, on the assumption that the human species evidences the capacity for reflexive reorganization of its relationship to the world in the face of problematics, the social theory of self and mind must be understood as a theory of the social process through which the reflexive capacity emerges, and not as a mechanistic, reductionistic theory of that capacity itself. In this sense, the accusation that the 'I' is *but* an *ad hoc* presupposition, misses the central and most important point – it is indeed a presupposition, but an essential one when placed within the perspective of emergence as a fact in nature.[130]

Furthermore, to speak of the reflexive capacity that self and mind introduce as but the 'unexpected' chance response of the organism, is to leave out of account the specific discussion of this capacity as entailing the intentional, hypothetical reconstruction of reality, in mind, before acting. In these terms, the unexpected character of a response, following the reflexive moment, is a matter of the individual acting differently than one would expect, knowing only the initial content of attitudes taken to the situation. The reflexive capacity is the ability to reorganize these present attitudes in the face of problematics; it is no longer conceived as simply a matter of chance discrepancy between an actual action and the action demanded by the 'me'. Thus, the essential argument is that while self and mind are social in origin and initial content, they constitute an emergent, reflexive capacity that is not, at least not necessarily, limited to the initial content internalized.

This point is admittedly not present with any clarity in *Mind, Self and Society*. Furthermore, it was noted that this was not the only difficulty to be dealt with. Mead also limits the 'creative process of mind in nature' within a conception of human history as a specific evolution in social form toward a predictable future of global attitudes (concepts and categories), and functional differentiation and integration of social elements.

It is not, of course, implied in any of Mead's writing that the human reflexive capacity that emerges is unlimited or totally free of constraint. Consistent with his desire to avoid idealism, Mead clearly accepts the reality of the 'world that is there' over and against mind, as has been noted. In order to survive and develop, men must continually 'adapt', but within broad limits, to this world and its passage. Human freedom inheres in the fact of passage in nature on the one hand, and in the capacity to reconstruct continually the selective relationship between self and nature on the other.[131]

However, though Mead argues that 'We are neither creatures of the necessity of an irrevocable past, nor of any vision given in the Mount',[132] his discussion of 'Society' clearly includes a limitation of man's ability to construct and reconstruct his reality within a specific, predicted social future. In very clear language, the ability to reflect is limited to problematics identified as those which the 'exigencies of evolution from time to time require'. Further, it is implied that the outcomes of such reconstructions will become the new reality-for-man only if consistent with the specific evolutionary movement towards greater globalization of functional differentiation and integration.

In contrast, however, it was argued in the previous section that Mead's framework contains the idea that reality-for-man is always the reality of *present* perspectives, and that both past and future are hypothetical constructions. Such constructions are therefore contingent; their truth inheres in their functionality, not for society, but for action in relation to species-needs. Their persistence is dependent at least on an absence of problematics in action. Thus Mead specifically holds that predictive 'knowledge' is highly probabilistic and time-bound. This position stands in direct contradiction to his own adherence to an extrapolation of his idea of evolution into a consideration of the future of social form.

Mead argues, at one point, that his prediction follows from, or is deducible from, the social behaviourist theory of self and mind that he develops.[133] However, if he is to remain consistent with his own epistemological stance and conception of science, this argument would have to hold only in so far as, and for as long as, the passing present remains unproblematic and calls forth no reflexive reconstruction of perspectives. And, given the assumptions of continual passage and emergence in nature, there is no warrant, within the theory itself, for such an expectation. Indeed, Mead himself argues at one point that

> Men in human society have come into some degree of control of the process of evolution out of which they arose.[134]

It is not inconsistent with his epistemology for Mead to reconstruct the past in terms of a specific notion of evolution; nor is it inconsistent for him to predicate intended future actions in these terms. It is inconsistent, however, to write as if this necessarily hypothetical and contingent future was rather a necessary outcome. He commits this error in so far as the character of future problematics and the valid reconstructions of men are described as defined and limited by such a future.

Mead not only argues that the future is hypothetical; in addition, he holds that man and environment (including the social environment) are mutually determinant. His hypostatization of the future, as a specific evolution of social form, contradicts this idea of reciprocal dependence, for it reduces mind to a determined and predictable role within this evolution.

Clearly, the basis of these contradictions is an inessential, indeed gratuitous, element of Mead's writing. The social theory of self and mind, given Mead's epistemological stance and conception of reality, can only be considered a theory of the *basis* and functions within action of the human reflexive capacity. To remain consistent, the theory cannot be predictive of the future form of conduct, for this depends on reflexion in the face of problematics; problematics that have not yet occurred, and that themselves are unpredictable as they involve the aspect of emergence.

Furthermore, there is nothing in the statement of the basis of mind and self that involves the necessity of such a predictable future. The reflexive, creative capacity is experienced in our present; it it taken as given. The past is always known from the perspective of the present and thus one can reconstruct the past in order to demonstrate how this capacity could have emerged; that is, one can state the conditions of its emergence and persistence.[135] One may then anticipate the future as including this capacity, in so far as one can maintain and foster those conditions that are essential to this capacity in the face of emergent problematics. The essential conditions that Mead speaks of involve the biological characteristics of the species on the one hand, and open, gestural communication as a part of social interaction on the other. The *specific* evolution of social form that is so much a part of the discussion of 'Society', is not an essential element in this basis.[136] In fact, as will be suggested below and developed in the subsequent chapter, Mead's predicted social future actually negates the very conditions necessary to the existence and perpetuation of the reflexive capacity of men.

In conclusion, it is clear that the criticisms of Mead's position, especially as developed in *Mind, Self and Society*, are only partially warranted. The over-socialized conception of man disappears with the elaboration of self and mind as emergent, functional capacities of the human species in relation to the 'world that is there'. The ambiguous 'I'/'me' distinction is more fully and clearly presented as a distinction between the internalized content of meanings on the one hand, and the emergent capacity for reflexive reorganization of attitudes on the other. In these terms, the 'me' aspect of the self is only a 'part' which stands in reciprocal dependence with the 'whole', which is characterized by the reflexive capacity. The apparent reduction of mind and self to the social process, in terms of a specific evolution of social form, also disappears on recognition that such a reduction contradicts Mead's own understanding of the future as hypothetical and contingent. The removal of this element does not, however, affect the basic social theory of man that Mead presents.

THE SOCIAL THEORY OF MIND AND THE SOCIOLOGY OF KNOWLEDGE

From the point of view of issues in the sociology of knowledge, Mead's perspective has usually been considered of importance primarily because it is understood as presenting a conceptualization of the 'mechanics' involved in how 'knowledge' is internalized from the social situation of individuals. In this interpretation, knowledge is understood as 'given' in the group and in its structure of relationships; that is, that meaning is inherent in the form of interaction. Mead's framework is apparently important because it provides conceptual clarity as to how the individual's ideas are tied to, and determined by, his social situation through the process of socialization.[137]

This approach to the possible importance of Mead's work is suggestive as far as it goes. However, in light of the interpretation developed above, it is rather narrow, and because of this, quite misleading. In the first place, Mead was *not* concerned solely with the internalization of a specific content of attitudes from the social situation into which individuals are born. This process must be understood as an essential aspect of the overall basis of the emergent and qualitatively different reflexive capacity of men – a capacity that enables men to react back on, and change intentionally, both the initial content of ideas internalized and, therefore, the initial interactional context.

Second, Mead did not identify knowledge with the content of

internalized meanings. He distinguished between information, which is more clearly associated with the internalization of existing attitudes, and knowledge as an active construction and reorganization of attitudes in relation to the solution of problematics that arise in experience. It is an assumption on Mead's part that the internalized meanings and the social context are 'two sides of the same coin'.[138] On this level, the self is precisely the social context and process internalized, and there would appear to be little in the way of a relationship to analyse, in so far as thought, as an internalized conversation of gestures and the social process, are identical.[139]

On both counts, then, a social study of consciousness involves more than simply an analysis of the relationships between specific social situations and the ideas (information) held by persons within these situations. This is so precisely because reflexive intelligence and knowledge are more and other than given attitudes and social patterns. In fact, Mead's perspective implies an analysis of the internalized content of mind as itself problematic or potentially so; indeed it implies a critical analysis of existing ideas as themselves an element in the existence and persistence of problematic situations.

Briefly, Mead understands all science as but the clearest expression of reflexive intelligence, and thus equates it with the general capacity of men to reorganize attitudes in the face of problematics. Thus, social science as well must be understood as basically problem-solving activity. However, the object of its investigation – the social context – is considered a set of interaction patterns which are, in large measure, interdependent with the organized and shared attitudes (information) of the individuals involved. It follows that, in so far as the patterns of action that are traditionally and habitually performed have become problematic in relation to the achievement of ends, so too are the organized attitudes involved in these patterns called into question. Thus, the reorganization of social activity implies the reorganization of attitudes involved in this activity. This in turn implies the necessity of critical reflexion on the adequacy of existing ideas in relation to species-needs.

None the less, having drawn this implication, it must be admitted that Mead's work does not fully elaborate nor deal with this notion of a critical analysis of ideas in relation to social form. His view of science does indeed entail critical analysis in so far as knowing, as opposed to being informed, is understood as an active process of constructing perspectives that enable men to overcome problematics that arise in experience. However, this critical orientation is not adequately carried over into social analysis and, in particular, is not pursued in relation to the analysis of the relationship between ideas and social factors. Mead does not explicitly view this relationship as itself potentially problematic, in terms, for example, of persistent ideas inhibiting social change, or of persistent social patterns inhibiting the reorganization of attitudes.

Instead, Mead's writing tends to concentrate on and emphasize the social being of men only in so far as it is considered a basis for the emergence of reflexive intelligence in the first place. The problematics that are generally of concern in his work are those that arise in the relationship between men, the fulfilment of their needs, and physical nature, which is the object of these needs.[140] Primarily by omission, his writing contains no clearly thought-out problematic entailed in the relationship between the emergent reflexive capacity, knowledge and the social forms and attitudes that are part of the basis of thought. The criticism that Mead's work is idealistic reflects this omission. As noted previously, he appears to view social change as ultimately unproblematic – through the interaction of groups with diverse perspectives, reciprocal role-taking is represented as relatively unproblematic, and as leading automatically to a common attitudinal structure, change in the thought and action of both groups, and an end to conflict.

However, there is no logical necessity for the exclusion of such a consideration, which, in Marx's perspective, was captured by the concept of alienation. Indeed, there are a number of suggestive passages in Mead's writing that demonstrate that he was not totally unaware of such problematics.[141] The fact that these implications *vis-à-vis* a critical social analysis are not made explicit by Mead himself is apparently related to the specific evolutionary assumptions discussed above. These aspects of Mead's writing will be considered in greater detail in the following chapter as they are of central importance in the investigation of compatibilities between the work of Marx and Mead.[142]

chapter 4

Marx and Mead: towards a critical sociology of knowledge

Of the two hypotheses guiding this study, the first has been established: both Marx and Mead clearly 'anticipate' the critique of the sociology of knowledge in terms at least of specific and central aspects of their work. Both writers develop basic presuppositions and concepts that are consistent with and detailed elaborations of the insight that social factors and ideas are integrally and reciprocally related. Furthermore, both perspectives propose the necessity of a critical mode of analysis; explicitly in the case of Marx, largely implicitly in the case of Mead.

At the same time, the analyses demonstrated particular inadequacies in both perspectives such that neither alone may be said to be fully adequate as a response to the critique. Mead's social theory of man and thought contains virtually no explicit appreciation of any problematic that would call forth or justify a sociology of knowledge of either critical or positivistic character. Though Marx introduces the necessary conceptualization of such a problematic, he fails to provide a theoretical basis for the process of alienation that is consistent with his fundamental and essential concept of human life as praxis.

The second hypothesis concerns these remaining inadequacies for it argues that the resolution of difficulties in the discipline lies not in either perspective alone, but in a synthesis of relevant ideas taken from both writers. If one rewords this hypothesis in terms of the analysis to this point, it is to suggest that the perspectives of Marx and Mead are fundamentally compatible and that the inadequacies of the one can be corrected or completed through specific emphases or developments found in the other.[1] The first task is therefore to delineate more explicitly the consistency that exists between the basic elements of the perspectives of these theorists. The second is to determine the degree to which their specific emphases are complementary in relation to the development of a fully adequate, critical sociology of knowledge.

INTERACTIONISM AND CRITICAL ANALYSIS: ASPECTS OF COMPATIBILITY

In relation to the basic questions involved in the development of the sociology of knowledge and to the contradiction between critics and proponents of the discipline, the presumed complementarity can be demonstrated in respect to at least four basic factors: conceptions of man, of the social, of knowledge, and of the relationship holding between these terms. Clearly both Marx and Mead presume the fundamental social nature of man and, indeed, they argue that it is only through their sociality that men can be individuals. For his part Marx includes sociality as a basic and interdependent element of praxis as reality-for-man. In his view, man does not exist as man except in terms of social interrelation and interdependence. This is held to be true whether or not it appears to be the case; for example, even where competitive relationships 'exist' from the superstructural point of view, and even where such a conception of man is supported by an individualistic metaphysic, productive life or praxis remains essentially co-operative; bourgeois and proletarian, lord and serf, master and slave, live by and through one another. Indeed, Marx continually emphasizes that despite the individualistic gloss that is part of capitalism's self-justification, the very system helps produce a national and global interdependence of men such as has never previously existed in human history.[2]

If there is a difference between Marx and Mead in this respect it is simply that Mead develops the conception of human sociality in much greater detail. In particular, Mead elaborates what is only stated in Marx's writing: that mind and self presuppose and emerge from the prior, social, communicative process into which individuals are born, through a process denoted by the term internalization. The essential point is to recognize an emphasis that is too often overlooked; both Marx and Mead adhere to the view that 'socialization' is *not* properly understood when simply interpreted as a process of bringing separate 'individuals' into a sufficient conformity with others so that community action is possible. In contrast, both these writers presume that the individual depends upon an on-going, interactional process for the realization of individuality, of those specific human characteristics which qualitatively distinguish him from other species.[3]

Despite this very specific emphasis on the social nature of persons, it is none the less clear that neither Marx nor Mead lapses into any necessary sociologistic or positivistic framework of analysis. This second point of compatibility concerns the fact that they both argue the essential sociality of persons without at the same time reducing the individual to 'society'. Though this argument is not fully clarified by either writer, it can be shown that their dialectical conceptions of man and social context capture both the experience of conformity and the experience of individual responsibility, creativity and freedom, without denying either side of the relationship.

Both writers regard sociality as predating mind, self-consciousness and language; both assume an historically prior and more primitive 'herd' situation out of which qualitatively different human characteristics have emerged. Further, both hold that the capacity for reflexive, problem-solving activity emerges in an individual's biography only through interaction with others. None the less, though the historical and biographical genesis and locus of mind is social, the focus of mental activity lies within the individual; both theorists clearly reject any conception of a 'group mind'.

Furthermore, the emergence of individual mindedness is understood by both writers as the emergence of a 'whole', which is reciprocally determinative in relation to the 'parts' that are its basis. In this sense, the emergence of the reflexive capacity, while still rooted in a social context, is an irreducible factor that must be adequately considered in any comprehension of the subsequent development of human life. In other words, it is evident that both Marx and Mead recognize that what the social context has become, subsequent to the emergence of mind, is inextricably bound up with that capacity. With the evolutionary emergence of reflexive intelligence, the passage of events becomes history and thereby becomes amenable to and reflective of a considerable degree of self-conscious control in relation to species' needs.

Thus, in neither perspective is there any conception of 'society', or of a social substratum, which can be legitimately or adequately considered apart from a dialectical or reciprocal relationship to the fact of individual mindedness. For Marx and for Mead, 'society' can only be properly understood as a 'form of co-operative activity', precisely the phrasing that they both utilize. In one sense, any given social form is an aspect of the 'solution' to specific, historically emergent problematics, a solution reflecting the necessity of some type of co-operative activity in relation to the fulfilment of species and individual needs *vis-à-vis* the 'world that is there'. Such organizational solutions are understood by both theorists as historically contingent and therefore as impermanent – they are subject to refutation and change in terms of subsequent problematics that arise in experience.

The third point of compatibility lies in the fact that both writers conceptualize thought as an essentially *functional* and dynamic, constructive process. It is important to recognize, moreover, that thought is understood as functional in relation to the life of the species, and not in relation to any externally given 'society' or specific form of sociality.[4]

The reflexive capacity does indeed have its origin in existing social relationships and will, therefore, to a considerable extent 'reflect' present social conditions in terms of the initial content internalized. However, mind is understood, by both, precisely as a capacity, and thus as a 'cause in itself' in terms of its function in relation to human need and problematics. To argue that this capacity has a social genesis need not imply a reduction to social factors; the genesis is understood as a 'meaningful genesis' discussed especially by Mead in terms of symbolic interaction or language, and it implies the potential for an *immanent* development beyond the point of emergence. As a capacity, reflexivity or thought implies the presence of an ability to transform the initial content internalized, to recognize and draw out possible implications and thereby to transform activity, its form and relational content. Both Mead and Marx assume the emergent existence and character of this capacity at a basic ontological level, although both subsequently lose this emphasis to some degree through the introduction of rather gratuitous elements.

Compared to Marx's structural emphasis, Mead presents a much more complete conceptualization of mindedness and knowing through his emphasis on the individual's symbolic or imaginative awareness of situations, on his selective perception of stimuli in the 'world that is there', and on his ability to reconstruct attitudes in the development of adequate response to needs. However, his conception is clearly consistent with Marx's insistence on the active character and role of thought in history. It should be noted that despite the attribution of an 'independent' role to thought in history, neither position becomes idealist. On the one hand, knowing and acting are limited by the fact of a 'world that is there' other than mind and, on the other hand, they are limited by human needs and their relationship to problematics that arise within 'present circumstances'.

The perspectives of these writers converge as well in respect to the character of the relationship posited between thought and social context. Both theorists regard thought and social interaction as 'two sides of the same coin'; yet, both 'sides' are understood as essential and quite irreducible to the other. Marx speaks of thought and sociality as integral and essential moments of the totality of human life, a life characterized as praxis. Mead speaks of these realms in like manner as aspects forming the basis of the reflexive capacity, which, congruent with the idea of praxis, is involved in the basic and essential problem-solving and need-fulfilling activity of the species.

In the absence of problematics, individuals are understood as acting habitually and non-reflexively and, for the most part, in terms of the structure of attitudes initially internalized from, and integral to, their social context. However, both writers assume change as an integral aspect of the 'world that is there', and thus they attribute an essential factor of contingency to the relationship between form and environment, between social, interactional patterns and attitudes and the 'world that is there'.

In the face of problematics, habitual action ceases to be adequate, and this implies that both the existing organization of attitudes and social patterns have become inadequate in some respect. In other words, the contingency of existing thought and forms of activity becomes evident; one can no longer act effectively in terms of initially internalized 'information'. However, under this condition one has the emergent capacity to hypothesize potentially effective 'knowledge', and to act on this basis of reflexive reconstruction and reorganization of attitudes. Such a reflexive reconstruction of attitudes is, concomitantly, a change in the relational pattern of action toward the world; it is a transformation, in at least some respect, of social form. Thus, with the emergence of mind, social forms or institutions can be understood as themselves objectifications of systems of ideas or as human products related to biological and social needs. Marx speaks of them as 'objectifications' of human capacities or powers; Mead speaks in similar vein of social actions as 'tests' of ideas formulated in the face of problematics. Both are consistent in emphasizing the contingency of any historically specific social form that is constructed. However, the primary point is that both writers presume that men have the capacity to intentionally change their social world in relation to the 'world that is there', through reflexively dealing with the difficulties that arise in experience.

Finally, both perspectives converge in respect to proposing a particular resolution of the issue of relativism, a resolution consistent with the basic insight of the sociology of knowledge. On the one hand, Marx and Mead agree in denying the possibility of achieving total, complete or absolute knowledge of nature or of any aspect of nature. Furthermore, they both refuse to accept any historically specific intellectual formula as the guarantor of truth precisely because they interpret the intellectual sphere as inextricably bound up with the social context. None the less, they both reject any totally relativistic stance through recourse to a particular 'absolute' or criterion of truth. Essentially, both theorists argue that thought is essentially a functional process involved in the maintenance of human life and its development. Thus they imply that ideas are to be judged in respect to their adequacy to and within human praxis.

Two points may be concluded at this point. First, both Marx and Mead clearly anticipated the critique and in a very fundamental manner as demonstrated in the separate analyses of their works. Second, in respect to most of the ideas shown to be basic to a sociology of knowledge, their perspectives are essentially compatible. Furthermore, both perspectives are rooted in a similar epistemological base which places the test of ideas squarely within praxis. However, in the analysis of Marx's perspective, it was demonstrated that the additional concept of alienation is of crucial importance, at least within the implied critical sociology of knowledge. This concept is virtually absent from Mead's writing and it therefore remains to determine if this concept is none the less consistent with his perspective as elaborated to this point. Only if the degree of compatibility extends to this idea as well is it then relevant to pursue the final question: that of the possible resolution of the difficulty that remains in respect of the basis of the phenomenon of alienation within praxis.

MEAD'S SOCIAL THEORY OF MAN AND THE PROBLEM OF ALIENATION

Earlier it was pointed out that Mead is often accused of 'sociological idealism' by critical theorists, precisely because his perspective demonstrates no appreciation of the issue of alienation. This is to say that while Mead's perspective may well present human life in a manner that parallels Marx's conception of praxis in many respects, it maintains a view of the relationship between thought and social context which entails no fundamentally problematic aspect. Thus Mead tends to assume that whenever problematics arise in the relationship between human needs and the 'world that is there' or between social form and physical environment, some adjustment automatically takes place and results in both changed ideas and changed forms of social activity.[5] In contrast, Marx maintained that existing ideas and social form are not readily changed; they become 'crystallizations', 'growing out of control, thwarting our expectations and bringing to naught our calculations'.[6]

One of the essential implications of this consideration of the relationship of thought and social factors as unproblematic in Mead's work, is that the very rationale for sociological analysis disappears, and, consequently, any rationale for a sociology of knowledge. Historically, sociology receives its primary motivation from a concern to comprehend the tension between the individual, his thought and social form.[7] Mead appears to deny this tension by conceptualizing the individual and the social context as 'two sides of the same coin', and by conceptualizing the change that does occur in both as proceeding smoothly and without problematics. By virtue of his collapse of the traditional duality, Mead apparently emasculates the discipline.[8]

The same argument could well be applied to Marx, but with one important exception. He, like Mead, develops an image of men as social beings who are active, intentional and creative problem-solvers in relation to nature. This is what men are, what their life as a species is – a continual 'dealing with' nature in relation to the needs of the species. Human life requires constant reformulation of ideas and thus, concomitantly, changes in social form. Marx understands human reality or praxis as basically this on-going, changing social process. Thus, it could be argued that in terms of the reality of praxis, a reality in which thought and sociality constitute an integral unity, Marx also collapses the individual/society duality and tension.

But unlike Mead, Marx is explicitly motivated, both theoretically and practically, by a concern with a problematic aspect or tension in this natural process of problem-solving in relation to a 'world that is there'. Specifically, though Marx presumes the on-going reality of praxis and though, at this level of praxis, he presumes that thought and social form constitute an 'integral unity'; he at the same time appreciates the fact that necessary social and ideational change is 'fettered' by existing social form and ideational structure. That is, he appreciates the extent to which existing form can be a 'system of alienation' characterized, for example, by persistent and unresolved problems of poverty, exploitation, labour strife and discrimination.

It is precisely in these terms that Marx retains a rationale for sociological analysis, though it is a specific rationale that explicitly demands a critical rather than positivistic mode of analysis. In his view, the tension between individual and society is improperly conceived as a tension between two separate realities for the 'individual is the social being'. To the contrary, such tension results from and signifies the inadequacy and contradictory nature of present, contingent interactional form.[9] Thus a critical investigation, both of the existing social form and of the ideas which rationalize its acceptance and perpetuation, is required – with a view to transforming actively the existing, problematic patterns of interaction. It is precisely Marx's intention to develop a mode of analysis that would enable one to pinpoint and transcend the specific, contingent limitation expressed in the concept of alienation, so that the 'natural problematics', on the level of praxis, could be handled on a rational, less trial-and-error basis, free of the paradoxical limitations of man's own products.

The essential point is that while Mead's perspective also suggests the critical orientation, it does not explicitly contain any comprehension of a problematic that would constitute the rationale in terms of which critical analysis would be necessary and meaningful. Mead stops short of any detailed consideration of a conceptual equivalent to Marx's ideas of alienation. His work is not explicitly a critical sociology; rather, it is a conceptualization of men, knowledge and the social, which appears, in itself, to be of little 'use'. One could argue that, as it stands, it is of 'ideological' relevance only, for in his failure to relate the perspective fully to any concrete problematics that might be associated with the active nature of man, Mead suggests a present world in which 'problem-solving' is an inevitable flow of evolutionary progress from one moment to the next.[10] Thus sociology, of both positivistic and critical persuasions, apparently loses any point in Mead's work, not simply because he collapses the individual/society distinction, but because, at the same time, he ignores all evidence of *persistent* tensions (of which even he is somewhat aware) by viewing them as but momentary and passing aberrations in an evolutionary transformation of social form.

Thus, the essential question is that of the extent to which Marx's appreciation of the issue of alienation is consistent with and can be utilized to complete the critical overtones of Mead's perspective. One way of approaching this question is to consider, from Mead's point of view, the impact of institutionalized divisions within an historical social form. For Marx, social divisions were understood as positive in respect to increased productivity, yet as eventually negative in relation to the basic sociality of men and the realization of further potentialities. In his view, the divisions of productive labour within capitalism were an integral aspect of this 'system of alienation', which must therefore be transcended. The vertical division into classes and status groups was also understood as a human social product that ultimately interfered with praxis, and therefore denied the realization of human potentialities implied in capitalistic organization.

In contrast, Mead deals minimally with social divisions as actually or potentially problematic aspects of social form, in relation to the fulfilment and development of needs. Indeed, it is apparent that he views such division in an almost totally positive light. As previously demonstrated, Mead predicts the future of society as involving greater and greater degrees of functional differentiation of tasks, or roles, within a gradually realized, global, democratic community. But it is not this alone which betrays Mead's positive orientation to social division. He also associates the 'growth of individuality' with this evolution of social form;

individuality is defined in this context by reference to the functional differences of one's task from those of others.[11]

However, this 'positive' view of differentiated social form is inconsistent with the basic aspects of Mead's thought that are relevant to the sociology of knowledge. In fact, these particular ideas entail precisely the opposite appreciation of social differentiation in relation to the emergent reflexive capacity that is central to Mead's image of man. Moreover, the inconsistency can be removed, for it is rooted in the gratuitous assumption of a specific evolutionary future. In the previous analysis of Mead, it was demonstrated that his specific evolutionary assumption, with its supposed behaviouristic justifications, contradicted his basic epistemological stance. This assumption entailed the prediction of a social future consisting of the development of global attitudes within a social structure characterized by increasing functional differentiation. In turn, this assumption involved a limitation and reduction of the emergent reflexive capacity to only a functional role within this social evolution. Two specific contradictions are entailed by this assumption. First, it contradicts Mead's epistemological stance; a conception of knowledge that denies his own attempt to predict the future of social form. Second, it contradicts his emphasis on the functionality of the reflexive capacity in relation to human species-needs as opposed to 'societal' needs. The future is always hypothetical, or contingent, and 'known' from the perspective of the present. The appearance of problematics demands the reconstruction of perspectives, and thus the reconstruction of both past *and* future.

The removal of this evolutionary assumption rendered the perspective consistent by removing the basis of the criticism that Mead fundamentally reduces the individual and his reflexive capacity to the on-going social process. As well, the removal of the assumption negates Mead's positive orientation toward social differentiation.

First, in terms of Mead's conceptions of social context and knowledge, the future of existing, differentiated social form may or may not involve increasing degrees of functional differentiation. The persistence and increase in this aspect of social structure is always contingent on the continued absence of any particular problematics that would demand transformation of those attitudes reflected in existing social form. Thus, it is inconsistent and contradictory for Mead to predict the persistence and expansion of social differentiation. His own conception of knowledge denies that present social form or present conceptual frameworks can be the basis of prediction of future social conditions.[12]

Second, the relationship between individuality and social, functional division also disappears. In terms of Mead's discussion of the reflexive capacity, individuality inheres in the fact that the focus of this capacity lies in the individual. Though a social being whose mind and self are genetically rooted in a social context, it is the individual who thinks, and who is capable of transcending initial contents internalized. This idea is distorted by the introduction of the evolutionary assumption. The assumption entails the idea of social history as a necessary and specific evolution of functional differentiation, and Mead adds to this, almost as an element of justification, the idea that the degree of individuality is rooted in functionally differentiated role-playing. However, the removal of the assumption leaves the basis of individuality squarely within the emergence of the reflexive capacity.

Thus it is argued that on removal of the gratuitous assumption of a predictable form of social evolution, the existence of societal division, as an example, needs no longer be considered 'positive' by any necessity within the Meadian perspective. As an aspect of present social form, particular social divisions are, if anything, 'neutral' in relation to the reflexive capacity and in relation to solutions to future problematics. On closer inspection, however, and in terms of Mead's own statements in respect to social conflict, the inadequacies of educational forms, relationships between classes and the tendency to reify ideas within science, the relationship between reflexive intelligence and existing social forms is only consistently understood as negative. To demonstrate that this is the case is to show that Mead's perspective further parallels Marx's ideas in respect to the concept of alienation.

For example, in the context of discussing the nature of institutions, Mead notes that 'there are, in the present

> oppressive, stereotyped and ultra-conservative social institutions – like the church – which by their more or less rigid and inflexible unprogressiveness crush or blot out individuality or discourage any distinctive or original expressions of thought and behavior in the individual selves or personalities implicated in and subjected to them.[13]

This insight reappears in his writing in various places, but it is continuously obscured by the implications of the evolutionary assumption. In this specific context, for example, Mead goes on immediately to argue that while such institutions or social forms are 'undesirable', they are, 'not necessarily outcomes of the general social process of experience and behavior'.[14] But while it may be the case in terms of Mead's perspective that such negative social forms are not necessary in any ontological sense, they do 'exist' in a present and by his own admission. That he so blithely passes over them is due, once again, to the fact that the 'general social process' referred to is obscured by Mead's own hope for the future – his inconsistent conception of it as a necessary, non-conflictual outcome of an evolutionary process.[15]

While Mead often admits of social forms as in some manner problematic, and of change as a 'struggle' requiring active reflexion and reconstruction, he continually down-plays this aspect of his writing. He seems content to argue that because it is 'better' that social forms or institutions are not oppressive, then it is necessary and inevitable that they will become 'very broad and general', 'affording plenty of scope for originality, flexibility and variety'.[16] However, to say that institutions may be oppressive is to say that they inhibit change and, therefore, that they inhibit the operation of the reflexive capacity that Mead indicates is so integral to such change.

There are several other brief, but suggestive, sections of Mead's writing that allude to what can be considered the problem of alienation and reification; to the problematic relationship between existing attitudinal organization, social form and the realization of the reflexive capacity. It was previously noted that Mead was extremely critical of the self-conception of science as positivistic, and of the 'copy-theory' of knowledge, which is its justification. Though he does not use the term, he is referring very clearly to what Marx would call reification – in this case, the distortion of the actual practice of science through the maintenance of an uncritically accepted and historically specific theory of science in the place of that practice and its development. In Mead's words, the copy-theory and other epistemologies have 'obscured it [science] with their tangled and forest growth'.[17]

Another discussion that very clearly points in the same direction concerns particular social problems: 'questions of property, of the family, or of the criminal'. Mead notes, but does not develop the point, that it is all too often the case that 'Our institutionalized past has determined for us what [these problems] are'.[18] Furthermore, 'the most serious obstacle to [their correction through reflexive reconstruction] lies in the failure of traditional ideas lying in our minds. . . '.[19]

> We live in a universe whose past changes with every considerable change in our scientific [in his sense] account of it, and yet *we are prone to look for the meaning of our biological and social life in fixed forms of historical institutions and the order of past events.* We prefer to understand the family, the state, the church and the school by forms which history has given to their social structures.[20]

In another context, Mead alludes to the fact that the process of overcoming these 'traditional' contents of mind, especially those that are operative in the conflicts between social groups, is not always an automatic process:

> The task, however, is enormous enough, for it involves not simply breaking down passive barriers such as those of distance in space and time and vernacular, but those of fixed attitudes of custom and status in which our selves are imbedded.[21]

The impact of such scattered points is minimal in relation to the overwhelming emphasis that Mead places on his belief that the future will indeed follow the course that he lays out for it. However, in that the evolutionary assumption stands in contradiction to the basic elements of his social theory of man, it is perhaps more accurate to say that the impact of the insights outlined are minimized rather than minimal. In fact there is nothing but the presence of this contradictory assumption to inhibit Mead from pursuing conceptual elaboration of the existence of a problematic within the relationship between existing attitudes, social forms and the operation of the reflexive capacity.

Thus, while it can be argued that his work is almost totally 'untouched by a concern with alienation', it cannot be maintained that such a concern is inconsistent with the most basic elements of his theory. Furthermore, in that the concept of alienation is consistent with Mead's theory, it then provides the rationale in terms of which sociological investigation on a Meadian basis is rendered meaningful. Basically, this entails a critical orientation to existing social form at both interactional and ideational levels in respect to the reciprocal and negative impact that such forms can have on the capacity to transcend existing, natural problematics. Thus, in respect to the issue of alienation, Mead's ideas, stripped of the gratuitous and contradictory evolutionary assumption, are quite consistent with and benefit from particular Marxian ideas.

PRAXIS AND ALIENATION: A MEADIAN CONTRIBUTION TO THE CRITICAL PERSPECTIVE

Having determined that the central idea of alienation is not inconsistent with the basic concepts and critical implications of Mead's perspective, it becomes feasible to consider the possiblity of utilizing Mead's insights in respect to the remaining deficiency of the critical sociology of knowledge. This deficiency concerns the unresolved and basic problem of adequately conceptualizing the nature of the relationship between the on-going reality of praxis and the recurring issue, within praxis, of alienation.

Marx failed to explain fully why it is that man, considered a being of praxis, should alienate himself; why, if men are active, social and self-conscious or reflexive producers of their world and of themselves, they should relate to what they themselves have produced in a manner which 'fetters' the very essence of their being. The lack of any complete elaboration of this crucial aspect of non-positivistic critical theory is the basis both of a misinterpretation of Marx's perspective as positivistic, and of his own recurring tendency to deprecate his conception of man as a self-productive being of praxis. On the one hand, this tendency involved an over-emphasis on the reciprocal effect of alienated products, an effect conceived almost mechanistically, and, on the other hand, it involved a lack of clarification of the extent to which alienation may be understood as a denial of praxis. If it may be said that Mead errs in the direction of viewing praxis itself as unproblematic, it may be said that Marx errs in the opposite direction of emphasizing the limitations of praxis to the point of denying the relevance of this initial conceptualization of human life. However, to remain consistent with the idea of praxis as reality-for-man, the critical perspective demands an integrated conceptualization of how men alienate their labour, and only then, of how this alienated labour has a reciprocal, limiting influence on praxis as a whole.

Previously, it was indicated that Marx's writing at least contains the suggestion that alienation is 'founded in the nature of human development', and since this is the central focus of Mead's efforts, it would appear reasonable to seek the resolution of this difficulty within his concept of socialization and the specific process of internalization.

To begin with, Mead argued that given the requisite physio-biological conditions, each person's mind and self are absent at birth on the qualitatively different human level. These properties emerge only through an internalization of other's responses to one's gestures, to others and to the environment. However, and most importantly, the *initial* development of mind and self is very largely a matter of internalizing *existing* meanings, attitudes and their organization. Thus Mead emphasizes the extent to which what an individual 'is' initially, is very largely a reflection of the existing and 'given' social situation of that particular individual.

Using Mead's distinction between levels of consciousness, this argument points to the predominance of 'information' over 'knowledge, at least during the initial stages of self-development. That is, it points to the fact that the child tends to comprehend and thus to respond to his world and to himself primarily in terms of 'information' internalized. This is to say that at least in the early stages there is a *potential for* rather than any necessary or immediate actualization of the critical, reflexive capacity through which knowledge, understood as construction in the face of problematics, becomes possible.

Essentially, precisely because self and mind are rooted in an internalization of a specific and given content and organization of attitudes, there is a tendency to respond to one's world and to the problematics that arise in one's experience in the very terms that have been rendered inadequate by these problematics. In other words there is a basic tendency towards reification and the perpetuation of existing ideas and action patterns and this tendency is rooted in the socialization process itself. Clearly, the degree to which initially internalized attitudes predominate in the definition of self and environment is, at least in part, the degree to which the individual is alienated from himself, from the realization of his own essential capacities as a reflexive being. Thus the very process of acquiring mind and self can be viewed as inherently limiting and as inherently paradoxical in nature.

On the one hand, through the emergent reflexive capacity, men become capable, self-consciously and intentionally, as Marx argued, of 'making their own circumstances'. However, on the other hand, they do so only on a basis of circumstances that they did not make and which in fact 'make them', in part at least, through socialization. At the most basic level, this implies that the very selves of persons are initially fashioned by and in the image of existing circumstances. Thus, to reflect critically on the adequacy of many existing ideas and their related social patterns is, fundamentally, to take on the difficult task of reflecting on and calling into question one's own self.[22]

To attack this point from a slightly different angle, one has only to recall the emphasis found in both Mead and Marx on the reciprocal influence of part and whole. For Marx, praxis is a totality greater than the sum of its constituent elements, yet dialectically interdependent with these elements. In similar fashion, Mead emphasized the fact that the reflexive capacity, though emergent from the interaction of biological and social components, none the less remains linked to these constituent elements. Thus, while the emergence of the reflexive capacity may yield the capacity consciously and intentionally to fashion new circumstances, it is a capacity that must none the less deal with its own basis; especially the attitudinal content that initiates the very possibility of reflexion.

Of course this limitation on emergent reflexivity is not presented nor meant in any absolute or total sense. Mead's comprehension of the paradoxical character of socialization simply indicates (often in spite of itself) the fact that reflexion, and thus the construction of knowledge adequate to both needs and to the 'world that is there', is an active process demanding effort. Reconstruction of perspectives and thus of social form is never an automatic nor a passive process. It is something that can only be accomplished actively against the opposition of one's previously internalized attitudes or images of reality and thus against one's very self. And though the focus of such reflexion is the individual, there is yet an additional problem involved in social change, the necessity of communicating to and convincing others, others whose selves, for the same reasons, are resistant to and not amenable to easy or automatic change.[23]

If nothing else, these emphases on the difficult and underlying self-criticism implied in reflexion and on the reciprocal, dialectical relationship between mind as capacity and mind as content indicate that reflexion and even the continuity of the process of 'taking the rôle of the other' are more problematic than even Mead was wont to believe. Thus, at this very basic level, socialization entails an alienation of men from the process of praxis in that it paradoxically fosters and yet inhibits the functioning of the self-consciousness or species-specific power that is an essential component of this process. Mead may not have been as aware as Marx that enormous difficulties intervene in the realization and effective use of human powers. None the less, his conceptualization of the emergence of reflexivity in terms of socialization contributes a more complete framework for adequately expressing and explaining such difficulties.[24]

It might be objected that this specific contribution to an understanding of the roots of alienation within praxis is not consistent with Marx's framework precisely because it emphasizes ideas and the reification of ideas instead of alienation in its broader sense. Certainly it is true that Marx emphasized a factor that Mead ignored, that of power in human relationships.[25] However, the concept of reification is not at all foreign to Marx's perspective as pointed out previously. In fact, though Marx failed to develop the concept in detail, the idea of reification must be viewed as central to his perspective and as an essential component of alienation in all its forms. In other words, even in Marx's writing, alienation cannot be fully and consistently comprehended apart from a consideration of an important and integral role played by reified or false consciousness.[26]

Earlier it was argued that alienation cannot be considered a total phenomenon if one is to remain consistent with the basic notion of human life as praxis.[27] It is therefore essential to view alienation as a condition coexistent with praxis as an on-going process – a factor of limitation rather than of total denial. Now in terms of the fact that human consciousness is an essential component of praxis, the notion of a coexistence of praxis and alienation can only mean that there are at least two levels of consciousness—the practical, a level integral to on-going praxis; and the abstract, a level in some sense divorced from praxis and at least potentially reified.

To elaborate and clarify this point by comparison, Marx clearly argued *vis-à-vis* the social moment of praxis that, appearances to the contrary, all human activity none the less remains social – meaning fundamentally co-operative.[28] Thus, even capitalist production depends on and expresses sociality, though in an alienated fashion involving superstructural competition, exploitation, and an ideology rooted in a conception of men as basically competitive and ego-centric. Similarly, in so far as consciousness is a concomitant and necessary moment of praxis, the same argument must be applicable to it. Thus it follows that a consistent development of Marx's position (in regard to the issue of relationship between praxis and alienation) requires this conceptualization of two levels of consciousness – the process itself and specific ideas as 'practical consciousness'; and the process and specific ideas at a purely theoretical, abstract and potentially reified level.[29]

This idea involves a corollary: that just as all products of praxis must, by definition, contain an essential element of consciousness, or must be considered meaningful phenomena, so too must the alienation of these products involve reified, unchanging ideas as an essential component. This consideration is often ignored, or at least not given sufficient emphasis in the analysis of alienation. Certainly Marx himself inadequately developed the significance of the reification of ideas in relation to the alienation of human products. However, if physically existent objects of nature, or more precisely, of transformed nature, are always objects-for-man,[30] then their alienation must involve a reification of their meaning.[31] This is more clearly the case in respect to institutions understood as human products or as specific forms of man's sociality. Institutions do not become nor remain alienated from men, nor acquire a determinative status, apart from an element of reification.[32]

Though admittedly implicit in Marx's writing, this point suggests that any complete, non-positivistic elaboration of the concept of alienation, and of the relationship between alienation and praxis, requires that more detailed attention be given to the importance of the reification of ideas. The central implication appears to be that a 'system of alienation' and its persistence are to be explained, at least in part, in terms of the reified conceptual structures of the persons involved. Thus, in so far as Mead's framework provides an explanation of the tendency toward reification in terms of socialization, it provides at least a partial explanation for the existence of alienation within praxis.

There is a second level on which Mead's perspective contributes to that of Marx, in regard to the relationship between alienation and the 'nature of human development' within praxis. This concerns Marx's emphasis on the character of the specific 'circumstances' which are internalized, and the nature of the 'effect' that these can have on the degree of realization of human capacities. The first contribution simply argues, and in very general terms, that a tension exists in the reciprocal relationship between content internalized and reflexivity, a tension that must be recognized and accorded due importance. The second contribution is an elaboration of the recognition that this tension can be more or less increased in the direction of maintaining existing circumstances.

To use a specific example, Marx was centrally concerned with the negative effects of the division of labour, and especially with the vertical division of class or power. However, as this concern is expressed in his work, it tends toward a theoretical reification of this 'social fact', such that the divisions of labour and class acquire ontological status as 'existential' determinants within and of historical development. It was noted that it is this tendency that allows an interpretation of alienation as a total denial of praxis. However, as indicated, such interpretation entails contradictions with the critical implications of Marx's ideas and the elaboration necessary to avoid this problem is absent from his work. The question therefore concerns whether or not Mead's insights can be utilized in a non-contradictory clarification of how such social factors have their 'effect', how they can apparently become self-perpetuating, or a 'power' in themselves, 'bringing to naught all our calculations'.

Marx himself expressed the view, if not always clearly, that such social-structural factors as the division of labour and the class hierarchy are contingent historical human products, just as much as are material objects worked up from natural elements, technologies, specific institutions, and so forth. They are, as well, part of the 'circumstances' into which individuals are born, which are internalized as a specific content of mind, and which thereby define the individual's self and 'determine' his actions.

Such 'circumstances' become problematic in themselves, in Marx's view, in that as 'solutions' to historical problems within praxis, they no longer contribute effectively to the development of the species. As part of the capitalist social system, for example, the division of labour has contributed to a tremendous increase in material productivity. At the same time, this increase has accrued to a minority to the point where even basic needs of the majority of individuals are met only at the whim and in terms of the self-defined interests of this minority.

Clearly, what is expected of men, as beings of praxis faced with such a problematic, is critical reflexion and action to change such social factors into forms that are more amenable to the fulfilment and development of needs. While certain actions have been taken historically, these actions have seldom fundamentally or successfully questioned the basic division of labour or class hierarchy; they have generally been actions that remain within the existing social form and ideology, and which have simply attempted to achieve a redistribution of the social product. However, that the basic structural patterns of the system are not persistently or effectively called into question cannot be understood as indicating the 'reality' of such patterns in any ontological sense.

From Mead's point of view the existing structure of relationships forms an integral part of the attitudinal structure that each individual internalizes; a part of his very definition of himself as an individual, and as a member of his community. This is to emphasize a point no less essential to Marx; that of the integral and interdependent unity between thought and social form. In these terms, the persistence of existing patterns of interaction is in part dependent on the very organization of common attitudes and, therefore, on the organization of common responses that have been internalized.[33] Thus, the lack of critical reflexion, and the lack of a reorganization of attitudes and social forms, reflects the tension that exists between the existing internalized content of attitudes and the emergent reflexive capacity discussed above.

However, though a specific, differentiated structure of activity reflects or manifests a particular organization of commonly held attitudes, it has further unintended consequences in practice that cannot be left out of account. Clearly, a differentiated structure involves the 'segmentation' of a population, and thus a narrowing of the specific, *concrete* activity or praxis of each 'functionally' differentiated group. This, in turn, can have negative consequences which flow from an institutionalization or crystallization of these differentiated contexts, for this implies a *narrowing* of the practical contexts in which socialization and subsequent development takes place. Thus, the very attitudes involved in the existence of differentiation have the consequence, in practice, of more or less isolating the concrete and practical contexts, or 'circumstances' of each group, from those of other groups.

Mead is clearly aware of the fact of differentiation and, in degree, is aware of the negative consequences that flow from such a structure.[34] He argues, for example, that individuals

> may belong to a *small community*. . . . We all belong to small cliques, *and we may remain simply inside them*. The organized other present in ourselves is then *a community of narrow diameter*. We are struggling now to get a certain amount of international mindedness.[35]

He then explicitly connects this factor of differentiation to the issue of problematics or conflicts in the relationships of groups within a 'community':

> A highly developed and organized human society is one in which the individual members are interrelated in a multiplicity of different and intricate and complicated ways whereby they all share a number of common social interests . . . *and yet* . . . *are more or less in conflict in relation to numerous other interests which they possess only individually or else share with one another in small and* limited groups. . . . [And there] . . . are conflicts among their respective selves or personalities, each with a number of social facets or aspects, a number of different sets of social attitudes constituting it. . . . [36]

Mead then connects this concern in regard to the differentiated aspect of social relationships, with the introduction into social structures of formal education, and this brings out the implications of his position much more clearly. First, he argues that the internalization of 'any institutionalized attitude organizes in some degree the whole social process'.[37] However, he points out that within a highly differentiated community this process is achieved only with the introduction of such elements as formal education:

> The getting of this social response into the individual constitutes the process of education which takes over the cultural media of the community *in a more or less abstract way*. Education is definitely the process of taking over a certain organized set of responses to one's own stimulation; and until one can respond

> to oneself as the community responds to him, he does not genuinely belong to the community.[38]

What Mead describes is a situation in which, *because* of differentiation, the existence of common attitudes necessary to the integration and maintenance of the social structure as a whole, comes to depend, in part at least, on the introduction of such means as a formal learning process, rather than on the existence of a common, concrete interactional context of activity in which all participate.[39] Thus, the division of labour and the attitudes that it reflects have, in this sense, a practical consequence not immediately present in the attitudes themselves.

But of greater importance is Mead's rather off-hand reference to the fact that common attitudes internalized through education are 'more or less abstract'. In terms of the distinction between levels of consciousness, this is an emphasis on the degree to which specific attitudes and their organization are learned and held outside of the concrete contexts in which they have (or have lost) their meaning. Given a division of labour – itself an aspect of existing structures or patterns of interaction reflecting attitudes internalized – a situation arises in which the attitudinal basis for action of any particular individual or group is, in greater or lesser part, 'abstract' in relation to the specific concrete context of action of that particular group. The concrete context of their lives and attitudes is rendered of 'narrow diameter' as a result of differentiation. The 'expansion' of this diameter to encompass the total community is accomplished only through the introduction of common attitudes on an abstract basis. As a consequence, specific persons are not directly in a position to 'test' the adequacy of these 'common' attitudes, and thus they are further limited as to the functioning of the reflexive capacity in relation to the broader community of which their concrete 'functional' role is only a part.[40]

For example, most persons are isolated from any intimate contact or involvement with the political process of their society. Their 'information' as to the nature of this process may diverge considerably from the actuality that the political institution has become over time; and yet they are seldom in a position to become directly aware, either of the discrepancy or of the relatedness of the problematics in their own lives, to what the political activity has actually become. The 'narrow diameter' of their concrete practice with others and with things makes it highly problematic that many of the common internalized attitudes will ever be directly questioned. This is precisely because, through the divisions of labour and class, individuals are isolated both practically and ideationally from concrete relationships with the context to which these common attitudes refer. Thus, the persistence of attitudes whose reification is witnessed by the persistence of problematic forms of interaction, is 'determined' by historical social forms that are internalized, but only 'determined by' in this very specific manner.[41] Specific social forms have no ontological status through which they could be considered direct 'causes' of alienation and reification.

In summary, Mead's ideas contain at least two basic and related emphases that can be utilized in developing a non-positivistic clarification of the process and nature of alienation within praxis. First, the very socialization process in which man's self-consciousness and critical-reflexive capacity is based, is itself paradoxical. Initial attitudes are internalized from others and become the definition of self and environment. Any problematics that arise may call forth reflexion as Mead argues, but such reflexion entails the potentially difficult process of what amounts to self-criticism on the one hand, and, on the other, to a reorganization of ideas as to the nature of reality and appropriate action which have, hitherto, been quite accepted and acceptable to both self and others.

The second emphasis involves a focus on the manner in which specific historical products may be understood as having a reciprocal effect on man, and may become 'self-maintaining', without, at the same time, having to treat this effect as mechanical in nature. In Mead's framework, this is basically a question of how the content of specific internalized attitudes, as well as their manifestations in action, increase the predominance of 'information' over 'knowledge'; the predominance of initially internalized ideas over the potential for reflexion and for reorganization in the face of problematics. The division of labour, as an example, is an aspect of interaction that itself is rooted in the persistence of particular common attitudes. The existence and persistence of these attitudes is, however, 'self-maintaining' in that, in action, they lead to an effective isolation of individuals and groups from each other, and from the concrete contexts to which many of their attitudes refer and in which the ideas may indeed be, or become, problematic.

In neither case is the limitation on human capacities conceptualized as in any sense a total limitation or denial of praxis. They are essentially understood as difficulties directly related to the social nature of mind and self. The framework focuses attention on these limitations with the intention of removing or gaining control of them, such that a more adequate appreciation of the nature and basis of problematics arising in experience may be achieved.

In conclusion, this chapter has dealt with three major questions. First, it was demonstrated that there is a basic compatibility between the perspectives of Marx and Mead in respect to those explicit elements of their writing that elaborate the basic insight of the sociology of knowledge: their conceptions of man, of the social, of knowledge, and of the relationship between these terms. Second, it was shown that the concept of alienation, which is central to the Marxian critical perspective, is consistent with the Meadian framework despite its relative absence on any explicit level from the latter's works. Finally, in terms of this degree and range of compatibility, it has been demonstrated that Mead's central concept of socialization and internalization can generate an explanation of the origins of alienation that is consistent with the basic presupposition of human life as praxis. It remains to summarize the basic elements of the critical sociology of knowledge in relation to the critique, and to draw out some of the implications of this study.

chapter 5

Conclusion: the critical perspective

In terms of the specific focus of this study, it can be concluded that particular insights developed by Marx and by Mead can indeed be brought together in relation to the basic issue faced by the effort to develop an adequate sociology of knowledge: the issue of relativism that seems to be implied by the insight that knowledge is fundamentally social in nature. Of course the particular resolution of this issue developed here is not consistent with the expectations of most of those who have proposed the possibility, for it involves a major reformulation of basic presuppositions and concepts that have traditionally informed both work in the discipline and the discipline's critics.

In the first place, the perspective that emerges from this study fully embraces the assumption that knowledge is social and historical in character. Far from bowing to the traditional, positivistic claim that this assumption must inevitably entail the genetic fallacy and the self-contradiction of relativism, the critical perspective involves a fundamental reformulation of those ontological and epistemological assumptions not in harmony with the view that ideas are radically social. The justification for this effort rests in the sense of the criticisms enumerated in the first chapter.

There it was pointed out that there is no real debate, but rather a thorough-going contradiction between the critique and the effort consistently to elaborate the conception of ideas as social phenomena, between positivism and the basic presuppositions of the sociological enterprise and of the sociology of knowledge in particular. The central aspect of this contradiction is that while sociology and the sociology of knowledge are rooted in a social conception of man and ideas, the critique is historically rooted in positivistic parameters and, in turn, in a basically individualistic, a-social conception of reality and of the appropriate mode of understanding this reality. It is not unfair to say that the haste with which sociology has sought the halo of scientific legitimacy has quite blinded many of its theorists and practitioners to any full appreciation of this contradiction – a contradiction that is entailed in their uncritical importation of a methodology developed in relation to another subject-matter entirely.

The failure to recognize and to deal with this contradiction has had considerable consequences for the discipline. In particular, it has meant a tendency to impose a conceptualization of man, thought and the social dimension in terms consistent with the demands of the method adopted, as opposed to developing a method consistent with an appropriate and prior conceptualization of the social dimension. In the effort to adhere to the positivistic canons of research, society has been divorced from man and treated as a 'thing', a reality or a force in itself causally related to man as its derivative. Within the sociology of knowledge, this has meant that social phenomena are generally treated as existential phenomena, which causally determine the ideational sphere.

It is ironic, to say the least, that the positivistic approach to the sociology of knowledge is most strongly criticized by those who themselves espouse the positivistic or naturalistic framework. Clearly, as the critique maintains, to interpret thought as existentially determined is indeed relativistic; it implies a devaluation of human reason and it calls into question an entire philosophical tradition with respect to our self-understanding. However, something is missed by the critics: the fact that the sociologists of knowledge who are brought to trial are accused and convicted of acting according to the very parameters or presuppositions in terms of which the critique itself is formulated. That is, the sociology of knowledge – positivistically conceived – is a theoretical and empirical impossibility, yet it is an effort that has sought consistency with precisely the methodological presuppositions maintained by its critics, and for this very reason is self-contradictory.

In terms of the critical perspective, this circumstance is recognized not as a negative but as a positive outcome of work in the sociology of knowledge. The very attempt to elaborate the insight within positivistic parameters brings the basic contradiction between sociology and positivism to its clearest and most obvious expression: to treat human reality according to the methodological canons of a science constructed with the physical universe in mind, is fundamentally to devalue that different reality; it is to transform 'rational man', the ultimate historical premise of positivism, into the irrational product of any number of forces supposedly external to himself. More than one sociologist has come to the conclusion that man is indeed irrational after all, or has redefined rationality in terms of adaptation to the externally conceived, social environment. However, neither shift resolves the basic contradiction.

The traditional search for a way out of this dilemma in the sociology of knowledge has involved some form of the argument that there are limits to the social determination of ideas. Social determination is said to be limited to those ideas not as yet founded in positivistic analysis and criteria of validity. However, while there is considerable merit in the desire to limit, there are no criteria within positivism that would enable one to determine when an idea or action is or is not socially determined. Furthermore, positivism is not self-validating and as 'knowledge about knowledge' it remains a matter of belief that it is itself not socially and historically specific.

The critical perspective clearly does not face this dilemma. Its basic virtue in relation to traditional difficulties in the discipline is that it involves an initial effort to define carefully the general nature of human life *prior to* consideration of the nature of an appropriate approach to a more detailed analysis of this life. That is, rather than casting life in the image of a methodology developed in relation to a particular and largely deterministic conceptualization of physical reality, the critical perspective is rooted in a prior effort to determine what it can possibly make sense to say about specifically human reality. Only then does it become relevant to construct an approach to analysis, a methodology appropriate to this reality.

Certainly Marx's early work and the larger part of Mead's efforts are oriented precisely to this question: what does it make sense to say about the particular 'reality' we are attempting to understand? Those who would criticize either writer for not providing empirically testable propositions about the nature of human life ignore the fundamental fact that much of what is important in their work concerns the pre-empirical, pre-analytical task of sketching out or conceptualizing the reality that is to be subjected to investigation. As a result, they overlook or ignore the character of analysis implied in the writing of both theorists.

One obvious characteristic of the critical perspective that emerges in the work of Marx and Mead is its acceptance and inclusion of the presupposition of rational man – the very premise in which positivism itself is historically rooted, but which is lost in the positivistic analysis of thought and action. This is not to say that the image of rational man contained within the critical perspective is the same as that underlying positivism; none the less, it is man and his powers or abilities that are made central, and not 'society' nor some other external determinant. Specifically, man is conceptualized as a being of praxis. This is to say that his reality is a reality of dialectical engagement with the world in an active, self-conscious and co-operative process of producing what is required to maintain the species or to fulfil needs. It is to recognize that man creates what he requires: conceptions of his physical world, objects of consumption, technologies, forms of co-operation or social, institutional structures. Furthermore, the idea of praxis contains the recognition that these products are and remain contingent and passing, and that man is capable, through his emergent reflexive capacity, of the necessary refashioning of his products whether this be as a result of the experience of problematics or of the recognition of new potentialities implicit in the present mode of production. This is not to say that man is totally free to produce as he pleases. Praxis is limited ultimately by the 'patience' of a nature of which man himself is a part; it is limited by human need and its gradual development; and it is limited from moment to moment by the existing products or circumstances on which man presently depends and which can therefore be changed only gradually.

The social and reflexive moments of praxis are both conceptualized as *means* within the critical perspective and are understood as dialectically related and thus inseparable aspects of human life. Social forms are particular patterns of action and interaction, which are fundamentally rooted in the conceptual frameworks of the persons involved. Of course these are bolstered and reinforced by differential rewards and power, but are none the less objectifications of the participants' consciousness. Furthermore, social forms are forms of co-operation in the general effort to fulfil needs – the larger process of praxis. Human consciousness is likewise interpreted as a tool. On one level the emergence of mind as a symbolic content enables and is expressed or objectified in an ever more complex social, productive process. On a second level, it is a reflexive capacity or ability, the capacity to question existing objectifications and ideas and to transform them in the resolution of problematic situations as they arise and are experienced. On the one hand, mindedness emerges through the internalization of meanings already objectified in both language and the interactional patterns or social circumstances into which each child is born. On the other hand, mindedness is the emergent ability to transform these very meanings and thus to transform the social forms and other objectifications in which they are embedded or through which they are expressed.

From this point of view, the demand for a critical mode of analysis as opposed to a strictly positivistic mode, reflects the recognition that science and social science in particular must itself be an aspect of praxis for it can be no more than a particular expression of man's reflexive capacity. Thus, social science must be a part of man's problem-solving activity. It must begin with the experience of problematics and it must involve a questioning of existing modes of interrelated action and thought in relation to those problematics if it is to remain consistent with the idea of praxis. The failure of positivistic methodology has been, in these terms at least two-fold. First, when applied to the human sphere, it has ignored the dialectical interdependence of thought and social form or of man and society, and has treated them, as it must, as separate and different phenomena. It has then reconnected them in strictly causal terms which do not capture the reciprocal 'determination' that is involved and which thereby devalue the reality in question. Second, it has reified the existing social context and, at best, has left man the task of adaptation to this 'environment' and to its autonomous evolutionary development. Positivism has not viewed itself as an aspect of praxis, as but an aspect inseparable from human life. It has viewed itself instead as a means of standing outside of praxis and has, in the process, distorted human reality.

This distortion is expressed most clearly in the positivistic interpretation of the one experience that would appear to justify its application to human reality: the experience of social constraint or control. Certainly there is considerable evidence amassed in positivistic research that would appear to support the view that persons are derivatives of their social milieux, that their thought is largely ideological or functional for social system maintenance and that conformity in thought and action, not rationality and freedom, is the primary human motivation. The argument that social 'facts' must be treated as things is very largely based on recognition of this very experience, as is the notion of a 'functional' study of 'society' as if it were a phenomenon separate from man.

However, the critical perspective rejects this interpretation of social constraint and the causal and functionalist modes of analysis which this interpretation would appear to call for. It does so precisely because this interpretation of constraint is not consistent with its prior conception of human life as praxis and because it is clearly not the only interpretation possible. In contrast, the critical perspective interprets social constraint as the central problematic to be dealt with within praxis itself: as the estrangement of persons from continued and conscious control over their own historical products. In other words, what is interpreted as social causality of action and thought within the positivistic framework, is interpreted as estrangement or alienation within the critical perspective. What is conceptualized as a fact of human existence by positivism, is understood as a problematic to be interpreted and overcome within critical sociology.

While maintaining that praxis is the underlying and persistent reality of human life, the critical perspective acknowledges that the various products or objectifications of praxis can and do become estranged from their producers and that, as a result, persons become subject to, rather than subjects in control of, their lives. The ongoing dialectic of man and object is fettered or limited in the direction of a predominance of product over process, of objectivity over subjectivity. This occurs in respect to objects treated as commodities, in respect to methods or technologies and particular social forms treated as the 'one best way', and in respect to conceptions of thought itself and to specific, supposedly 'self-evident' beliefs accepted uncritically. The roots of this estrangement are interpreted as lying within and not outside of praxis itself: within the socialization process in the dialectic of content and capacity, and within the reciprocal and largely unintended consequences of particular social forms that have been developed.

From this point of view, positivistic analysis at best achieves a useful description of the current form of praxis, including, if not recognizing, the degree of estrangement within it. Its basic error lies in its distortion of the social circumstances that are described through the assumption that explanation must consist of the determination of causal or functional relationships between the various components of the social situation as they presently appear. As Marx argued, this error amounts to presupposing as a fact what yet has to be explained: the historical emergence of these particular forms on the one hand, and, on the other, their perpetuation in spite of the problematics they entail in relation to human need and development. In other words, beyond the element of description, positivistic analysis reifies or de-historicizes a particular stage of development and, as a result, contributes to its perpetuation.

In contrast, as a part of praxis itself, the task of social science goes beyond description and becomes critique. It becomes the task of unmasking human alienation, the task of demonstrating the relationship between the experience of persistent problematics and the persistence of particular and largely unquestioned ideas and the social forms in which they are embedded and reinforced. Within this programme it is the role of a critical sociology of knowledge to consider the adequacy of existing thought and institutional structure in relation to both present need and potentiality. It is the effort to discover the degree to which persistent problems are a consequence of an unreflexive or a-critical adherence to particular, abstract ideas, and to discover how, in turn, the predominance of existing information is rooted in the reciprocal relationship between attitudes and specific, historically developed patterns of action.

The aim of such research is clearly not the achievement of disinterested, value-free knowledge of the laws governing the relationship between thought and social form. To the contrary, its goal is praxis itself, ultimately the resolution of problems of alienation and reification which limit fulfilment and development of human need. Thus, to be consistent with the concept of human life as praxis, social analysis must view itself as subject to and as a functional moment within the very process and its development. It is perhaps in this respect more than any other that the critical perspective so clearly differs from the sociology of knowledge positivistically conceived.

Finally, it is within this notion of social analysis as an aspect within and inseparable from praxis that a particular resolution of the traditional issue of relativism emerges, and with it, a final response to the critique. Obviously, in strictly positivistic terms, the critical perspective does remain relativistic; it virtually embraces relativism as a fact of human life. Human consciousness and ideas are interpreted as but tools in the life and development of the species, as a functional moment within praxis and thus inseparable from the social dimension. Furthermore, the entire range of concepts and even the basic categories are considered contingent and thus ever subject to refutation and reformulation as problematics emerge in the passage of time and as new possibilities are recognized within present circumstances. In consequence, the very study of the dialectic of social form and idea is construed as an aspect of man's effort to specify his alienation, especially the reification of ideas in relation to social form. It is therefore itself but a tool ultimately oriented to the reassertion of control over and change in the structure of present circumstance.

But though the critical perspective explicitly rejects the possibility of absolute knowledge in the traditional sense, it none the less rejects any total relativism of thought and does provide a fundamental criterion of judgment. This criterion is obviously man himself, or more precisely, man's life understood as praxis. If social analysis is to be considered itself an aspect of praxis, then clearly the test of its pronouncements must ultimately be their functionality for praxis, for the resolution of problematics, the fulfilment of species-needs and thus for the continued realization of praxis itself.

Notes

1 THE CRITIQUE OF THE SOCIOLOGY OF KNOWLEDGE

1 At least twenty-five years of literature in the area abounds with indications not only of the need to formulate an adequate framework which counters the critique, but that the promise of such a response lies in a sociology of knowledge constructed on the basis of compatible elements of Marxian and Meadian sociologies. H. Gerth and C. W. Mills in their text *Character and Social Structure* (New York: Harbinger, 1964), p.xv, Mills himself in I. L. Horowitz (ed.), *Power, Politics and People* (London: Oxford, 1963), pt 4, A. Gouldner in his *The Coming Crisis in Western Sociology* (New York: Equinox, 1966), p. 116, and J. Israel in his *Alienation: From Marx to Modern Sociology* (New York: Basic Books, 1966), p. viii and p. 20 all suggest that there is considerable potential in a synthesis of their writings. Other writers such as W. Stark, *The Sociology of Knowledge* (London: Routledge & Kegan Paul, 1958), A. Child, 'The Problem of Imputation in the Sociology of Knowledge', *Ethics*, LI (June 1940–41), pp. 153–85, B. Bauman, 'G. H. Mead and Luigi Pirandello: Some Parallels' in P. Berger (ed.), *Marxism and Sociology* (New York: Appleton-Century-Crofts, 1969), E. Urbanek, 'Roles, Masks and Characters: a Contribution to Marx's Idea of Social Role', *Social Research*, XXXIV (1967), J. McKinney, 'The Contribution of G. H. Mead to the Sociology of Knowledge', *Social Forces*, XXXIV (1955) and K. Wolff, 'The Sociology of Knowledge in the United States of America', *Current Sociology* (1966), have placed specific emphasis on the relevance of Mead's work in relation to the epistemological problems of the discipline raised by the critics. The efforts of P. L. Berger and T. Luckmann in *The Social Construction of Reality* (New York: Doubleday, 1966), imply a complementarity of the Marxian and Meadian perspectives in so far as they claim to draw their 'anthropological presuppositions' and their 'dialectical' modification of Durkheim's image of society from Marx, and their 'social-psychological' presuppositions from Mead. They suggest in particular that problems associated with the concepts of alienation and reification might be effectively dealt with in terms of Mead's

approach to the socialization process. In contrast to Berger and Luckmann, one finds much more detailed if yet incomplete efforts to deal with the suggested compatibilities in recent efforts by R. Lichtman, 'Symbolic Interactionism and Social Reality: Some Marxist Queries', *Berkeley Journal of Sociology*, XV (1970), R, Ropers, 'Marx, Mead and Modern Sociology', *Catalyst*, no. 7 (1973), G. F. Cronk, 'Symbolic Interactionism: A "Left-Meadian" Interpretation', *Social Theory and Practice* (1972) and I. M. Zeitlin, *Rethinking Sociology* (New Jersey: Prentice-Hall, 1973). There are of course other efforts to construct an adequate sociology of knowledge in the face of the critique such as those of W. Stark, *The Sociology of Knowledge*, Berger and Luckmann, *Social Construction*, N. Elias, 'Sociology of Knowledge: New Perspectives', *Sociology* (May 1971) and S. Taylor, *Conceptions of Institutions and the Theory of Knowledge* (New York: Bookman Associates, 1956), but none proceed in precisely the direction of this study in an attempt to consider the hypotheses in respect to the importance of Marx and Mead.

2 It may appear to be a fruitless task to return to such classical thinkers for guidance in respect to contemporary issues and debates. However, in Nisbet's words, it is assumed here that 'in the same way that a novelist will always be able to learn from a study of Dostoevski or James – to learn a sense of development and form as well as to draw inspiration from the creative source – so the sociologist can forever learn from a rereading of such men as Weber and Simmel'. Current efforts of re-evaluation of various classical writers have not gone unrewarded in relation to the 'crisis of Western sociology' and complement Nisbet's early suggestion. It is hoped that this study constitutes a modest addition to these efforts in relation to the development of a valid sociology of knowledge and, more generally perhaps, to a valid sociology. See R. A. Nisbet, *The Sociological Tradition* (New York : Basic Books, 1966), p. 20.

3 I refer here for example to the work of the Frankfurt school, which is discussed, particularly in regard to the critical implications of Marx's work, by T. Schroyer, *The Critique of Domination* (New York: G. Braziller, 1973). See also F. Hearn, 'The Implications of Critical Theory for Critical Sociology', *Berkeley Journal of Sociology* XXVIII (1973), and C. Fletcher, *Beneath the Surface* (London: Routledge & Kegan Paul, 1974).

4 As Nisbet has argued, in *Sociological Tradition*, p. viii, 'In the history of ideas, influences always demand counter-influences for their nourishment. . . . So long as these conflicts [of ideas] continue, will the sociological tradition remain the evocative and relevant tradition that it has been for more than a century.' Counter-influences to various social theories of knowledge exist in profusion but adequate response to this 'nourishment' has not been forthcoming within the field. An effort to transcend the current impasse needs once again to be undertaken.

5 R. K. Merton, 'The Sociology of Knowledge', in G. Gurvitch and W. E. Moore (eds), *Twentieth Century Sociology* (New York: The Philosophical Library, 1945), pp. 366–405.

6 These reservations are the subject of the following discussion. They concern the extent to which this 'general' statement is indeed not as general as it might be and thus the degree to which Merton prejudges the character of a possible sociology of knowledge, especially in his use of the term 'existential'.

7 Merton, 'The Sociology of Knowledge', pp. 379–80, suggests that, in regard to the term knowledge, 'Even a cursory summary is enough to show that the term . . . has been so broadly conceived as to refer to every type of assertion and every mode of thought ranging from folk belief to positive science [and these] . . . are more or less indiscriminantly held to be "existentially conditioned". See also F. E. Hartung, 'Problems of the Sociology of Knowledge', *Philosophy of Science*, XIX (January 1952), A. Child, 'The Existential Determination of Thought', *Ethics*, LII (1942), pp. 200–49 and J. Plamenatz, *Ideology* (Toronto: Macmillan, 1971), chs 1–3.

8 On this criticism, see especially A. Child, 'The Problem of Imputation in the Sociology of Knowledge', pp. 200–49, V. Hinshaw, 'The Epistemological Relevance of Mannheim's Sociology of Knowledge', *Journal of Philosophy*, XL (1943), S. Taylor, *Conceptions* and R. K. Merton, 'Paradigm for the Sociology of Knowledge', in J. R. Curtis and J. W. Petras (eds), *The Sociology of Knowledge : A Reader* (New York: Praeger, 1972), pp. 342–72.

9 This central criticism of the discipline appears in almost every comment in the field. See in particular Merton, 'Paradigm', Taylor, *Conceptions*, B. Walter, 'The Sociology of Knowledge and the Problem of Objectivity', in L. Gross (ed.), *Sociological Theory: Inquiries and Paradigms* (New York: Harper & Row, 1967), Hinshaw, 'Relevance', R. H. Coombs, 'Karl Mannheim, Epistemology and the Sociology of Knowledge', *Sociological Quarterly*, VII (1966) and Child, 'The Existential Determination of Thought'.

10 Hartung, 'Problems', p. 21.

11 G. Remmling, *The Road to Suspicion* (New York: Appleton-Century-Crofts, 1967).

12 K. Mannheim, *Ideology and Utopia* (New York: Harvest Books, n.d.), pp. 64–85.

13 A. Child, 'The Theoretical Possibility of the Sociology of Knowledge', *Ethics*, LI (July 1941), pp. 392–441. Child is the one critic who impugns the discipline to this fundamental extent and, in fact, denies the traditional meaning of the insight entirely. His argument, its basis and implications, will be discussed in more detail below.

14 We refer here basically to the tendency for the sociology of knowledge to be conceived primarily as analysis of communication,

media impact, propaganda or the study of the social distribution of ideas within the functional divisions of a society; generally the study of the 'functional' interrelationships of ideas taken as such and social-structural elements or characteristics. As an example, see F. Znaniecki, *The Social Role of the Man of Knowledge* (New York: Columbia University Press, 1940).

15 E. Durkheim, *The Rules of the Sociological Method* (New York: Free Press, 1966), chap. 1.

16 E. Durkheim, 'The Dualism of Human Nature and Its Social Conditions', in K. Wolff (ed.), *Emile Durkheim: 1858–1917* (Columbus, Ohio: Ohio State University Press, 1960).

17 E. Durkheim, *The Elementary Forms of Religious Life*, J. Swain (trans.) (New York: Free Press, 1969), especially introduction and conclusion. See also E. Durkheim and M. Mauss, *Primitive Classification*, R. Needham (trans.) (Chicago: Phoenix Books, 1967).

18 E. Durkheim, 'Individualism and the Intellectuals' in S. Lukes, 'Durkheim's Individualism and the Intellectuals', *Political Studies*, XVII (1969).

19 Durkheim, *Elementary Forms*, pp. 26–32, 479–95.

20 *Ibid.*, p. 483.

21 Mannheim, *Ideology and Utopia*, chap. 1, pt 1 and chap. 5.

22 *Ibid.*, p. 276.

23 *Ibid.*, pp. 306–9.

24 *Ibid.*, pp. 282–3.

25 *Ibid.*, pp. 147–64.

26 See, for example, Hartung, 'Problems', Merton, 'Paradigm', Walter, 'Objectivity' and Taylor, *Conceptions.*

27 Hartung, 'Problems, p. 31 and P. Hamilton, *Knowledge and Social Structure* (London: Routledge & Kegan Paul, 1974), pp. 132–4.

28 P. L. Berger and T. Luckmann, *The Social Construction of Reality* (New York: Doubleday, 1967), pp. 13–14.

29 *Ibid.*, p. 17. They describe their work as an effort to synthesize insights of Marx, Durkheim, Weber, Mannheim and Mead.

30 *Ibid.*, pp. 30–1, 56–7.

31 *Ibid.*, p. 61.

32 *Ibid.*, pp. 56–62.

33 Objectification or institutionalization and internalization become the two processes of basic concern in their writing.

34 Berger and Luckmann, *Social Construction*, pp. 59, 62, 63, 174–80.

35 *Ibid.*, pp. 101–4. The same point is made somewhat more clearly by Berger in an article with S. Pullberg, 'Reification and the Sociological Critique of Consciousness', *History and Theory*, V. 4 (1965), pp. 196–211.

36 P. L. Berger and T. Luckmann, *Social Construction*, pp. 87, 108–9, 163–73.

37 For example, Franz Adler, among others, argues that, 'If the sociology of knowledge is to develop healthily . . . and if it is to

take its place with dignity among the other branches of sociology, the sociologies of knowledge will have to . . . abide by the canons of scientific research and the methods of verification accepted in this culture . . . ; they will have to throw off the ballast of inflated language and the esoteric metaphysical speculations with which past authors have encumbered the field' ('The Sociology of Knowledge Since 1918', *Midwest Sociologist*, XVII (1955), p. 12). See also 'Werner Stark's Sociology of Knowledge,' *Kyklos*, XII (1959) and *idem* 'The Range of the Sociology of Knowledge', in H. Becker and A. Boskoff (eds), *Modern Sociological Theory in Continuity and Change* (New York: Holt, Rinehart & Winston, 1957). Cf., Hinshaw, 'Relevance', Hartung, 'Problems', Coombs, 'Mannheim' and Merton, 'Paradigm'.

38 M. Scheler, 'The Sociology of Knowledge: Formal Problems', R. Kochne (trans.) in J. E. Curtis and J. W. Petras (eds), *The Sociology of Knowledge: a Reader* (New York: Praeger, 1972), pp. 177, 182.

39 These points will be taken up in more detail in the subsequent analyses of Marx and Mead.

40 S. Taylor, *Conceptions*, chap. 4.

41 Berger and Luckmann, *Social Construction*, pp. 13–15.

42 E. Durkheim, *Rules of the Sociological Method*, conclusion, *Elementary Forms*, p. 13 and Mannheim, *Ideology and Utopia*, pp. 306–9.

43 Child, 'Theoretical Possibility', p. 405.

44 Child, 'The Problem of Imputation Resolved', *Ethics*, LIV (1943), pp. 108–9, emphasis added.

45 Child does leave room for a type of sociology of knowledge, if it can still be called that. The discipline becomes the statement of what specific ideas are in fact held and expressed by specific groups, especially groups organized around some explicit ideology. Also, it becomes but the beginning of a study of the empirically demonstrable impact of ideologically organized groups on the more amorphous categories of persons these groups attempt to influence. In general, the discipline is left with the study of a presumed functional correlation between specific ideas and specific aspects of social structure. *Ibid.*, p. 104.

46 Plamenatz, *Ideology*, p. 70.

47 *Ibid.*, p. 61.

48 Hartung, 'Problems', p. 18.

49 *Ibid.*, p. 27.

50 *Ibid.*, pp. 20–1.

51 L. Kolakowski, *The Alienation of Reason* (New York: Anchor Books, 1969), esp. pp. 1–10. For other critical analyses of positivism in respect to social analysis, see H. Marcuse, *One-Dimensional Man* (London: Routledge & Kegan Paul, 1966), esp. chs 5–7, F. Matson, *The Broken Image* (New York: Anchor Books, 1966), J. E. Hanson, 'A Dialectical Critique of Empiricism',

Catalyst, no. 3 (Summer 1967), A. Dawe, 'The Role of Experience in the Construction of Sociological Theory', *Sociological Review*, XXI (1973), A. Dawe, 'The Relevance of Values', in A. Sahay (ed.), *Max Weber and Modern Sociology* (London: Routledge & Kegan Paul, 1971), and Schroyer, *Critique of Domination*, chap. 3.

52 Kolakowski, *Alienation*, p. 9.

53 It is well to remember that the debate over positivism within sociology has a history as long as the discipline itself. This alone is enough to support the effort to achieve some alternative basis of objectivity within the sociology of knowledge. See A. Giddens (ed.), *Positivism and Sociology* (London: Heinemann, 1974), J. O'Neill (ed.), *Modes of Individualism and Collectivism* (London: Heinemann, 1973), pp. 3–26, P. Winch, *Idea of a Social Science* (London: Routledge & Kegan Paul, 1958) and B. Fay, *Social Theory and Political Practice* (London: Allen & Unwin, 1975).

54 For example, the founder of sociological positivism, Auguste Comte – see 'The Positive Philosophy' in K. Thompson and T. Tunstall, *Sociological Perspectives* (Harmondsworth: Penguin, 1971), pp. 18–32.

55 See, for example, T. Kuhn, *The Structure of Scientific Revolutions* (Chicago: University of Chicago Press, 1962) and P. K. Feyerabend, 'Problems of Empiricism', in R. G. Colodny (ed.), *Beyond the Edge of Certainty* (New Jersey: Prentice-Hall, 1965).

56 See Lavine's works, in particular T. Z. Lavine, 'Naturalism and the Sociological Analysis of Knowledge', in Y. H. Krikorian (ed.), *Naturalism and the Human Spirit* (New York: Columbia University Press, n.d.), pp. 183–209. Also 'Reflections on the Genetic Fallacy', *Social Research*, XXIX (1962), pp. 321–36, 'Note to Naturalists on the Human Spirit' and 'What is the Method of Naturalism?', *The Journal of Philosophy*, XL (February 1953), 'Sociological Analysis of Cognitive Norms', *Journal of Philosophy*, XXXIX (1942) and 'Karl Mannheim and Contemporary Functionalism', *Philosophy and Phenomenological Research*, XXV (1965).

57 Lavine 'Sociological Analysis of Cognitive Norms', p. 350. Lavine's argument is expressly 'in behalf of an *unrestricted* sociological analysis of knowledge', which would thus include the very validating norms of positivistic science.

58 Lavine, 'Note to Naturalists on the Human Spirit', pp. 258–9. There are severe problems with Lavine's thesis beyond this point in her argument, for she then proceeds to develop a justification for the need to study the very social-historical rootedness of positivistic science via the presumption and utilization of that very methodology. See M. Natanson (ed.), *Philosphy of the Social Sciences* (New York: Random House, 1963), pp. 271–85. None the less, the significant point for this study is that she points out – and emphasizes – the very lack of empirically demonstrable grounds in terms of which the insight can be rejected in favour of the canons of empirical science, themselves but presuppositions or rooted in

presuppositions.

59 This point is, ironically, better appreciated and understood in the natural sciences than in sociology. As John O'Neill notes in *Individualism and Collectivism*, p. 22, 'even in mathematics Gödel and Tarski have shown that it is not possible to develop a self-validating logic which relieves us of the choice of axioms and the assumption of responsibility for the particular grammar in which we frame a problem.'

60 Taylor, *Conceptions*. See also Taylor, 'Social Factors and the Validation of Thought', *Social Forces*, XLI (October 1962).

61 Taylor, *Conceptions*. The central thesis of Taylor's work is that individualistic epistemologies and the insight of the sociology of knowledge are ultimately not incompatible (p. 14), and his argument is primarily based on demonstrating that the classical theory is itself but one, and indeed a partial, response to the persistent historical issue of relativism.

62 *Ibid*., p. 18.

63 *Ibid*., p. 124. See also L. Kolakowski, *Alienation*.

64 Taylor, *Conceptions*, pp. 38–9, 96, 119.

65 *Ibid*., p. 53.

66 *Ibid*., p. 40.

67 *Ibid*., p. 42.

68 'Kant does not regard his categories as resting upon an agreement, as having been built up in a social process, but as the conditions universally necessary for rational thought. If Kant has not taken from the past the conception of an absolute ontology, or truth, resting upon a stadium such as God, he has none the less made the forms according to which one judges just as absolute. . . . Kant goes so far as to say that in order to eliminate all elements of contingency from knowledge – to render it truly scientific – the validating criteria must be a priori. To this the sociology of knowledge must take exception. It would hold that the validating framework is built up in the social process, and hence, the view of an absolute rationality is untenable. If, as the sociology of knowledge would hold, the categories have a history, this would mean that the objectivity given by the Kantian categorical scheme, like that given by the sacred society, has its basis in agreement. To say this is to indicate that knowledge validated on the basis of the Kantian criteria is perspectival knowledge, is knowledge from one point of view' (*ibid*., p. 47).

69 *Ibid*., p. 46.

70 Cf. I. M. Zeitlin, *Ideology and the Development of Social Theory*, (New Jersey: Prentice-Hall, 1968), ch. 1.

71 Taylor, *Conceptions*, p. 40.

72 *Ibid*., pp. 33, 46–7, 119–20.

73 See for example, Nisbet, *Sociological Tradition*, pt 1, Zeitlin, *Ideology and Development*, pts 1 and 2; Gouldner, *Coming Crisis*, ch. 2 and A. Dawe, 'The Two Sociologies', in K. Thompson and J.

Tunstall (eds), *Sociological Perspectives* (Harmondsworth: Penguin Books, 1971), pp. 542–54.

74 Writers such as Comte, Durkheim, Parsons, etc., clearly emphasize the importance of the social context for the individual, yet, in each case, the orientation to analysis is positivistic in character – it is held that there are no fundamental distinctions between the studies of physical and social reality. Indeed, the majority of modern textbooks begin by defining sociology as an empirical science of society, and express this idea in the language of observation and experiment.

75 Taylor, *Conceptions*, pp. 32–3, 7–88, 119–20. Taylor argues that the classical theory of knowledge 'is distinguished by its antithetical separation of the free, rational individual from the external, restrictive institution. It is true that the effort is made, but rarely, to carry out the principle of individualism in a complete way. Only a few attempt the reduction to anarchism. . . . But generally speaking, the discussion of the self-sufficient individual is based upon the intellectual conviction that egoism is a universal fact of human life. . . . More often than not the literary expression of the time is infused with a high regard for mankind who, it is felt, requires only the independence, the intrepidity and the courage to oppose its rationality to slavish obedience, tyranny and hypocrisy in order to liberate itself from institutional bondage' (p. 87).

76 *Ibid.*, pp. 32, 36.

77 *Ibid.*, pp. 36–7, 47, 53–4, 126.

78 *Ibid.*, pp. 16–17. It is Taylor's contention that the 'faith' in reason was not totally denied by the recognition of institutional bias. But reason alone was not enough; individualistic thinkers 'hastened to establish a mode of thought that would be detached from the distorting influence of social factors . . . ; while it was the philosopher's conception that bias and error are intrinsic to institutions, they, nevertheless, believed that it was possible to reach the reasoning process as such, and having accomplished this end, to find ways to eliminate, or control the virus of error, constituted, so to speak, by social existence' (p. 17).

79 This emphasis, on the 'search for a rational method' necessary to counteract the 'negative influence' of various factors, including social factors, on reason in search of truth, is admirably brought out by Stanley Taylor, *Conceptions*, ch. 2 and by Kolakowski, *Alienation*. Discussion of the forerunners of the discipline, with specific emphasis on Enlightenment thinkers, include G. Remmling, *Towards the Sociology of Knowledge* (London: Routledge & Kegan Paul, 1973), pt 2, Remmling, *Road to Suspicion*, chs 11–13, Stark, *Sociology of Knowledge*, P. Hamilton, *Knowledge and Social Structure*, ch. 1 and Curtis and Petras (eds), *The Sociology of Knowledge*, pt 1, no. 1. It is interesting that the so-called 'forerunners' of the discipline were writers whose primary concern lay in comprehending, *in order to remove*, the influence of social

factors. Despite the fact that a consistent adherence to the sociological insight implies, to the contrary, a 'positive' conception of the relationship, the influence of the forerunners remains as an influence of method on conceptual elaboration. Thus, for example, Hamilton argues that the problems of the sociology of knowledge simply amount to a 'need for a *scientific* test of the concepts and theories that [sociologists of knowledge] employ: interests and value [social factors] may play a highly significant role in the choice of issues for scientific study, *but they must and can be separated out from actual methods of investigation and explanation*. . . . The sociology of knowledge . . . ought to be involved in *the study of the extent to which the processes of knowledge production, validation, distribution and change are inter-penetrated by social phenomena and work towards a precise determination of the effects of that inter-penetration*' (pp. 147–8, emphasis added). In other words, he, for one, conceives the discipline as an attempt to understand and control the 'negative' intrusion of social factors, and, thereby, contradicts the traditional sociological meaning of the insight.

80 *Taylor*, *Conceptions*, pp. 45–6.

81 *Ibid.*, pp. 48, 128. 'a leading characteristic of all forms of individualism was its repudiation of institutional structure as a validational base for either thought or conduct. Yet this institutional structure was but the product of an earlier stage of the social process, and expressed an earlier form of the conceptual system. Individualism in denying the reality of institutions did not recognize that the object of its denial was in fact an outworn categorical order. Moreover, individualism did not at first view itself as an institution, or as the matrix of a new institutional complex. In its assertion of the profound nature and finality of the individual as opposed to society . . . it failed to recognize that this, too, was a socially formulated "perspective" ' (p. 128).

2 MARX: ELEMENTS OF A SOCIOLOGY OF KNOWLEDGE

1 See, for example, P. Hamilton, *Knowledge and Social Structure* (London: Routledge & Kegan Paul, 1974), introduction. These criticisms are not always made together by the same author of course. Often Marx is indeed interpreted as attempting a 'scientific sociology of knowledge and is criticized simply for his failure, for his infusion, into empirical analysis, of value judgment. But it is argued as well that he failed to exempt 'scientific method' from social penetration: 'On the basis of his theory of the division of labor, Marx begins to suspect that inevitably man's total outlook as distinguished from its details must be distorted. At this point the particular conception of ideology merges with the total conception of ideology and Marx discredits the total structure of man's consciousness, considering him no longer capable of thinking

correctly.' G. Remmling, *Road to Suspicion* (New York: Appleton-Century-Crofts, 1967) p. 162. Remmling is arguing that Marx totally discredits reason, for, while he goes on to note that Marx has a conception of the basis of truth, this requires the metaphysical acceptance of Marxism itself as truth. This not only misses Marx's point, as will be brought out below, it is an argument that can be used against Remmling himself in terms of his own acceptance of quantitative method as the answer to relativism and to the 'abyss of commercialized nihilism' (p. 48).

2 For example: 'In the social production which men carry on they enter into definite relations that are indispensable and independent of their will; these relations of production correspond to a definite stage of development of their material powers of production. The totality of these relations of production constitute the economic structure of society – the real foundation on which legal and political superstructures arise and to which definite forms of social consciousness correspond. The mode of production of material life determines the general character of the social, political and spiritual processes of life. It is not the consciousness of men that determines their being, but, on the contrary, their social being determines their consciousness.' K. Marx, *A Contribution to the Critique of Political Economy* (Moscow: Progress, 1970), pp. 20–1. 'Consciousness is therefore from the very beginning a social product and remains so as long as men exist at all', *The German Ideology* (Moscow: Progress, 1968), p. 427, 'Dominant ideas are nothing more than the ideal expression of the dominant material relationships, the dominant relationships grasped as ideas . . .' (*ibid*, p. 61). 'My dialectic method is not only different from the Hegelian, but its direct opposite. To Hegel, the life-process of the human brain, e.g. the process of thinking, which, under the name of "the idea", he even translated into an independent subject, is the demiurgos of the real world, and the real world is only the external, phenomenal form of "the idea". With me, on the contrary, the ideal is nothing else than the material world reflected in the human mind, and translated into forms of thought' (Marx, *Capital I*, Moscow: Foreign Languages Publishing House, 1954, p. 19). As to the apparent relativism of Marx's position, he argues that, 'The same men who establish social relations in conformity with their material power of production also produce principles, laws and categories in conformity with their social relations. Thus, these categories are no more eternal than the relations which they express. They are historical and transient products' (Marx, *The Poverty of Philosophy*, New York: International Publishers, 1963, pp. 109–10).

3 L. Dupré, *The Philosophical Foundations of Marxism* (New York: Harcourt, Brace World, 1966). See esp. chap. 8 for a summary of his argument.

4 S. Avineri, *The Social and Political Thought of Karl Marx* (Cambridge: Cambridge University Press, 1969), epilogue.

5 'Marx's career reveals throughout an implicit tension between his conviction that the revolution is immanent and his disinclination to be implicated in a coup that would try violently to usher in the millenium. . . . Marx disregarded the possibilities open to his own theory; and therein lies his major intellectual blunder.' (*ibid.*, p. 58). See also p. 251 and T. Schroyer, *Critique of Domination* (New York: G. Braziller, 1973) pp. 92–7.

6 See chap. 1, note 13.

7 Avineri, *Social and Political Thought* and Dupré, *Philosophical Foundations*.

8 Cf., 'Marx is neither materialist (matter is fundamental to consciousness) nor an idealist (consciousness is fundamental to matter). He adheres to a position in which nature is basic to mind, but man's activities mediate the natural processes and create a unity that is in neither the subject nor the object. The subject–object schema of materialism and idealism is transcended in a radicalization which conceives the humanization of nature and the naturalization of man as proceeding via the synthetic "fire" of human labor which constitutes an objective world that man can comprehend reflectively, thereby recognizing new human potentialities.' (Schroyer, *Critique of Domination*, p. 76). See also J. Habermas, *Knowledge and Human Interests* (Boston: Beacon Press, 1971), Avineri, *Social and Political Thought*, Dupré, *Philosophical Foundations*', McLellan, *The Thought of Karl Marx: An Introduction* (London: Macmillan, 1971), McLellan, *Marx Before Marxism* (Harmondsworth: Penguin, 1970), G. Petrovic, *Marx in the Mid-Twentieth Century* (New York: Doubleday, 1967), L. Kolakowski, *Toward a Marxist Humanism: Essays on the Left Today* (New York: Grove Press, 1969) and B. Ollman, *Alienation: Marx's Conception of Man in Capitalist Society* (Cambridge: Cambridge University Press, 1973).

9 In particular, see D. McLellan, *Marx Before Marxism*, Avineri, *Social and Political Thought*, Dupré, *Philosophical Foundations* and J. O'Malley (ed.), *Karl Marx: Critique of Hegel's Philosophy of Right* (Cambridge: Cambridge University Press, 1970), introduction. Like these other writers who Marx criticizes, Marx was writing in response to the problematic character of social life in post-revolutionary Europe. He, however, could accept neither materialist nor idealist 'solutions' and used others' work as a foil against which to develop his own ideas. It is often overlooked that much of his writing is indeed a criticism of the ideas of others – especially the idealists (Hegel and the Young–Hegelians) and the 'abstract' materialists such as Feuerbach and the political economists. This is clearly the case, for example, in the early writings where the descriptions of social conditions are taken directly from the political economists. An essential part of Marx's critical approach involves the demonstration that it is precisely the attempt by these writers to follow materialist canons of 'objectivity' that inhibits their ability to see the *meaning* for persons of the

descriptions they themselves give of conditions.

10 T. B. Bottomore (ed.), *Karl Marx: Selected Writings in Sociology and Social Philosophy* (Toronto: McGraw-Hill, 1964), pp. 67–9. Emphasis added.

11 Pursuing the conclusion of chapter 1, the intention here is to elaborate this 'other' position in terms of which Marx develops his critical stance.

12 'It is, in practice, much easier to discover by analysis the earthly core of the misty creations of religion than, conversely, to infer from the actual relations of life at any period the corresponding "spiritualized" forms of these relations. But the latter method is the only materialistic, and therefore the only scientific one. The inadequacy of the abstract materialism of natural science, which leaves out of consideration the historical process, is at once evident from the abstract and ideological conceptions of its spokesmen, whenever they venture beyond the bounds of their own specialism' (K. Marx, *Capital I*, Moscow: Foreign Languages Publishing House, 1964, p. 372, n. 3). Even in this passage however, it is already clear that what he means by these terms must include reference to 'practice' and 'human relationships' which he implies natural science (so often the model for social science) does not include.

13 T. B. Bottomore (ed.), Karl Marx, *Early Writings* (Toronto: McGraw-Hill, 1964), p. 157.

14 *Ibid.*, pp. 163–4, emphasis added. See also K. Marx, *German Ideology* (Moscow: Progress Publishers, 1968), pp. 57–61.

15 K. Marx, *Early Writings*, pp. 159–61, 164, 207–8.

16 Marx, *German Ideology*, p. 39, emphasis added.

17 *Ibid.*, p. 31, emphasis added.

18 'Man is the direct object of natural science, *because* directly perceptible nature is for man directly human sense experience. . . . But nature is the direct object of the science of man. The first object for man – man himself – is nature, sense experience. . . . The social reality of nature and human natural science, or the natural science of man, are identical expressions' (Marx, *Early Writings*, p. 164).

19 Marx, *German Ideology*, p. 40, emphasis added.

20 *Ibid.*, pp. 40–1, emphasis added. See also *Early Writings*, p. 157.

21 Marx, *German Ideology*, p. 42, emphasis added.

22 Marx argues that the elements of praxis or 'aspects of social activity are not of course to be taken as . . . different stages, but just as aspects or, . . . "moments", which have existed simultaneously since the dawn of history and the first men, and which still assert themselves in history today' (*ibid.*, pp. 40–1). Each of these elements is an essential functional aspect of and for the whole of species-life which Marx summarizes in the term praxis. It must be emphasized that they are not understood as functional for 'Society'; rather, the social is itself but a functional aspect of human life.

23 If Marx seems often to deprecate the importance of consciousness

and human reason, it is because his writing in this context is a critique of the German idealists and 'abstract materialists' and the over-emphasis placed on ideas in interpreting human history. The argument here demands that these aspects, including consciousness, be interpreted as concomitant and interpenetrating; none being given priority.

24 Marx, *German Ideology*, p. 38.

25 The same type of argument is present in the *Manuscripts* where Marx asks his 'questioner' to consider the implications of not considering man as a self-creative being as the starting point of analysis, *Early Writings*, pp. 165–6. See also *Capital I*, pp. 183–4. This type of approach parallels M. Natanson's argument against the validity of nihilism in *Philosophy of the Social Sciences*, pp. 21–3, and is reflected in A. Camus's argument against suicide in *The Myth of Sisyphus* (New York: Vintage Books, 1955), pp. 3–4.

26 K. Marx, *Poverty of Philosophy* (New York: International Publishers, 1963), pp. 109–10. The fact that Marx presumes change as fundamental to reality-for-man can not be emphasized too strongly. Because of this, Marx does not construct any theory of change – change itself is not problematic to him; rather, the absence of change, especially in social form and ideas which direct activity, becomes the essential factor which requires explanation. Cf., A. Dawe, 'The Two Sociologies', *British Journal of Sociology*, XXI (1970), pp. 207–18.

27 K. Marx, *German Ideology*, pp. 89–90.

28 One essential element of praxis is that man is a social being – the individual exists through others and they through him. Thus Marx assumes that there is no essential opposition between the demands of the individual and the demands, minimally, of living in harmony with others – the problem for Marx is not that of order. His effort is not spent contemplating the perfect state which, as an institution, would balance the individual and common good without infringing on either. Nor is he concerned with the second option – that of considering the manner in which 'society' constrains the individual. If Marx is concerned with order at all, it is a concern directed at the 'order', the 'society', that exists, how it comes to be, and how it is maintained at all given the presupposition of constant change, and given the negative character of any specific 'order' for social man that has lasted beyond its historical usefulness.

29 Marx, *Early Writings*, p. 158, emphasis added.

30 Marx, *German Ideology*, p. 41, emphasis added.

31 K. Marx, *A Contribution to the Critique of Political Economy*, (Moscow: Progress, 1970), pp. 20–1.

32 See, for example, R. K. Merton, *A Paradigm for the Sociology of Knowledge*, in Curtis and Petras (eds), *The Sociology of Knowledge*, (New York: Praeger, 1972), A. Child, 'The Problem of Imputation in the Sociology of Knowledge', *Ethics* (January 1941), pp. 200–15.

33 See B. Ollman, *Alienation* (Cambridge: Cambridge University

Press), ch. 1.

34 From the *Grundrisse* as translated by T. B. Bottomore in *Selected Writings* (New York: McGraw-Hill, 1964), p. 91. Cf., 'man is not merely a natural being; he is a human natural being. He is a being for himself, and, therefore, a species-being; and as such he has to express and authenticate himself in being as well as in thought. . . . And as everything natural must have its origin so man has his process of genesis, history, which is for him, however, *a conscious process and thus one which is consciously self-transcending*', Marx, (*Early Writings*, p. 208, emphasis added), and, 'The animal is one with its life activity. It does not distinguish the activity from itself. It is its activity. But man makes his life activity itself an object of his will and consciousness. He has a conscious life activity. It is not a determination with which he is completely identified. Conscious life activity distinguishes man from the life activity of animals. . . . Only for this reason is his activity free activity' (*ibid.*, p. 127). See also *ibid.*, p. 52.

35 Avineri, *Social and Political Thought*, p. 71.

36 L. Kolakowski, *Toward a Marxist Humanism* (New York: Grove Press, 1968), chap. 2.

37 In these terms it must be mentioned that the critique of the sociology of knowledge hardly misses the mark in so far as it is directed at the 'Marxist' interpretation of Marx – i.e. in so far as it is directed at a positivistic gloss on Marx's insights. Continuously, in the criticisms of the sociology of knowledge, as well as in direct criticisms of Marx's ideas, references are made not to Marx but to Engels and Lenin. A classic in this regard is L. Feuer, 'Alienation: The Career of a Concept', *New Politics*, II (1962), pp. 116–34.

38 Kolakowski, *Toward a Marxist Humanism*, p. 40.

39 *Ibid.*, p. 41.

40 The quotation is from the 'third manuscript' of 1844 as translated by R. C. Tucker in his *The Marx-Engels Reader* (New York: Norton, 1972), p. 93, emphasis added. The definition of 'suffering' as 'experiencing' is included in the translation of the same section used by Bottomore in Marx, *Early Writings*, p. 208.

41 Marx *Early Writings*, p. 206.

42 'The way in which consciousness is, and in which something is for it, is knowing. Knowing is its only act. Thus something comes to exist for consciousness so far as it knows this something. Knowing is its only objective relation' (*Ibid.*, p. 209).

43 *Ibid.*, p. 217.

44 See especially, Kolakowski, *Towards a Marxist Humanism*, Avineri, *Social and Political Thought*, ch. 4 and G. Petrovic, *Marx in the Mid-Twentieth Century*, pt 3, sect. 2.

45 S. Taylor, *Conceptions of Institutions and the Theory of Knowledge* (New York: Bookman Associates, 1956), argued against Kant that his categories did not include that of value – however, with such inclusion he accepts the 'ideal' nature of the categorical framework

and thus tends to reify this aspect of consciousness. Recognizing this as a problem, as ignoring the historical element, Marx tried to ground the categories in praxis – including the category of value. This resulted in the understanding of values in terms of needs – specifically the needs revolving around the social character of praxis. Thus Marx was able to dissolve the fact/value distinction not by arguing naïvely that objects contain value in themselves, but by arguing that objects, facts, are always human facts, objects-for-man: 'sensuous objects'.

46 Marx, *Early Writings*, p. 164, emphasis added.

47 Marx, *Critique of Political Economy*, p. 21.

48 To this extent, but without considering the issue of alienation, this conclusion parallels Taylor's – that the 'relation between the forms of thought and institutions is that between a concept and the process by which it is produced and expressed. . . . Thus there is a *logical* nexus between forms of thought and institutions . . .' (*Conceptions*, p. 129).

49 Marx, *Early Writings*, p. 158.

50 Avineri, *Social and Political Thought*, p. 76.

51 Most of the argument above is based on what were originally unpublished works. However, there has been considerable analysis done that demonstrates the lack of fundamental difference between these works and his later studies. See Avineri, *Social and Political Thought*, Kolakowski, *Towards a Marxist Humanism*, Dupré, *Philosophical Foundations* and McLellan, *Thought of Karl Marx*.

52 Marx, *Selected Writings*, p. 97.

53 See, for example, the article by J. Horton, 'The Dehumanization of Anomie and Alienation', in J. E. Curtis and J. W. Petras (eds), *The Sociology of Knowledge* (New York: Praeger, 1972), p. 586. An educative example of the positivistic use of the term is R. Blauner's *Alienation and Freedom* (Chicago: University of Chicago Press, 1968), or M. Seeman, 'On the Meaning of Alienation', *American Sociological Review*, XXIV (1959), pp. 783–91.

54 Durkheim conceived of the social as a 'reality sui generis', an entity and a force necessary for civilized, normative, individual, yet co-operative existence. Anomie refers to a problematic for individuals and groups of a lack of clarity in norms which results from the normal evolutionary change of 'society' from mechanical to organic forms, i.e. from a transition period in which contradictory norms from each form co-exist. The 'solution' to this problematic lies in the evolutionary emergence of a single, organic order. Durkheim's emphasis thus tends toward a reification of the social. On the other hand, Weber's emphasis is clearly on the individual. For him, the social, in its various forms, is a rational product of individuals, which, through the medium of a means–end reversal, becomes a force in itself, i.e. a rational system which negates or denies the rationality of its base – individual, rational persons. The 'solution' in terms of this conceptualization clearly demonstrates Weber's

'existentialist' bias for it involves a central role for the charismatic individual who overturns traditionally accepted beliefs and develops another belief base, which, in turn, is objectified in social forms. Weber's position is closer to that of Marx, but his view does not incorporate a fully positive conception of social man nor any clearly developed conception of human life as on-going praxis.

55 Marx, *Early Writings*, p. 121.

56 In other words, reality is always human reality or reality-for-man. Thus, a condition of alienation is a situation in which all the various elements of reality, from physical products to social forms to ideas, are estranged from men or treated as somehow having a life of their own. Marx uses various terms to refer to this situation, the most general being that of alienation. The terms reification and false-consciousness refer to the crystallization and estrangement of ideas in particular; that of fetishization, to the treatment of physical products as of value in themselves. Each term, however, refers to the same phenomenon, albeit, particular aspects of the general condition as discussed below.

57 Marx clearly speaks of the 'laws' of capitalism, of definite patterns that do exist and can be discerned. On the other hand, he calls capitalism 'anarchistic'. The two statements are, however, not contradictory when it is realized that they refer to different angles of vision on the contradictory, alienated character of this mode of production.

58 Marx, *Early Writings*, p. 121.

59 Alienation is not specific to capitalism in Marx's view though it is most thoroughly developed in that system: 'What requires explanation is not the unity of living and active human beings with . . . nature, and therefore their appropriation of nature; nor is this the result of a historical process. What we must explain is the separation . . . a separation which is only fully completed in the relation between wage-labour and capital' (quoted in Ollman, *Alienation*, p. 133, from *Pre-Capitalistic Economic Formations*).

60 Thus Marx criticizes political economy which 'conceives the material process of private property, as this occurs in reality, in general and abstract formulas which then serve it as laws', precisely because 'It does not comprehend these laws' (Marx, *Early Writings*, p. 102). Thus, 'political economy has merely formulated the laws of alienated labor' (*ibid.*, p. 132), i.e. political economy has merely grasped the regularities in a system of alienation and mistakenly passed these off as natural laws governing behaviour. In Marx's view, it is important to understand these regularities; but only as a prelude to changing them in respect to their negative aspects – aspects which the political economists themselves are aware of. 'The philosophers have only interpreted the world in different ways; the point is to change it' (Marx, *Selected Writings*, p. 205. The same point is made in all of Marx's writing, cf., N. Geras, 'Essence and Appearance: Aspects of Fetishism in Marx's Capital', *New Left*

Review, LXV (1971), pp. 69–86.

61 Marx, *Early Writings*, pp. 122–3, emphasis added.

62 Cf., Ollman, *Alienation*, p. 132.

63 Even in *Capital I*, Marx argues, 'Political Economy has indeed analysed, however incompletely, value and its magnitude, and has discovered what lies beneath these forms. But it has never once asked the question why labour is represented by the value of its product and labour-time by the magnitude of that value. These formulae, which bear stamped upon them in unmistakable letters, that they belong to a state of society, in which the process of production has the mastery over man, instead of being controlled by him, such formulae appear to the bourgeois intellect to be as much a self-evident necessity imposed by Nature as productive labour itself' (pp. 80–1).

64 Marx, *Early Writings*, p. 126.

65 Marx, *Economic and Philosophic Manuscripts of 1844* (Moscow: Foreign Language Publishing House, 1961), p. 72, emphasis added.

66 *Ibid.*, p. 72.

67 *Ibid.*, p. 70.

68 Marx, *Capital I*, p. 310.

69 Marx, *Early Writings*, pp. 125–6.

70 *Ibid.*, p. 129.

71 The practical construction of an objective world, the manipulation of inorganic nature, is the confirmation of man as a conscious species-being, i.e. a being who treats the species as his own being or himself as a species–being. . . . While, therefore, alienated labor takes away his species-life, his real objectivity as a species-being, and changes his advantage over animals into a disadvantage insofar as his organic body, nature, is taken from him . . .' (*ibid.*, pp. 127–8).

72 *Ibid.*, p. 127. Cf., H. Marcuse, *One-Dimensional Man* (London: Routledge & Kegan Paul, 1966), sect. 2, 'One-Dimensional Thought', L. Kolakowski, *Alienation*, and G. Grant, 'The University Curriculum', in *Technology and Empire* (Toronto: Anansi, 1969).

73 Marx, *Early Writings*, p. 130. Marx continues, 'through alienated labor the worker creates the relation of another man, who does not work and is outside the work process, to this labor. The relation of the worker to work also produces the relation of the capitalist . . . to work' (p. 131).

74 'Society, as it appears to the economist, is civil Society, in which each individual is a totality of needs and only exists for another person, as the other exists for him, insofar as each becomes a means for the other' (*ibid.*, p. 181).

75 Once again it is important to recognize that Marx's work is, at once, a critique of 'material conditions', and a critique of the interpretations of these conditions by others; interpretations that have the effect of contributing to the maintenance of the situation in

so far as they are believed.

76 Cf., 'Contribution to the Critique of Hegel's Philosophy of Right', in Marx, *Early Writings*, p. 44.

77 'Political economy has merely formulated the laws of alienated labor.' Thus, various 'solutions' to negative social conditions that are put forward by the political economists on the basis of these 'laws' are not solutions at all. For example, an 'enforced increase in wages . . . would be nothing more than a better remuneration of slaves, and would not restore, either to the worker or to the work, their human significance and worth. Even the equality of incomes which Proudhon demands would only change the relation of the present-day worker to his work into a relation of all men to work. Society would then be conceived as an abstract capitalist' (*ibid.*, p. 132). Cf., the discussion of 'vulgar communism' (*ibid.*, pp. 152–5).

78 See S. Avineri, *Social and Political Thought*, 'Epilogue: The Eschatology of the Present' and T. Schroyer, *Critique of Domination* (New York: Braziller, 1973), pp. 92–100.

79 The same criticism is directed at Mead but concerns precisely the opposite 'error'. The 'I' concept in Mead's work is said to be a residual, *ad hoc* addition (as will be developed later), an addition necessary to account for creativity, freedom and responsibility of specifically human life in an otherwise reductive, deterministic theoretical framework. Without developing the link between alienation and praxis, or without explaining how men alienate themselves despite their praxical being, Marx could be accused of introducing the idea of alienation to account for the 'reductive', 'deterministic' and limiting elements of human existence in an otherwise idealistic theory of human life. The failure to develop this connection clearly is a major problem of the Marxian sociology of knowledge.

80 See, for example, Marx, *German Ideology*, pp. 46–7.

81 Typical of such interpretations see Merton, 'A Paradigm for the Sociology of Knowledge', and in Curtis and Petras, *The Sociology of Knowledge* (New York: Praeger, 1972), and P. Hamilton, *Knowledge and Social Structure*.

82 Schroyer, *Critique of Domination*, pp. 92–7.

83 See, for example, L. Althusser, *For Marx* (New York: Vintage Books, 1970), chap. 2, 'On the Young Marx'.

84 For example, 'The individual is the social being. The manifestation of his life – even when it does not appear directly in the form of a communal manifestation, accomplished in association with other men – is, therefore, a manifestation and affirmation of social life.' K. Marx, *Early Writings*, p. 158. 'Productive life [praxis], now appear(s) to man only as a means for the satisfaction of a need. . . . Productive life is, however, species-life. It is life creating life.' *Ibid.*, p. 127. 'It can be seen that the history of industry and industry as it objectively exists is an open book of the human faculties. . . . Everyday material industry . . . shows us, in the form of sensuous

useful objects, in an alienated form, the essential human faculties transformed into objects.' *Ibid.*, p. 163. 'The whole of what is called world history is nothing but the creation of man by human labor, and the emergence of nature for man.' *Ibid.*, p. 166. This is not to imply that alienation is not 'real' in its consequences; only that it is not presented as a total denial of praxis – alienation is a 'distortion' and not a total negation.

85 *Ibid.*, pp. 157–8, emphasis added.

86 Marx, *German Ideology*, p. 44.

87 'A certain mode of production, or industrial stage, is always combined with a certain mode of co-operation, or social stage, and this mode of co-operation is itself a "productive force" ' (*ibid.*, p. 41).

88 Marx, *Early Writings*, p. 133.

89 *Ibid.*, p. 131, emphasis added.

90 'We have already done much to solve the problem in so far as we have transformed the question concerning the origin of private property into a question about the relation between alienated labor and the process of development of mankind. For in speaking of private property one believes oneself to be dealing with something external to mankind. But in speaking of labor one deals directly with mankind itself. This formulation of the problem already contains its solution' (*ibid.*, p. 133). It should be noted that here again one finds the emphasis on alienation as only an 'apparent' denial of praxis—private property, as a mode of alienation, has historically emerged out of 'human development', out of praxis itself.

3 G. H. MEAD: THE PERSPECTIVE OF SOCIAL BEHAVIOURISM AND THE SOCIOLOGY OF KNOWLEDGE

1 Certainly the 'Symbolic Interactionist' school, a major outgrowth of Mead's insights, tends to be quite descriptive and a-critical. Concentration has been placed on the ability of the theory to account for the moulding of self and mind in social situations, with little or no emphasis on the negative aspects of such moulding. Cf., P. L. Berger and T. Luckmann, *Social Construction of Reality* (New York: Doubleday, 1966), chap. 3, E. Goffman, *The Presentation of Self in Everyday Life* (New York: Doubleday Anchor Books, 1959) and J. G. Manis and B. N. Meltzer (eds), *Symbolic Interaction: A Reader in Social Psychology* (Boston: Allyn & Bacon, 1972), pt v, 'Research Implications and Applications'. For a brief discussion of the limitations of this development of Mead's ideas, see H. P. Dreitzel (ed.), *Recent Sociology No. 2* (London: Macmillan & Co., 1970), editor's introduction. See also W. W. Mayrl, 'Ethnomethodology: Sociology Without Society', *Catalyst*, no. 7 (1973), pp. 15–28.

2 Cf., R. W. Hornosty, 'Conceptions of Human Nature in the Sociological Tradition' (unpublished Ph.D. dissertation, State University of New York at Buffalo, 1973), esp. chap. 5, 'Dissolution of the Inner Dialectic and the Birth of "Homo Sociologicus" '.

3 For the basis of this argument, see D. Wrong, 'The Oversocialized Conception of Man', *American Sociological Review*, XXVI (1961).

4 This may especially be said of the chapter entitled 'Society' in G. H. Mead, *Mind, Self and Society*, edited and introduced by C. W. Morris (Chicago: University of Chicago Press, 1972). The point will be considered in detail below.

5 See R. Lichtman, 'Symbolic Interactionism and Social Reality', *Berkeley Journal of Sociology*, XV (1970), T. Schroyer, 'Toward a Critical Theory for Advanced Industrial Society', in Dreitzel (ed.) *Recent Sociology No. 2*, Maryl, 'Ethnomethodology' and I. M. Zeitlin, *Rethinking Sociology* (New York: Appleton-Century-Crofts, 1973).

6 Unlike Marx, Mead clearly does not often direct his attention to analysis of social problematics, and, indeed, as is discussed below, there is an overall tendency to assume an 'automatic' process of change in social form when problems arise. Mead's early writing does consider the problematic nature of education as a social form and its negative impact; he wishes a transformed educational process which would recognize and be based in the social character of actual development, *but*, only in order to better achieve the development of a person who conforms to the values and interests of his society. Already in these writings there is a contradiction present between the implications of a presupposed ability on the part of persons to transform social form, and the desire to do so in the interest of existing institutions. See Mead's address, 'The Psychology of Consciousness Implied in Instruction', in A. J. Reck (ed.), *Mead: Selected Writings* (New York: Bobbs-Merrill, 1964), pp. 114ff. It is interesting to note, however, that in spite of Mead's 'conservative' emphasis in respect to social form and social change, his perspective has been utilized in an entirely opposite direction – after being shorn of certain aspects. See, for example, J. Taylor, 'Anthrocracy', *Catalyst*, no. 2 (Summer 1966).

7 It is generally recognized that the perspectives of these writers differ considerably, none the less, and that the compatibility is therefore not a matter of simple 'addition'. 'Dialectical materialism' and 'social behaviourism' are rooted in somewhat different presuppositions, and considerably different intellectual traditions. Thus, whatever 'use' either perspective can make of the other will require fundamental transformations. Cf., R. Ropers, 'Mead, Marx and Social Psychology', *Catalyst*, no. 7 (Winter 1973); R. Lichtman, 'Symbolic Interactionism and Social Reality, Some Marxist Queries'; G. F. Cronk, 'Symbolic Interactionism: A "Left-Meadian" Interpretation' in *Social Theory and Practice* (1972); and Zeitlin, *Rethinking*

Sociology.

8 In particular, 'The Genesis of Self and Social Control', 'The Social Self' and 'A Behavioristic Account of the Significant Symbol', in Reck (ed.), *Mead*.

9 Clearly, the central emphasis in *Mind, Self and Society* is on the development of a conceptual framework that can be a basis for the interpretation of self and mind as emerging within the on-going social process into which each individual is born. The basic ontological and epistemological presuppositions remain largely, though not totally, implicit in that work and are more completely developed in themselves, in *The Philosophy of the Act* (Chicago: University of Chicago Press, 1967), *The Philosophy of the Present* (La Salle, Illinois: The Open Court Publishing Co., 1959) and in various articles – those reprinted in A. J. Reck (ed.), *Mead*, and two articles introduced by David Miller, 'Relative Space-Time and Simultaneity' and 'Metaphysics', both in *Review of Metaphysics*, XVII (1964), pp. 524–35. For some idea of the background to the development of Mead's basic ideas see *Movements of Thought in the Nineteenth Century* (Chicago: University of Chicago Press, 1967).

10 This fundamental question must constantly be kept in mind in any adequate interpretation of Mead's perspective and its limitations – the development of an answer to the question is the fundamental intention behind his work, and he repeatedly insists that any adequate conception of men must combine both the reality of nature, and yet the significance of the emergence of mind in nature. For example, he holds that: 'Nature – the external world – is objectively there, in opposition to our experience of it, or in opposition to the individual thinker himself . . . nevertheless [objects] possess certain characteristics by virtue of their relationship to . . . mind, which they would not possess otherwise or apart from those relations. . . . Experienced objects have definite meanings for the individuals thinking about them' (*Mind, Self and Society*, p. 131). Cf., M. Natanson, *The Social Dynamics of G. H. Mead* (Washington, D. C.: Public Affairs Press, 1956).

11 Mead, *Mind, Self and Society*, pp. 1–8. The same criticism reappears throughout his writing: see, for example, *Philosophy of Act* 'The Nature of Scientific Knowledge', pp. 45–62, 'Mechanism and Contingency', pp. 313–20, 'Categorical Fragments', pp. 626–63, 'The Process of Mind in Nature', pp. 357–444. Also *Philosophy of Present* pp. 14–15.

12 Mead, *Mind, Self and Society*, 'A Contrast of Individualistic and Social Theories of the Self', pp. 222ff. Again, this criticism is repeatedly stressed throughout Mead's writing: see, for example, *Philosophy of Act*, 'The Process of Mind in Nature', *passim* and *Philosophy of Present*, pp. 14–15, 38–9.

13 Mead, *Mind, Self and Society*, p. 131.

14 Thus Mead criticizes positivistic behaviourists, such as Watson, who ignore these differences or rule them non-existent simply because

they are not observables. *Ibid.*, pp. 1–13.

15 See, for example, Mead's discussion of 'Form and Environment', *Philosophy of Act*, pp. 308–12.

16 That is, consciousness in the sense of awareness, not self-consciousness: see 'The Self and the Process of Reflection', in *Mind, Self and Society*, pp. 354–78.

17 *Ibid.*, pp. 371–3. See also *Philosophy of Present*, pp. 69–70.

18 Mead, *Mind, Self and Society*, p. 136.

19 *Ibid.*, pp. 198, 328–36. The concept of emergence is only fully developed in *Philosophy of Act* and, especially, in *Philosophy of Present*, and will be discussed in detail below.

20 'In the type of temporary inhibition of action which signifies thinking, or in which reflection arises, we have presented in the experience of the individual, tentatively and in advance and for his selection among them, the different possibilities or alternatives of future action open to him within the given social situation. . . . Reflection . . . arises only under the conditions of self-consciousness and makes possible the purposive control and organization by the individual organism of its conduct, with reference to its social and physical environment . . . ' (*Mind, Self and Society*, pp. 90–1). See also *ibid.*, pp. 42–3, 62–6, 73, 94–5, 122–5 and *Philosophy of Act*, pp. 372–3.

21 In one sense this dual criticism is quite 'encouraging' in the context of Mead's intentions and in respect to the basic concerns of this study. On the one hand, writing in opposition to both positivism and idealism, Mead parallels Marx's concern to achieve synthesis of these positions in response to their separate inadequacies. On the other hand, to be accused of erring in both directions at least suggests that the critics misinterpret particular ideas; e.g. what appears sociologistic may more aptly be seen as a step on Mead's part away from what are seen by him as idealist pitfalls. In similar fashion, Marx's arguments, against the idealist position of the Young–Hegelians, are often misinterpreted as an embrace of the opposite pole. See chap. 2, note 23.

22 See, for example, 'Evolution Becomes a General Idea', in G. H. Mead, *Movements of Thought*, pp. 153–68, in particular p. 168 where both emphases are present.

23 *Ibid.* Also Mead, *Mind, Self and Society*, *passim.*

24 Mead, *Mind, Self and Society*, pp. 98–100.

25 'The Self and the Process of Reflection', *ibid.*, p. 363, *ibid.*, p. 249. Cf., D. L. Miller, *G. H. Mead: Self, Language and the World* (Austin, Texas: University of Texas Press, 1973), pp. 60–5.

26 'The Self and the Process of Reflection'.

27 *Ibid.*

28 *Ibid.* See also 'The Function of Imagery in Conduct' and 'The Biologic Individual', *ibid.*, pp. 337–53.

29 *Ibid.*

30 This idea is an early statement of the idea of emergence in the essay

'The Self and the Process of Reflection', *ibid.*, where Mead contrasts the situation of other animals with that of men. Particular species may be more developed in some aspects than is the case for the human species, but do not evidence the same unique combination of aspects.

31 Mead, *Philosophy of Present*, pp. 70–2.

32 Mead, *Mind, Self and Society*, pp. 150–2.

33 It must be emphasized that in Mead's view, self and mind are absent at birth, and thus, that initial 'gestures' of the child are not 'significant' or meaningful in the sense of reflective intelligence. On the other hand, as noted, these gestures are not the result of specific and clearly defined instincts as is the case with other animals at birth. Cf., 'The Self and the Process of Reflection' and 'The Biologic Individual', in Reck (ed.), *Mead*.

34 This is not to say that the infant does not contribute in some way to the interaction and pattern established. The colicky infant, for example, would affect the character of the relationship – but, in a non-meaningful, non-intentional manner from the standpoint of the infant itself. Meaningfulness inheres initially in the interpretation of the gesture by the adult – the gesture only subsequently becomes 'significant' for the child.

35 'The situation in which one seeks conditioning responses is, I think, as far as effective intelligence is concerned, always present in the form of a problem. When a man is just going ahead, he seeks the indications of the path, but he does it unconsciously. . . . But when he reaches the chasm [a problematic], this onward movement is stopped by the very process of drawing back. . . . That conflict, so to speak, sets him free to see a whole set of other things . . . the characters which present various possibilities of action under the circumstances. The man holds onto these different possibilities of response in terms of the different stimuli which present themselves, and it is this ability to hold onto them there that constitutes his mind' (Mead, *Mind, Self and Society*, p. 124).

36 *Ibid.*, 'The Self and the Process of Reflection', pp. 360–1, emphasis added.

37 'Meaning is . . . a development of something objectively there as a relation between certain phases of the social act; it is not a psychical addition to that act and it is not an "idea" as traditionally conceived. A gesture by one organism, the resultant of the social act in which the gesture is an early phrase, and the response of the other organism to the gesture, are the relata in a threefold relationship of gesture to first organism, of gesture to second organism, and of gesture to subsequent phases of the given social act; and this threefold relationship constitutes the matrix within which meaning arises or which develops into the field of meaning' (*ibid.*, p. 76).

38 'It is . . . the relationship of . . . this vocal gesture, to such a set of responses in the individual himself as well as in the other that makes

of that vocal gesture . . . a significant symbol. A symbol does tend to call out in the individual a group of reactions such as it calls out in the other, but there is something further that is involved in its being a significant symbol: this response within one's self to such a word as "chair" or "dog" is one which is a stimulus to the individual as well as a response. This is what is involved in what we term the meaning of a thing, or its significance. . . . When we speak of the meaning of what we are doing we are making the response itself, that we are on the point of carrying out, a stimulus to our action. It becomes a stimulus to a later stage of action which is to take place from the point of view of this particular response' (*ibid.*, pp. 71–2).

39 Mead repeatedly speaks of two aspects of this development which he tends not to separate clearly: on the one hand, a content of mind is internalized but, on the other, mind is an ability or capacity of awareness of meaning or significance. This lack of clear distinction will be discussed in detail later and is essential to a comprehension of the contradictions in Mead's framework.

40 'There is an organization of the various parts of the nervous system that are going to be responsible for acts, an organization which represents, not only that which is immediately taking place, but also the later stages that are to take place. When one approaches a distant object he approaches it with reference to what he is going to do when he arrives there. . . . The later stages of the act are present in the early stages – not simply in the sense that they are all ready to go off, but in the sense that they serve to control the process itself. . . . The act as a whole can be there determining the process' (Mead, *Mind, Self and Society*, p. 11).

41 'The human animal is an attentive animal. . . . Our whole intelligent process seems to lie in the attention which is selective of certain types of stimuli. . . . Not only do we open the door to certain stimuli and close it to others, but our attention is an organizing process as well as a selective process. . . . Our attention enables us to organize the field in which we are going to act. Here we have the organism as acting and determining its environment. It is not simply a set of passive senses played upon by the stimuli which come from without' (*ibid.*, p. 25).

42 See Mead's contrast of the human situation with that of the dog-fight, *ibid.*, pp. 42–3.

43 *Ibid.*, p. 132.

44 'If we seek the ideal character of a horse in the central nervous system we would have to find it in all those different parts of the initiated acts. . . . We can find in that sense in the beginning of the act just those characters which we assign to "horse" as an idea, or if you like, as a concept' (*ibid.*, p. 12).

45 'The Self and the Process of Reflection', *ibid.*, pp. 368–71.

46 *Ibid.*, p. 47.

47 See Mead's contrast of the situation of man and animal in the face of

a problematic situation, *ibid.*, pp. 122–5.

48 *Ibid.*, pp. 92–4.

49 'The self has the characteristic that it is an object to itself, and that characteristic distinguishes it from other objects and from the body. . . . The apparatus of reason would not be complete unless it swept itself into its own analysis or the field of experience or unless the individual brought himself into the same experiential field as that of other individual selves in relation to whom he acts in any given social situation. . . . For the individual organism is obviously an essential and important fact or constituent element of the empirical situation in which it acts; and without taking objective account of itself as such, it cannot act intelligently or rationally' (*ibid.*, pp. 136, 138).

50 *Ibid.*, pp. 144–64. See also 'The Genesis of Self and Social Control', in Reck (ed.), *Mead*, pp. 267–93.

51 Mead, *Mind, Self and Society*, pp. 150–1.

52 *Ibid.*, pp. 151–2.

53 *Ibid.*, pp. 156–8.

54 *Ibid.*, pp. 164, 219.

55 'An institution is . . . nothing but an organization of attitudes which we all carry in us, the organized attitudes of others that control and determine conduct.' (*ibid*, p. 211). Cf., J. W. Petras (ed.), *G. H. Mead: Essays on his Social Philosophy* (New York: Teacher's College Press, 1968), pp. 8–9.

56 'All social interrelations and interactions are rooted in a certain common socio-physiological endowment of every individual involved in them. The physiological bases of social behaviour – which have their ultimate seat or locus in the lower part of the individual's central nervous system – are the bases of such behaviour, precisely because they consist in drives or instincts or behaviour tendencies, on the part of the given individual, which he cannot carry out or give overt expression and satisfaction to without the co-operative aid of one or more other individuals' (Mead, *Mind, Self and Society*, p. 139, f.n. 2*a*).

57 'There are what I have termed "generalized social attitudes" which make an organized self possible. In the community there are certain ways of acting under situations which are essentially identical, and these ways of acting on the part of anyone are those which we excite in others when we take certain steps. . . . There are then a whole series of such common responses in the community in which we live, and such responses are what we term institutions. The institution represents a common response on the part of all members of the community to a particular situation' (*ibid.*, pp. 260–1); 'Human society as we know it could not exist without minds and selves, since all its most important characteristic features presuppose the possessions of minds and selves by its individual members; but its individual members would not possess minds and selves if these had not arisen within or emerged out of the human social process in

its lower stages of development . . . ' (*ibid.*, p. 227); 'Human society . . . does not merely stamp the pattern of the individual's self; it also, at the same time, gives him a mind, as the means or ability of consciously conversing with himself in terms of the social attitudes which constitute the structure of his self and which embody the pattern of human society's organized behavior as reflected in that structure. And his mind enables him in turn to stamp the pattern of his further developing self (further development through his mental activity) upon the structure of organization of human society, and thus in a degree to reconstruct and modify in terms of his self the general patterns of social and group behavior in terms of which his self was originally constituted' (*ibid.*, p. 263, f.n. 10). The 'conservatism' that remains in Mead's work, despite such passages, is investigated below.

58 In other words, Mead emphasizes the character of social forms, in contrast to the notion of the underlying social process, as 'means' in the relationship of human form and physical environment.

59 Mead, *Mind, Self and Society*, p. 173.

60 *Ibid.*, p. 175.

61 *Ibid.*, p. 173.

62 *Ibid.*, p. 174.

63 *Ibid.*, p. 176.

64 *Ibid.*, p. 177.

65 *Ibid.*, p. 178, emphasis added.

66 *Ibid.*, p. 174.

67 *Ibid.*

68 'If it [self] did not have these two phases ["I" and "Me"] there could not be conscious responsibility, and there would be nothing novel in experience' (*ibid.*, p. 178). Mead himself labelled the 'I' a 'fictitious' element in an early article, 'The Mechanism of Social Consciousness', in Reck (ed.), *Mead*, pp. 134–41. The argument here is that the larger part of his writings rejects such a view. Cf., Hornosty, 'Conceptions of Human Nature', W. L. Kolb, 'A Critical Evaluation of Mead's "I" and "Me" Concepts', in Manis and Meltzer (eds), *Symbolic Interaction*, pp. 253–61.

69 However, as will be argued, it is only 'apparently' the case that the 'I' has no basis in the socialization process.

70 As already mentioned, Mead speaks of man's qualitative differences as involving the ability to reorganize reality systematically and reflexively and thus to control intentionally the course of action in the face of problematics. To pin these differences solely to the concept of the 'I' and, in turn, to the notion of chance, is to lose sight of this broader notion of the differences between the human species and other animals.

71 In other words, human reflexive intelligence must then be comprehended as only quantitatively different from animal intelligence – a more complex phenomenon perhaps, but reducible to stimulus-response patterns, a position Mead himself explicitly

rejected and sought to transcend.

72 Mead, *Mind, Self and Society*, pp. 122–5, 308–9, *Philosophy of Act*, p. 68.

73 Mead, *Mind, Self and Society*, pp. 122–5, 308–9.

74 *Ibid.*, pp. 309–10, 324.

75 Mead, *Mind, Self and Society*, pp. 214–15, *Philosophy of Act*, 'Mechanism and Contingency', pp. 313–20.

76 This particular problem is most clearly evident in the section 'Society', Mead, *Mind, Self and Society*, pp. 227–336.

77 *Ibid.*, p. 324.

78 *Ibid.*, p. 308, emphasis added.

79 *Ibid.*, pp. 309–10, emphasis added.

80 *Ibid.*, p. 208.

81 Earlier, as noted, Mead clearly uses the term 'impulse' to capture the differences between the animal and man, i.e. the lack of any defined instinctual patterning in the human infant. Here he tends to contradict that differentiation by attributing to man specific biological tendencies, in order to explain social conflicts. As will be shown, however, Mead could have explained such conflict in terms of his social theory of self and mind, and avoided the contradictory recourse to instincts.

82 Mead, *Mind, Self and Society*, p. 208.

83 *Ibid.*

84 *Ibid.*, p. 323.

85 See R. Lichtman, 'Symbolic Interactionism and Social Reality', and T. Schroyer, 'Toward a Critical Theory'.

86 See 'The Limits of the Problematic', Mead, *Philosophy of Act*, pp. 26–44.

87 See, for example, Mead, *Mind, Self and Society*, pp. 119–20.

88 *Ibid.*, pp. 303–5.

89 *Ibid.*, pp. 284–5.

90 *Ibid.*, p. 309.

91 *Ibid.*, p. 309, f.n. 19, emphasis added.

92 *Ibid.*, p. 323. See also *Philosophy of Act*, p. 655.

93 Mead, *Mind, Self and Society*, p. 325.

94 *Ibid.*, p. 328.

95 *Ibid.*, p. 262.

96 *Ibid.*, p. 310. From another point of view, Mead's 'idealism' in respect to social change and in relation to his intentions, is a matter of not dealing adequately with any problematic that might be entailed by the very 'existence' of social forms, institutions, habits or attitudinal structures. Mead nods to the existence of this 'problem', as will be shown below, but in this section of his work he speaks clearly as if, given problems in the relationships between men and in the relation between men and the 'world that is there', change 'automatically' occurs in the patterns of interaction and in the structure of the selves involved.

97 It is not necessary to go into Mead's lengthy discussion of this

concept here, but only to emphasize that it is a basic presupposition of his work which has important consequences for the interpretation of various ideas in his perspective that cannot be ignored in relation to the difficulties under discussion.

98 Mead, *Philosophy of Act*, p. 641, emphasis added.
99 Mead, *Philosophy of Present*, p. 24.
100 *Ibid.*, p. 35.
101 *Ibid.*, pp. 33–4. See also 'The Objective Reality of Perspectives', *ibid.*, pp. 161–75 and *Philosophy of Act*, 'Consciousness and the Unquestioned', p. 71.
102 Mead, *Philosophy of Present*, pp. 70–7, 84–5.
103 Cf., Miller, *G. H. Mead: Self, Language and the World*, pp. 46–7.
104 *Ibid.*, p. 148, emphasis added.
105 In other words it is mind, individual mind, that presupposes an on-going social, interactional context. The emergent whole is not 'Society', in any ontological sense, but a mind whose locus, as Mead puts it, is social, but whose focus lies in the individual. Cf., E. Durkheim, *Rules of Sociological Method* (New York: Free Press, 1964) pp. xlvii–xlviii.
106 Mead, *Mind, Self and Society*, p. 227.
107 Mead, *Philosophy of Present*, p. 68, *Philosophy of Act*, p. 68.
108 *Philosophy of Present*, pp. 70–1.
109 *Ibid.*, p. 68, emphasis added.
110 See *ibid.*, p. 38 and *Philosophy of Act*, 'The Nature of Scientific Knowledge', esp. pp. 50–1 and 'The Process of Mind in Nature', p. 359.
111 Mead, *Philosophy of Act*, p. 8.
112 *Ibid.*, p. 3.
113 *Ibid.*, p. 25, emphasis added.
114 See Mead, 'The Objective Reality of Perspectives', in Reck, *Mead*, pp. 306–19.
115 Mead, *Philosophy of Act*, p. 25.
116 *Ibid.*, pp. 54–5, emphasis added. See also *Philosophy of Present*, p. 68.
117 'The Process of Mind in Nature', *Philosophy of Act*, p. 424.
118 See esp. 'The Limits of the Problematic' and 'The Nature of Scientific Knowledge', *ibid.*, pp. 26–62, *passim*.
119 *Ibid.*, p. 62.
120 *Ibid.*, p. 53. See also 'The Process of Mind in Nature', *ibid.*, pp. 398–9.
121 *Ibid.*, pp. 59–60, emphasis added.
122 *Ibid.*, p. 64, emphasis added.
123 *Ibid.*, 'Consciousness and the Unquestioned', pp. 65–6.
124 See Mead, *Philosophy of Present*, pp. 6–14, 23–5.
125 'A Pragmatic Theory of Truth', in Reck (ed.), *Mead*, pp. 320–44. See also Mead, *Philosophy of Present*, p. 68.
126 Mead, *Philosophy of Act*, pp. 30–3; *Philosophy of Present*, 'The Objective Reality of Perspectives'.

127 Mead, *Philosophy of Act*, p. 88. See also pp. 412–20 and *Philosophy of Present*, p. 173.
128 Mead, *Philosophy of Act*, 'Fragments on the Process of Reflection', pp. 87–90 and 'The Process of Mind in Nature', pp. 412–20.
129 *Ibid.*, pp. 90–1.
130 In other words, the 'I' concept captures the emergent characteristic of man, his ability self-consciously to control himself and his environment; whereas, the 'me' aspect refers to the internalization of the communicative process, which is but a part of the emergent whole. In these terms, both 'I' and 'me' are integral parts of the social theory of mind and self.
131 Mead, *Philosophy of Act*, pp. 662–3.
132 Mead, *Philosophy of Present*, p. 90.
133 Mead, *Mind, Self and Society*, p. 323.
134 Mead, *Philosophy of Act*, p. 511, 'A Philosophy of History'. See also *Mind, Self and Society*, pp. 251–2.
135 Mead, *Philosophy of Present*, pp. 14–16.
136 At most, Mead could speak consistently only in terms of this social form as a possible value to be achieved, or an end to be striven for.
137 Cf., J. C. McKinney, 'The Contributions of G. H. Mead to the Sociology of Knowledge' *Social Forces*, XXXIV (December 1955), and T. V. Smith, 'The Social Philosophy of G. H. Mead', *American Journal of Sociology*, XXXVII (November 1931).
138 Mead, *Mind, Self and Society*, p. 140.
139 The same problem was noted in respect to Marx, see above, chap. 2, 'Alienation and the Social Analysis of Ideas'.
140 Beyond the brief discussion of problematics in the relationships between men in the section on 'Society' in *Mind, Self and Society*, and in scattered early articles, Mead tends to concentrate only on conceptualizing the process of problem-solution in the relationship between men and the 'world that is there'.
141 These will be discussed in detail in the following chapter. See, for example, 'The Relation of Play to Education', in Petras, *Mead: Essays*, chap. 2, pp. 27–34, esp. pp. 28–9.
142 As there is no explicit rationale for critical social analysis in Mead's work, it is necessary to demonstrate the compatibility of the concept of alienation with his framework.

4 MARX AND MEAD: TOWARDS A CRITICAL SOCIOLOGY OF KNOWLEDGE

1 Once again it should be pointed out that those who have proposed the Marx/Mead synthesis have most often done so in positivistic terms. For example, J. C. McKinney, 'The Contributions of G. H. Mead to the Sociology of Knowledge' *Social Forces* XXXIV (1955), pp. 144–9, views Mead as providing the 'researchable mechanisms' involved in the relation between thought and social-existential factors which are supposedly omitted by Marx. Such writers

therefore propose an important hypothesis, but for the wrong reasons. cf., A. Child, 'The Problem of Imputation Resolved', *Ethics*, LIV (1943), pp. 96–109 and 'The Existential Determination of Thought', *Ethics*, LII (January, 1942), pp. 153–85, and J. Israel, *Alienation* (Boston: Allyn & Bacon, 1971).

2 K. Marx *Manifesto* (New York: Appleton-Century-Crofts, 1955) and *Selected Writings* (New York: McGraw-Hill, 1964), pp. 127–45.

3 It is not unfair to say that sociology has largely 'imported' its theory of socialization from psychology, with the result that the process is understood narrowly in terms simply of 'domesticating' the child. In other words, socialization is usually thought of as bringing the child into conformity with existing culture; non-conformity is then understood as deviance resulting from, in part, incomplete socialization. This misses Mead's point, and the implications of Marx's position as well; for them, socialization is a much broader process, a process necessary to the emergence of specifically human characteristics. Yet it is understood by them both as a paradoxical and limiting process, and this point becomes important in the elaboration of the basis of alienation.

4 What is fundamental for both writers is human life itself and human self-development. The 'social' is but a necessary aspect of this life, understood as essential to or 'functional' for specifically human existence. Equally, self-consciousness is an aspect of human life or functional for that life and in relation to the social aspect. Priority is given to human being and becoming, and not to any of the aspects that lie at the basis and are part of this life.

5 One way of expressing this problem is to say that Mead places such complete emphasis on the unity of parts in the whole, on the unity, for example, of person and the social, that he ignores the importance of his own scattered insights into the problematics that arise in this unity. Thus R. Lichtman, 'Symbolic Interactionism and Social Reality', *Berkeley Journal of Sociology*, XV (1970), p. 81, argues: 'Society and persons are *dialectical* aspects of each other, and their *distinctiveness* must be maintained along with their continuity. If their continuity alone is emphasized, the self becomes a passive and even trivial aspect of social life'. Yet, as noted, it is the individual that is reflexive in Mead's view, and, therefore, he cannot hold consistently to this over-emphasis on the non-problematic character of the relationship between aspects of the emergent mind.

6 Marx, *Selected Writings*, p. 97.

7 See R. A. Nisbet, *The Sociological Tradition* (New York; Basic Books, 1966), I. M. Zeitlin, *Ideology and the Development of Sociological Theory* (New Jersey: Prentice–Hall, 1968), A. Dawe, 'The Two Sociologies', *British Journal of Sociology*, XXI (1970), L. Bramson, *The Political Context of Sociology* (Princeton, New Jersey: Princeton University Press, 1970), C. W. Mills, *The Sociological Imagination* (London: Oxford University Press, 1972) and A. Gouldner, *Coming Crisis* (New York: Avon Books, 1970).

8 R. W. Hornosty, 'Conceptions of Human Nature', (unpublished Ph.D. dissertation, SUNY at Buffalo, 1973), chap. 5.

9 Thus capitalism, while historically a development of human potentialities, must be transcended if further possibilities (which it has in part made possible) are to be realized.

10 Cf., Mead, *Mind, Self and Society* (Chicago: University of Chicagc Press, 1934), 'Society' and G. Chasin, 'G. H. Mead: Social Psychologist of the Moral Society', *Berkeley Journal of Sociology*, IX (1964), pp. 95–117.

11 Mead, *Mind, Self and Society*, pp. 325–8.

12 Mead's understanding of 'knowledge' implies that the absolute, in terms of which statements and actions are judged, is that of functionality for the continuance and development of specifically human life. However, his tendency to 'predict' the future social form is also expressed as a tendency to utilize this 'future' to judge present activities – thus shifting the criteria of objectivity from functionality to an acceptance of specific forms as the way of the future. This he cannot do if his position is to remain consistent, for it implies the granting of ontological status to society.

13 Mead, *Mind, Self and Society*, p. 262.

14 *Ibid.*

15 For example, Mead argues that social conflicts at one time resulted in one group 'wiping out' the other. This situation gradually 'evolved' as 'domination' of one group over another and, finally, the 'achievement on the part of the individual of a higher self . . . passes over, under what we consider high conditions, into the just recognition of the capacity of the individual in his own field. The superiority which the person has is not a superiority over the other but is grounded in that which he can do in relation to the functions and capacity of others' (*ibid.*, pp. 284–5).

16 *Ibid.*, p. 262.

17 Mead, *Philosophy of Act*, p. 53. See also 'Scientific Method and the Individual Thinker', in A. J. Reck (ed.), *Mead, Selected Writings* (New York: Bobbs-Merrill, 1974), pp. 190–1.

18 'Back of Our Minds', in Mead, *The Philosophy of the Act* (Chicago: University of Chicago Press, 1938), p. 488.

19 *Ibid.*, p. 492.

20 *Ibid.*, pp. 492–3, emphasis added.

21 'The Genesis of Self and Social Control', in Reck (ed.), *Mead*, p. 292.

22 'The relations between social reconstruction and self or personality reconstruction are reciprocal and integral or organic; social reconstruction . . . entails self or personality reconstruction . . . , for, since their selves or personalities are constituted by their organized social relations to one another, they cannot reconstruct their selves . . . without also reconstructing, to some extent, the given social order . . . , in short, social reconstruction and self or personality reconstruction are two sides of a single process. . . . '

Mead, *Mind, Self and Society*, p. 309. Thus Mead provides a conceptualization of the considerable depth to which social control, or the limitations of present social form, penetrates the existence of each individual. Cf., G. F. Cronk, 'Symbolic Interaction', *Social Theory and Practice* (1972). Even R. Lichtman, 'Symbolic Interactionism and Social Reality', *Berkeley Journal of Sociology*, XV (1970), nods to this element as Mead's important contribution to critical theory.

23 Mead, *Mind, Self and Society*, pp. 215–22, 324.

24 Marx himself made several statements related to 'human development' which have a very Meadian ring to them. For example, in *Capital I* (Moscow: Foreign Languages Publishing House, 1964), p. 52, 'In a sort of way, it is with man as it is with commodities. Since he comes into the world neither with a looking glass in his hand, nor as a Fichtian philosopher, to whom "I am I" is sufficient, man first sees and recognizes himself in other men. Peter only establishes his own identity as a man by first comparing himself with Paul as a being of like kind. And thereby Paul, just as he stands in his pauline personality, becomes Peter to the type of the genus homo'. And, earlier, in the *Manuscripts*, 'the relation of man to himself is first realized, objectified, through his relation to other men'. (*Early Writings*, New York: McGraw-Hill, 1964, p. 130). However, while suggestive, such statements clearly do not constitute a developed conception of socialization such as is found in Mead's writing.

25 Two points must be mentioned with respect to Marx's emphasis on power. First, such emphasis in relation to alienation is not inconsistent with the critical perspective, for to speak of power is to speak of the control some have over others and therefore of the action of man on man within praxis. Unlike the positivistic tendency to look to technology or 'social facts' as the determinants of alienation, a consideration of the role of power is a consideration of the activity of men themselves. Second, Marx's concern with power is not opposed to a concern with the importance of reification within alienation. On the one hand, the false-consciousness of the majority is central to the legitimation of power and the perpetuation of power structures. On the other hand, Marx emphasized that the powerful are themselves alienated and falsely-conscious and that they act within a reified framework of ideas. Finally, it must be remembered that Marx placed alienation before power: 'the worker creates the relation of another man, who does not work and is outside the work-process, to this labor. The relation of the worker to work also produces the relation of the capitalist . . . to work. Private property is therefore the product, the necessary result of alienated labor, of the external [abstract] relation of the worker to nature and to himself' (*Early Writings*, p. 131). The basic question is, again, why man alienated himself, and this returns one to Meadian insights.

26 For example, Marx argues, again without the necessary conceptual elaboration, that the historical succession of generations within praxis 'can be speculatively distorted so that later history is made the god of earlier history . . . thereby history receives its own special aims and becomes a person "ranking with other persons" . . . , while what is designated by the words "destiny", "goal", "germ", "idea" of earlier history is nothing more than an abstraction from later history, from the active influence which earlier history exercises on later history', *German Ideology*, (Moscow: Progress Publishers, 1968), p. 60. Clearly, Marx is stressing the fact that alienation, and especially the reification of ideas, intervenes in the historical process of praxis.

27 See above pp. – .

28 'The division of labour implies the contradiction between the interest of the separate individual or the individual family and the communal interest of all individuals who have intercourse with one another. And, indeed, this communal interest *does not exist merely in the imagination*, as the "general interest", *but first of all in reality*, as the mutual interdependence of the individuals among whom labour is divided' (Marx, *German Ideology*, p. 44, emphasis added).

29 These levels of consciousness, largely implicit in Marx's work, correspond to Mead's distinction between knowledge as practical constructive thought on the one hand, and information or internalized attitudes prone to reification on the other.

30 See above, pp. 50–2.

31 Cf., S. Avineri, *The Social and Political Thought of Karl Marx* (Cambridge: Cambridge University Press, 1968), p. 76: ' "productive forces" are not objective facts external to human consciousness. They represent the organization of human consciousness and human activity. . . . Consequently, the distinction between "material base" and "superstructure" is not a distinction between "matter" and "spirit" . . . but between conscious human activity . . . and human consciousness . . . '.

32 Cf. Marx, *Selected Writings*, pp. 218–20.

33 Mead, *Mind, Self and Society*, pp. 262–3 and f.n. 10, p. 263.

34 See, for example 'Industrial Education, the Working Man, and the School', in J. W. Petras, *Mead: Essays on his Social Philosophy* (New York: Teachers College Press, 1968), pp. 55–8, where Mead openly objects to the division of labour in terms of the narrowness of mind it entails. The theoretical basis of this criticism is developed in the following pages.

35 Mead, *Mind, Self and Society*, pp. 264–5, emphasis added.

36 *Ibid.*, pp. 307–8, emphasis added.

37 *Ibid.*, p. 264.

38 *Ibid.*, pp. 264–5, emphasis added.

39 Mead directed considerable criticism at the school system precisely because he saw it as contributing to the very problems it might help

overcome. For example, Mead objected to the positivistic, correspondence theory of knowledge of truth which he saw as a reified version of what actually occurs, in the long run, in science. He saw the same thing in an educational process which emphasizes an uncritical acceptance of ideas taught, and their rote application to 'reality'. Not only are many ideas held in separation from the contexts in which they have their meaning, the self-understanding and practice of education reinforces the confusion between information and knowledge. See *Philosophy of Act*, pp. 50, 52, 'The Teaching of Science in College', pp. 60–72, and 'The Psychology of Social Consciousness Implied in Instruction', pp. 114–22, both in Reck (ed.), *Mead*. See also 'Industrial Education, the Working Man, and the School', in Petras (ed.), *Mead: Essays*, pp. 50–62.

40 Returning to the Marxian emphasis on power, it becomes obvious that this problem of 'narrowness' and reification is doubly problematic with respect to the vertical structure of class differentiation and especially the situation of the ruling class. On the one hand, the perspective of the ruling class 'narrowly' develops within interaction most divorced and isolated from the basic productive process in which problematics between men and nature continually arise. As Marx himself argues, 'consciousness *can* really flatter itself that it is something other than consciousness of existing practice . . . [precisely because] . . . the division of labour implies . . . the fact that intellectual and material activity – enjoyment of labour, production and consumption – devolve on different individuals . . . ' (*German Ideology*, pp. 43–4, emphasis in original). On the other hand, this ruling class has the power to enforce its narrow perspective 'in all good conscience' despite its irrelevance to concrete problematics.

41 Marx himself argued that through the division of labour, 'the productive forces appear to be completely independent and severed from the individuals and to constitute a self-subsistent world alongside the individuals. The reason for this is that the individuals whose forces they are, *themselves exist separated and in opposition to one another*, while on the other hand these forces are only real forms in the intercourse and association of these individuals' (*Selected Writings*, p. 174, *German Ideology*, pp. 83–4, emphasis added).

Select bibliography

Adler, Franz, 'A Quantitative Study in the Sociology of Knowledge', *American Sociological Review*, 19 (February 1954).
Adler, Franz, 'The Sociology of Knowledge Since 1918', *Midwest Sociologist*, XI (Spring 1955), 3–12.
Adler, Franz, 'The Range of Sociology of Knowledge' in *Modern Sociological Theory in Continuity and Change*. Edited by Becker and Boskoff. Dryden Press, 1957, pp. 396–423.
Adler, Franz, 'Werner Stark's Sociology of Knowledge: A Critique', *Kyklos*, XII, no. 2 (1959), 216–21.
Adler, Franz, 'Werner Stark's Sociology of Knowledge: A Further Comment', *Kyklos*, XII, no. 3 (1959), 500–6.
Althusser, Louis, *For Marx*. Translated by Ben Brewster. New York: Random House, 1969.
Avineri, Shlomo, *The Social and Political Thought of Karl Marx*. Cambridge University Press, 1968.
Bales, Robert F., 'Comments on Herbert Blumer's Paper', *American Journal of Sociology*, LXXI (1966), 545–7.
Barber, Bernard, 'Sociology of Science – A Trend Report and Bibliography', *Current Sociology*, V, no. 2 (1956), 91–153.
Bauman, Z., 'On the Philosophical Status of Ethnomethodology', *Sociological Review*, XXI, no. 1 (1973), 5–23.
Baumann, Bedrich, 'George H. Mead and Luigi Pirandello: Some Parallels Between the Theoretical and Artistic Presentation of the Social Role Concept', in *Marxism and Sociology*. Edited by P. Berger, New York: Appleton-Century-Crofts, 1969.
Becker, Howard and Dahlke, Helmut Otto, 'Max Scheler's Sociology of Knowledge', *Philosophy and Phenomenological Research*, V, 2, (1942), 310–22.
Berger, Brigitte, 'Vilfredo Pareto and the Sociology of Knowledge', *Social Research*, XXXIV (1967), 265–81.
Berger, Peter L., *Invitation to Sociology: A Humanistic Perspective*. New York: Doubleday, 1963.
Berger, Peter L., ed. *Marxism and Sociology*. New York: Appleton-Century-Crofts, 1969.
Berger, Peter and Kellner, Hansfried, 'Marriage and the Construction of Reality', *Diogenes*, XLVI (Summer 1964), 1–24.

Berger, Peter L. and Luckmann, Thomas, *The Social Construction of Reality: A Treatise in the Sociology of Knowledge*. New York: Doubleday, 1966.

Berger, P. L. and Pullberg, S., 'Reification and the Sociological Critique of Consciousness', *History and Theory*, IV (1965).

Berghe, Pierre L. Van Den, 'Dialectic and Functionalism: Towards a Theoretical Synthesis', *American Sociological Review*, XXVIII, no. 5 (October 1963), 695–705.

Berlin, Isaiah, *Karl Marx: His Life and Environment*. 3rd edn. London: Oxford University Press, 1963.

Bierstedt, Robert, 'A Critique of Empiricism in Sociology', *American Sociological Review*, XIV (1949), 584–92.

Birnbaum, Norman, 'The Sociological Study of Ideology (1940–60): A Trend Report and Bibliography', *Current Sociology* 9 (1960), 91–172.

Blauner, R., *Alienation and Freedom*. University of Chicago Press, 1968.

Blum, Alan F., 'The Corpus of Knowledge as a Normative Order', *Theoretical Sociology*. Edited by John C. McKinney and Edward A. Tiryakian. New York: Appleton-Century-Crofts, 1970, pp. 320–36.

Blumberg, Albert E., 'Science and Dialectics: A Preface to a Re-examination', *Science and Society*, XXII (1958), 306–29.

Blumer, Herbert, 'Sociological Implications of the Thought of George Herbert Mead', *American Journal of Sociology*, LXXI (1966), 535–44.

Blumer, Herbert, 'Reply', *American Journal of Sociology*, LXXI (1966), 547–8.

Blumer, Herbert, 'Society as Symbolic Interaction', in *Human Behaviour and the Social Process*. Edited by A. M. Rose. Boston: Houghton Mifflin, 1962, 179–92.

Blumer, Herbert, 'Comments on Mr. Chasin's Article', *Berkeley Journal of Sociology*, IX (1964), 118–22.

Bottomore, T. B., 'Some Reflections on the Sociology of Knowledge', *British Journal of Sociology*, VII (March 1956), 52–8.

Bottomore, T. B., ed. *Karl Marx*. Makers of Modern Social Science. Englewood Cliffs, New Jersey: Prentice-Hall, 1973.

Bottomore, T. B., 'Karl Marx: Sociologist or Marxist?', *Science and Society*, XXX (1966), 11–24.

Bramson, Leon, *The Political Context of Sociology*. Princeton, New Jersey: Princeton University Press, 1961.

Braybrooke, David, *Philosophical Problems of the Social Sciences*. Sources in Philosophy Series. New York: Macmillan, 1965.

Brodbeck, May, ed., *Readings in the Philosophy of the Social Sciences*. New York: Macmillan, 1968.

Chall, Leo. P., 'The Sociology of Knowledge', in *Contemporary Sociology*. Edited by J. S. Roucek. New York: Philosophical Library, 1958.

Chasin, Gerald, 'George Herbert Mead: Social Psychologist of the Moral Society', *Berkeley Journal of Sociology*, IX (1964), 95–117.

Chasin, Gerald, 'Reply to Professor Blumer's Comments', *Berkeley*

Journal of Sociology, IX (1964), 123–6.
Child, Arthur, 'The Existential Determination of Thought', *Ethics*, LII (January 1942), 153–85.
Child, Arthur, 'The Problem of Imputation in the Sociology of Knowledge', *Ethics*, 51, no. 2 (Jan. 1941), 200–15.
Child, Arthur, 'The Problem of Imputation Resolved', *Ethics*, LIV (1943), 96–109.
Child, Arthur, 'The Problem of Truth in the Sociology of Knowledge', *Ethics*, 58, no. 1 (Oct. 1947), 18–34.
Child, Arthur, 'The Theoretical Possibility of the Sociology of Knowledge', *Ethics*, LI (July 1941), 392–441.
Child, Arthur, 'On the Theory of the Categories', *Philosophy and Phenomenological Research*, II (December 1946), 316–35.
Child, Arthur, 'Toward a Functional Definition of the *A Priori*', *The Journal of Philosophy*, XLI (1944), 155–60.
Cohen, P., 'Discussion: The Very Idea of a Social Science', *Problems in Philosophy of Science*. Edited by I. Lakatos and A. Musgrave. Amsterdam: North Holland Publishing Co., 1968, pp. 407–23.
Cohen, S., Martin P., and Johnson, R., 'Toward the Development of Dialectics', *Science and Society*, XXII (1958), 21–43.
Coombs, Robert H., 'Karl Mannheim, Epistemology and the Sociology of Knowledge', *Sociological Quarterly*, VII, no. 2 (Spring 1966), 229–33.
Coser, Lewis A. and Rosenburg, Bernard, 'Sociology of Knowledge', in *Sociological Theory: A Book of Readings*. Edited by Coser, L. A. and Rosenburg, B., New York: Macmillan, 1957, chapter 15.
Cronk, George Francis, 'Symbolic Interactionism: A "Left-Meadian" Interpretation', *Social Theory and Practice*, 2 (Spring 1973).
Curtis, James E. and Petras, John W., eds., *The Sociology of Knowledge: A Reader*. New York: Praeger, 1972.
Dahlke, H. Otto, 'The Sociology of Knowledge', in *Contemporary Social Theory*. Edited by H. E. Barnes and H. Becker. New York: Appleton-Century-Crofts, 1940.
Davis, Kingsley, 'Final Note on a Case of Extreme Isolation', The Bobbs-Merrill Reprint Series in the Social Sciences. Indianapolis: Bobbs-Merrill. Reprinted by permission of *The American Journal of Sociology*, LII (March 1947), 432–7.
Dawe, Alan, 'The Relevance of Values', in *Max Weber and Modern Sociology*. Edited by A. Sahay. London: Routledge & Kegan Paul, 1971, 37–66.
Dawe, Alan, 'The Role of Experience in the Construction of Social Theory: An Essay in Reflexive Sociology', *Sociological Review*, XXI, no. 1 (1973), 25–55.
Dawe, Alan, 'The Two Sociologies', *British Journal of Sociology*, XXI (1970), 207–18.
Dickenson, John, 'Towards an Epistemological Development of Dialectics', *Science and Society*, XXII (1958), 207–17.
Diggins, J. P., 'Reification and the Cultural Hegemony of Capitalism:

the Perspectives of Marx and Veblen', *Social Research*, 44 (1977), 354–83.

Diggins, J. P., 'Thoreau, Marx and the Riddle of Alienation', *Social Research*, 39, no. 1 (1972).

Doan, F. M., 'Notations on G. H. Mead's Principle of Sociality with Special Reference to Transformations', *Journal of Philosophy*, LIII (1956), 607–15.

Dreitzel, Hans Peter, ed., *Recent Sociology No. 1: On the Social Basis of Politics*. London: Macmillan, 1969.

Dreitzel, Hans Peter, ed., *Recent Sociology No. 2: Patterns of Communicative Behaviour*. London: Collier-Macmillan, 1970.

Dupré, Louis, *The Philosophical Foundations of Marxism*. New York: Harcourt, Brace & World, 1966.

Durkheim, Emile, *The Division of Labour in Society*. Translated by George Simpson. Chicago: Free Press, 1933.

Durkheim, E., 'The Dualism of Human Nature and its Social Conditions', in *Emile Durkheim, 1858–1917*. Edited by K. Wolff. Columbia: Ohio State University Press, 1960, pp. 325–40.

Durkheim, E., *The Elementary Forms of the Religious Life*. Translated from the French by Joseph Ward Swain. New York: Free Press, 1965.

Durkheim, E., and Mauss, Marcel. *Primitive Classification*. Translated from the French and edited, with an introduction, by Rodney Needham. University of Chicago Press, 1963.

Durkheim, E., *The Rules of Sociological Method*. Translated by Sarah A. Solovay and John H. Mueller. Edited by George E. G. Catlin. 8th edn. New York: Free Press, 1964.

Durkheim, E., *Selected Writings*. Edited, translated and with an introduction by Anthony Giddens. Cambridge University Press, 1972.

Durkheim, E., *Suicide: A Study in Sociology*. Translated by John A. Spaulding and George Simpson. Edited, with an introduction by George Simpson. New York: Free Press, 1966.

Easton, L. D., 'Alienation and History in the Early Marx,' *Philosophy and Phenomenological Research*, 22 (1961–2).

Easton, L., 'Alienation and Empiricism in Marx's Thought', *Social Research*, 37 (1970).

Eldridge, J. E. T., ed., *Max Weber: The Interpretation of Social Reality*. London: Michael Joseph, 1971.

Elias, Norbert, 'Sociology of Knowledge: New Perspectives, Part One', *Sociology*, V, no. 2 (1971), 149–68.

Elias, Norbert, 'Sociology of Knowledge: New Perspectives, Part Two', *Sociology*, V, no. 3 (1971), 355–70.

Emmet, Dorothy and MacIntyre, Alasdair, eds, *Sociological Theory and Philosophical Analysis*. New York: Macmillan, 1970.

Engelmann, Hugo O., 'Sorokin and the Sociology of Knowledge', in *Sorokin and Sociology*. Edited by G. C. Hallen. Agra, India: Satish Book Enterprises, 1972.

Fay, Brian, *Social Theory and Political Practice*. London: Allen & Unwin, 1975.

Feuer, L., 'Alienation: The Career of a Concept', *New Politics*, 2 (1962).
Feyerabend, P. K., 'Problems of Empiricism' in *Beyond the Edge of Certainty*. Edited by R. G. Colodny. Englewood Cliffs, New Jersey: Prentice-Hall, 1965.
Fletcher, C., *Beneath the Surface*. London: Routledge & Kegan Paul, 1974.
Frank, A. G., 'Functionalism, Dialectics and Synthetics', *Science and Society*, XXX (1966), 136–48.
Friedman, Jonathan, 'Marxism, Structuralism and Vulgar Materialism', *Man: The Journal of the Royal Anthropological Institute*, IX, no. 3 (September 1974), 444–69.
Fuse, Toyomasa, 'Sociology of Knowledge Revisited: Some Remaining Problems and Prospects', *Sociological Inquiry*, XXXVI – XXXVII (1966–7), 241–53.
Gellner, Ernest, 'The New Idealism – Cause and Meaning in the Social Sciences', *Problems in Philosophy of Science*. Edited by I. Lakatos and A. Musgrave. Amsterdam: North Holland Publishing Co. (1968), 377–406.
Geras, N., 'Essence and Appearance: Aspects of Fetishism in Marx's Capital', *New Left Review*, LXV (1971).
Gerth, H. H. and Mills, C. Wright, *Character and Social Structure*. New York: Harbinger, 1964.
Gerth, H. H. and Mills, C. Wright, eds, *From Max Weber: Essays in Sociology*. Translated, and with an introduction, by H. H. Gerth and C. Wright Mills. New York: Oxford University Press, 1958.
Giddens, Anthony, 'Durkheim's Political Sociology', *Sociological Review*, XIX (1971), 477–519.
Giddens, Anthony, *Politics and Sociology in the Thought of Max Weber*. Studies in Sociology Series. London: Macmillan, 1972.
Giddens, Anthony, ed., *Positivism and Sociology*. London: Heinemann, 1974.
Gillen, C. T., 'Freedom and the Limits of Social Behaviourism', *Sociology*, IX, 1975, 29–47.
Gouldner, A. W., *The Coming Crisis of Western Sociology*. New York: Avon Books, 1970.
Grant, George P., *Philosophy in the Mass Age*. Vancouver: Copp Clark, 1966.
Grant, George P., *Technology and Empire: Perspectives on North America*. Toronto: Anansi, 1969.
Green, M., 'Alienation Within a Problematic of Substance and Subject', *Social Research*, 33 (1966).
Gregor, A. James, 'Marx, Feuerbach and the Reform of the Hegelian Dialectic', *Science and Society*, XXIX (1965).
Habermas, J., *Knowledge and Human Interests*. Boston: Beacon Press, 1971.
Hallen, G. C., ed., *Sorokin and Sociology*. Agra, India: Satish Book Enterprises, 1972.
Hamilton, Peter, *Knowledge and Social Structure: An Introduction to the*

Classical Argument in the Sociology of Knowledge. London: Routledge & Kegan Paul, 1974.

Hansen, James E., 'A Dialectical Critique of Empiricism', *Catalyst* (Summer 1967), 1–19.

Hartung, Frank E., 'Problem of the Sociology of Knowledge', *Philosophy of Science*, XIX (January 1952), 17–32.

Hartung, Frank E., 'The Sociology of Positivism', *Science and Society*, VIII (1944), 328–41.

Hearn, Francis, 'The Implications of Critical Theory for Critical Sociology', *Berkeley Journal of Sociology*, XXVIII (1973–4), 127–58.

Hinshaw, Virgil, G., Jr., 'Epistemological Relativism and the Sociology of Knowledge', *Philosophy of Science*, XV, no. 1 (January 1948), 4–10.

Hinshaw, Virgil, G., Jr., 'The Epistemological Relevance of Mannheim's Sociology of Knowledge', *Journal of Philosophy*, XL, no. 3 (February 4, 1943), 57–72.

Hodges, Donald Clark, 'The Method of Capital', *Science and Society*, XXXI (1967), 505–14.

Holzner, Burkart, *Reality Construction in Society*. Revised ed. Cambridge, Mass.: Schenkman, 1968.

Horton, J., 'The Dehumanization of Alienation and Anomie', *British Journal of Sociology*, XV (December 1964).

Huber, Joan, 'Symbolic Interaction as a Pragmatic Perspective: The Bias of Emergent Theory', *American Sociological Review*, XXXVIII (April 1973), 274–84.

Hughes, H. Stuart, *Consciousness and Society: The Reorientation of European Social Thought 1890–1930*. New York: Vintage, 1958.

Israel, Joachim, *Alienation: From Marx to Modern Sociology*. Boston: Allyn & Bacon, 1971.

Jay, Martin, 'The Frankfurt School's Critique of Marxist Humanism', *Social Research*, XXXIX, no. 2 (1972), 285–305.

Jay, Martin, 'Some Recent Developments in Critical Theory', *Berkeley Journal of Sociology*, XXVIII (1973–74), 27–44.

Josephson, Eric and Mary, eds, *Man Alone: Alienation in Modern Society*. New York: Dell, 1962.

Kamenka, Eugene, *Marxism and Ethics*. London: Macmillan, 1969.

Kaplan, Abraham, *The Conduct of Inquiry: Methodology for Behavioral Science*. San Francisco: Chandler, 1964.

Kelsen, Hans, 'Causality and Imputation', *Ethics*, LXI, no. 1 (October 1950), 1–11.

Kolakowski, Leszek, *The Alienation of Reason: A History of Positivist Thought*. Translated by Norbert Guterman. New York: Doubleday, 1968.

Kolakowski, Leszek, *Toward a Marxist Humanism: Essays on the Left Today*. Translated from the Polish by Jane Zielonko Peel. New York: Grove Press, 1968.

Kruger, M., 'Sociology of Knowledge and Social Theory', *Berkeley Journal of Sociology*, XIV (1969), 152–63.

Kuhn, Thomas S., *The Structure of Scientific Revolutions*. 2nd edn, enlarged. International Encyclopedia of Unified Science, vol 2, no. 2. University of Chicago Press, 1970.

Lavine, T. Z., 'Karl Mannheim and Contemporary Functionalism', *Philosophy and Phenomenological Research*, XXV, no. 4 (1965), 560–71.

Lavine, T., 'Naturalism and the Sociological Analysis of Knowledge', in *Naturalism and the Human Spirit*. Edited by Y. H. Krikorian. New York: Columbia University Press, n.d.

Lavine, T., 'Note to Naturalists on the Human Spirit', *Journal of Philosophy*, XL (1953).

Lavine, T., 'Reflections on the Genetic Fallacy', *Social Research*, XXIX, no. 3 (Autumn 1962), 321–36.

Lavine, T., 'Sociological Analysis of Cognitive Norms', *Journal of Philosophy*, XXXIX (1942), 342–56.

Lavine, T., 'What is the Method of Naturalism', *Journal of Philosophy*, XL (1953).

Layne, Neville, 'Durkheim as Pacifist', *Sociological Inquiry*, XLIII, no. 2 (1973) 99–103.

Layne, Neville, 'Durkheim as a Social Actionist', *Sociological Inquiry*, XLII, no. 2 (1972) 105–7.

Lefebvre, Henri, *Dialectical Materialism*. Translated from the French by John Sturrock. London: Jonathan Cape, 1968.

Lefebvre, Henri, *The Sociology of Marx*. Translated from the French by N. Guterman. New York: Random House, 1968.

Lichtman, Richard, 'Symbolic Interactionism and Social Reality: Some Marxist Queries', *Berkeley Journal of Sociology*, XV (1970), 75–94.

Light, I. H., 'The Social Construction of Uncertainty', *Berkeley Journal of Sociology*, XIV (1969), 189–99.

Loewith, Karl, 'Weber's Interpretation of the Bourgeois-Capitalistic World in Terms of the Guiding Principle of "Rationalization" ', in *Max Weber*. Edited by Dennis Wrong. Makers of Modern Social Science Series. Englewood Cliffs, New Jersey: Prentice-Hall, 1970, pp. 101–22.

Ludz, P. C., 'Alienation as a Concept in the Social Sciences', *Current Sociology*, XXI (1973).

Lukes, Steven, 'Durkheim's "Individualism and the Intellectuals" ', *Political Studies*, XVII, no. 1 (1966), 14–30.

Lukes, Steven, 'Alienation and Anomie' in *Philosophy, Politics and Society*. Edited by P. Laslett and P. Runciman. Oxford: Basil Blackwell, 1967.

Mandel, Ernest and Novack, George, *The Marxist Theory of Alienation*. New York: Pathfinder Press, 1970.

Manis, Jerome G. and Meltzer, Bernard N., *Symbolic Interaction: A Reader in Social Psychology*. 2nd edn. Boston: Allyn & Bacon, 1972.

Mannheim, Karl, *Essays on the Sociology of Knowledge*. Edited by Paul Kecskemeti. London: Routledge & Kegan Paul, 1952.

Mannheim, Karl, *Ideology and Utopia: An Introduction to the Sociology of Knowledge*. Translated from the German by Louis Wirth and

Edward Shils. New York: Harcourt, Brace & World, 1936.
Maquet, J. J., *The Sociology of Knowledge*. Westport, Connecticut: Greenwood Press, 1951.
Marcuse, Herbert, *One-Dimensional Man: Studies in the Ideology of Advanced Industrial Society*. Boston: Beacon Press, 1966.
Markovic, Mihails, *From Affluence to Praxis: Philosophy and Social Criticism*. Foreword by Erich Fromm. Ann Arbor: The University of Michigan Press, 1974.
Marx, Karl, *Capital: A Critical Analysis of Capitalist Production*. Vol. 1. Moscow: Foreign Languages Publishing House, 1964.
Marx, Karl, *Capital: A Critique of Political Economy*. Vol. 2. Edited by I. Lasker. Moscow: Progress Publishers, 1967.
Marx, Karl, *Capital: A Critique of Political Economy*. Vol. 3. Moscow: Progress Publishers, 1966.
Marx, Karl, *A Contribution to the Critique of Political Economy*. Moscow: Progress Publishers, 1970.
Marx, Karl, *Critique of the Gotha Programme*. Edited by C. P. Dutt. A revised translation. New York: International Publishers, 1966.
Marx, Karl, *Critique of Hegel's 'Philosophy of Right'*. Edited, with an Introduction and Notes by Joseph O'Malley. Translated from the German by Annette Jolin and Joseph O'Malley. Cambridge University Press, 1970.
Marx, Karl, *Early Writings*. Edited and translated by T. B. Bottomore. Foreword by Erich Fromm. New York: McGraw-Hill, 1964.
Marx, Karl, *Economic and Philosophic Manuscripts of 1844*. Translated by Martin Milligan. Moscow: Foreign Languages Publishing House, 1961.
Marx, Karl, *The Grundrisse*. Edited and translated by David McLellan. New York: Harper & Row, 1971.
Marx, Karl, *Grundrisse: Foundations of the Critique of Political Economy*. Translated with a foreword by Martin Nicolaus. Harmondsworth, Middlesex, England: Penguin Books Ltd in association with New Left Review, London, 1973.
Marx, Karl and Engels, Friedrich, *The Communist Manifesto*. Edited by Samuel H. Beer. New York: Appleton-Century-Crofts, 1955.
Marx, Karl and Engels, Friedrich, *The German Ideology*. Edited by S. Pyazanskaya. Moscow: Progress Publishers, 1968.
Marx, Karl and Engels, Friedrich, *Selected Works*. 3 vols. Moscow: Progress Publishers, 1969–70.
Marx, Karl and Engels, Friedrich, *The Poverty of Philosophy*. Introduction by Engels. New York: International Publishers, 1963.
Marx, Karl and Engels, Friedrich, *Selected Writings in Sociology and Social Philosophy*. Edited, with an introduction and notes, by T. B. Bottomore and Maximilien Rubel. Translated by T. B. Bottomore. Foreword by Erich Fromm. New York: McGraw-Hill, 1964.
Maryl, W. W., 'Ethnomethodology: Sociology Without Society'. *Catalyst*, no. 7 (1973).
Matson, Floyd W., *The Broken Image: Man, Science and Society*.

Garden City, New York: Doubleday, 1966.
McGill, V. J., and Parry, W. T. 'The Unity of Opposites: A Dialectical Principle', *Science and Society*, XII (1948), 418–44.
McKinney, John C., 'The Contribution of George H. Mead to the Sociology of Knowledge', *Social Forces*, XXXIV (1955), 144–9.
McKinney, John., 'George H. Mead and the Philosophy of Science', *Philosophy of Science*, XXII (October 1955), 264–71.
McLellan, David, *Marx Before Marxism*. Harmondsworth: Penguin, 1970.
McLellan, David, *The Thought of Karl Marx: An Introduction*. London: Macmillan, 1971.
Mead, G. H., 'Bibliographic Notes', *American Journal of Sociology*, LXXII, no. 5 (March 1967), 551–7.
Mead, G. H., *The Conscientious Objector*. Patriotism Through Education, Series No. 33. New York City: National Security League, 1917.
Mead, G. H., *Mind, Self and Society: From the Standpoint of a Social Behaviourist*. Edited, with an introduction, by Charles W. Morris. Chicago and London: University of Chicago Press, 1934.
Mead, G. H., *Movements of Thought in the Nineteenth Century*. Edited by Merrit H. Moore. Chicago and London: University of Chicago Press, 1936.
Mead, G. H., *The Philosophy of the Act*. Edited, with an introduction by Charles W. Morris in collaboration with John M. Brewster, Albert M. Dunham, David L. Miller. Chicago and London: University of Chicago Press, 1938.
Mead, G. H., *The Philosophy of the Present*. Edited by Arthur E. Murphy with prefatory remarks by John Dewey. The Paul Carus Lectures, Third Series. La Salle, Illinois: Open Court, 1959.
Mead, G. H., *Selected Writings*. Edited, with an introduction, by Andrew J. Reck. Indianapolis: Bobbs-Merrill, 1964.
Mead, G. H., 'Two Unpublished Papers'. Introduction by David L. Miller. *Review of Metaphysics*, XVII (1964), 514–56.
Merton, Robert K., 'The Sociology of Knowledge' in *20th Century Sociology*. Edited by G. Gurvitch and Wilbert E. Moore. New York: Philosophical Library, 1945.
Merton, Robert K., 'Paradigm for the Sociology of Knowledge' in *The Sociology of Knowledge: A Reader*. Edited by J. E. Curtis and J. W. Petras. New York: Praeger, 1972.
Merton, Robert K., 'Sorokin's Formulations in the Sociology of Knowledge' in *Sorokin and Sociology*. Edited by G. C. Hallen. Agra, India: Satish Book Enterprises, 1972.
Meszaros, Istvan, *Marx's Theory of Alienation*. London: Merlin Press, 1970.
Miller, David L., *George Herbert Mead: Self, Language and the World*. Austin, Texas: University of Texas Press, 1973.
Mills, C. Wright, *The Sociological Imagination*. London: Oxford University Press, 1959.

Mills, C. Wright, *Power, Politics and People*. Edited by I. L. Horowitz. New York: Oxford University Press, 1967.

Mommsen, Wolfgan J., 'Max Weber as a Critic of Marxism', *Zeitschrift fur Soziologie*, III, no. 3 (June 1974), 256–78.

Natanson, Maurice, *The Social Dynamics of George H. Mead*. Introduction by Horace M. Kallen. Washington: Public Affairs Press, 1956.

Natanson, Maurice, 'Alienation and Social Role', *Social Research*, 33 (1966).

Natanson, Maurice, ed., *Philosophy of the Social Sciences: A Reader*. New York: Random House, 1963.

Nettler, G., 'A Test for the Sociology of Knowledge', *American Sociological Review*, X (1945), 393–9.

Nisbet, Robert A., *Emile Durkheim*. Makers of Modern Social Science. Englewood Cliffs, New Jersey: Prentice–Hall, 1965.

Nisbet, Robert A., *The Sociological Tradition*. New York: Basic Books, 1966.

Notestein, Robert B., 'William Graham Summer: An Essay in the Sociology of Knowledge', *American Journal of Economics and Sociology*, XVIII (July 1959), 397–413.

Ollman, Bertell, *Alienation: Marx's Conception of Man in Capitalist Society*. Cambridge University Press, 1971.

O'Neill, John, ed., *Modes of Individualism and Collectivism*. London: Heinemann, 1973.

O'Rourke, James J., *The Problem of Freedom in Marxist Thought*. Boston: D. Reidel, 1974.

Pappenheim, Fritz, *The Alienation of Modern Man*. New York: Monthly Review Press, 1959.

Petras, John W., ed., *G. H. Mead: Essays on His Social Philosophy*. New York: Teachers College Press, Teachers College, Columbia University, 1968.

Petras, John W., 'George Herbert Mead's Theory of Self: A Study in the Origin and Convergence of Ideas', *Canadian Review of Sociology and Anthropology*, X (1973), 148–59.

Petrovic, Gajo, *Marx in the Mid-Twentieth Century*. Garden City, New York: Doubleday, 1967.

Pfuetze, Paul E., *Self, Society, Existence: Human Nature and Dialogue in the Thought of George Herbert Mead and Martin Buber*. Foreword by H. Richard Niebuhr. New York: Harper, 1961.

Piccone, Paul, 'Functionalism, Teleology and Objectivity', *Monist* (Summer 1968), 408–23.

Plamenatz, J., *Ideology*. Toronto: MacMillan, 1971.

Primbs, Edward R. J., 'Contemporary American Criticism of Dialectical Materialism', *Science and Society*, XXIX, no. 2 (Spring 1965), 129–72.

Reck, A. J., 'The Constructive Pragmatism of George Herbert Mead', *Recent American Philosophy: Studies of Ten Representative Thinkers*, chapter 3, New York: Pantheon Books, 1964.

Remmling, Gunter W., *Road to Suspicion: A Study of Modern Mentality and the Sociology of Knowledge*. New York: Appleton-Century-Crofts, 1967.

Remmling, Gunter W., ed., *Towards the Sociology of Knowledge: Origin and Development of a Sociological Thought Style*. London: Routledge & Kegan Paul, 1973.

Rex, John, 'Typology and Objectivity: A Comment on Weber's Four Sociological Methods', in A. Sahay, ed., *Max Weber and Modern Sociology*, pp. 17–36. London: Routledge & Kegan Paul, 1971.

Reynolds, Larry T. and Janice M., eds, *The Sociology of Sociology: Analysis and Criticism of Thought, Research And Ethical Folkways of Sociology and Its Practitioners*. New York: David McKay, 1970.

Ropers, R., 'Mead, Marx and Social Psychology', *Catalyst*, no. 7 (Winter 1973), Trent University.

Rose, Arnold M., 'A Systematic Summary of Symbolic Interaction Theory', *Human Behaviour and the Social Processes*, pp. 3–19. Edited by A. M. Rose. Boston: Houghton Mifflin, 1962.

Sahay, Arun, 'The Importance of Weber's Methodology in Sociological Explanation' in *Max Weber and Modern Sociology*, pp. 67–81. Edited by A. Sahay. London: Routledge & Kegan Paul, 1971.

Sallach, David L., 'Critical Theory and Critical Sociology: The Second Synthesis', *Sociological Inquiry*, XLIII, no. 2, 131–40.

Schacht, R., *Alienation*. New York: Anchor, 1971.

Schaff, Adam, 'Marxist Dialectics and the Principle of Contradiction', *Journal of Philosophy*, LVII (1960), 241–50.

Schroyer, Trent, *The Critique of Domination*. New York: G. Braziller, 1973.

Schuetz, Alfred, 'Common-Sense and Scientific Interpretation of Human Action' *Philosophy and Phenomenological Research*, XIV, no. 1 (September 1953), 1–37.

Seeley, John R., 'Thirty-Nine Articles: Toward a Theory of Social Theory', *The Critical Spirit: Essays in Honour of H. Marcuse*, pp. 150–71. Edited by K. H. Wolff and B. Moore. Boston: Beacon, 1967.

Sklair, Leslie, *Organized Knowledge: A Sociological View of Science and Technology*. St Albans, Herts: Paladin, 1973.

Smith, T. V., 'The Social Philosophy of G. H. Mead', *American Journal of Sociology*, XXXVII (November 1931).

Stark, Werner, *The Sociology of Knowledge: An Essay in Aid of a Deeper Understanding of the History of Ideas*. London: Routledge & Kegan Paul, 1958.

Stark, Werner, 'Reply', *Kyklos*, XII, no. 2 (1959), 221–6.

Stark, Werner, 'A Second Reply', *Kyklos*, XII, no. 2 (1959), 506–9.

Stevens, Edward, 'Sociality and Act in George Herbert Mead', *Social Research*, XXXIV (1967), 613–31.

Stone, Gregory P., 'On the Edge of Rapprochement: Was Durkheim Moving Toward the Perspective of Symbolic Interaction?', *Sociological Quarterly*, VIII (1967), 149–64.

Strauss, Anselm, ed., *George Herbert Mead on Social Psychology: Selected Papers*. Introduction by Anselm Strauss. The Heritage of

Sociology Series. Chicago and London: University of Chicago Press, 1964.
Taylor, Stanley, *Conceptions of Institutions and the Theory of Knowledge*. New York: Bookman Associates, 1956.
Taylor, Stanley, 'Social Factors and the Validation of Thought', *Social Forces*, XLI (October 1962), 76–82.
Tenbruck, Friedrich H., 'Max Weber and the Sociology of Science: A Case Reopened', *Zeitschrift fur Soziologie*, III, no. 3 (June 1974), 312–21.
Tillman, Mary Katherine, 'Temporality and Role-Taking in G. H. Mead', *Social Research*, XXXVII (1970), 533–46.
Tiryakian, Edward A., *Sociologism and Existentialism: Two Perspectives on the Individual and Society*. Englewood Cliffs, New Jersey: Prentice-Hall, 1962.
Tucker, Robert C., *The Marx-Engels Reader*. New York: W. W. Norton, 1972.
Urbanek, E., 'Roles, Masks and Characters: A Contribution to Marx's Idea of Social Role', *Social Research*, XXXIV (1967).
Urry, John, 'Thomas S. Kuhn as Sociologist of Knowledge', *Sociological Inquiry*, XLII (1972), 462–73.
Walter, Benjamin, 'The Sociology of Knowledge and the Problem of Objectivity', in *Sociological Theory: Inquiries and Paradigms*. Edited by L. Gross. New York: Harper & Row, 1967.
Weber, Max, *The Methodology of the Social Sciences*. Translated and edited by Edward A. Shils and Henry A. Finch. Foreword by Edward A. Shils. Chicago Free Press, 1949.
Willer, Judith, *The Social Determination of Knowledge*. Englewood Cliffs, New Jersey: Prentice-Hall, 1971.
Winch, Peter, *The Idea of a Social Science and its Relation to Philosophy*. London: Routledge & Kegan Paul, 1958.
Wolff, Kurt, H., 'Ernest Grunwald and the Sociology of Knowledge: A Collective Venture in Interpretation', *Journal of History of the Behavioral Sciences*, I (1956), 152–64.
Wolff, Kurt, H., ed., *From Karl Mannheim*. New York: Oxford University Press, 1971.
Wolff, Kurt, H., 'A Preliminary Inquiry into the Sociology of Knowledge from the Standpoint of the Study of Man', in *Scritti di Sociologia e Politica in Onore di Luigi Sturzo*. Bologna: Zanichelli, 1953, III, pp. 583–618.
Wolff, Kurt, H., 'On the Scientific Relevance of "Imputation" ', *Ethics*, VLXI (1950), 69–73.
Wolff, Kurt, H., 'The Sociology of Knowledge: Emphasis on an Empirical Attitude', *Philosophy of Science*, X (April 1943), 104–23.
Wolff, Kurt, H., 'The Sociology of Knowledge and Sociological Theory', in *Symposium on Sociological Theory*, pp. 567–602. Edited by L. Gross. Evanston, Illinois: Row, Peterson, 1959.
Wolff, Kurt, H., 'The Sociology of Knowledge in the United States of America', *Current Sociology*, XV (1967), 1–56.

Wolff, Kurt, H., 'The Unique and the General: Toward a Philosophy of Sociology', *Philosophy of Science*, XV, no. 3 (July 1948), 192–210.
Wolff, Kurt, H., *Trying Sociology*. Toronto: John Wiley, 1974.
Worsley, P. M., 'Emile Durkheim's Theory of Knowledge', *Sociological Review*, IV (1956), 47–62.
Wrong, D., 'The Oversocialized Conception of Man in Modern Sociology', *American Sociological Review*, XXVI (April 1961), 183–93.
Zeitlin, Irving M., *Ideology and the Development of Sociological Theory*. Prentice-Hall Sociology Series. Englewood Cliffs, New Jersey: Prentice-Hall, 1968.
Zeitlin, Irving M., *Rethinking Sociology: A Critique of Contemporary Theory*. New York: Appleton-Century-Crofts, 1973.
Znaniecki, F., *The Social Role of the Man of Knowledge*. New York: Columbia University Press, 1940.

Index

Adler, F., 121n.37
alienation, 37–44, 45, 48, 84–5, 91–2, 94, 100ff, 133n.56; and reification, 102ff; as central problematic, 38, 44, 46–7, 115; and power, 149n.25
anomie, 39, 132n.54
attention, 61, 141n.41
attitudes, 61
authenticity, 48, 50
Avineri, S., 23, 33, 128n.5, 150n.31

Berger, P., 8, 10, 118n.1, 121n.29, n.33
Blauner, R., 132n.53

categories, 9, 16–17, 19, 34–5
change, evolutionary theory of, 66–7, 78, 85, 95; assumption of, 30, 90, 105, 130n.26; *see also* passage
Child, A., 12, 15, 120n.13, 122n.45
class, 94, 104
conflict, 68–9
consciousness, levels of, 107, 150n.29; *see also* mind, thought
correspondence theory of truth, 34, 35, 74
critique of the sociology of knowledge, 3–10, 17, 21, 32, 118n.1; and contradiction, 10–21, 111; grounds of, 11–13

dialectical relationship, 35, 48–9, 90, 115
division of labour, 94ff, 104ff, 150n.34
Dupre, L., 23
Durkheim, E., 6, 10–11, 39, 132n.54

emergence, 70ff, 79, 89
Engels, F., 23
existential, 3

false consciousness, 45, 102

generalized other, 62
genesis, meaningful, 89
genetic fallacy, 4–6, 9, 12, 110
gesture, 58–60

Hamilton, P., 125n.79, 126n.1
Hartung, F., 13
history, historical, 30, 88

idealism, 24–5, 55, 57, 90
I/me distinction, 63–5, 70–2, 78–9, 143n.68, n.69, 146n.130
imputation, 3, 12
individualism, *see* positivism
individuality, 67, 94–6
information (as distinct from knowledge), 75, 77, 100, 151n.39
intentionality, 60–1, 65, 80, 91
internalization, 59ff, 83

Kant, I., 16, 17, 25, 34, 124n.68
knowing, act of, 34, 101, 131n.42; as opposed to information, 75, 77, 100, 151n.39
knowledge, Meadian theory of, 73–8; Marxian theory of, 22, 32–7; correspondence theory of, 34–5, 74; *see also* positivism
Kolakowski, L., 23, 33–4

language, 28, 63
Lavine, T., 14–15, 122n.57, n.58
legitimation, 9
Lichtman, R., 147n.5
Luckmann, T., 8, 10

McKinney, J. C., 146n.1
Mannheim, K., 7, 10, 11

Marx, K., 2, 10, 22ff, 86ff, 128n.9; criticisms of, 47–54, 127n.2; traditional interpretation of, 22–3, 36
materialism, 24–5, 55, 57
Mead, G. H., 2, 10, 55ff, 86ff; criticisms of, 55, 64–70, 78, 81–3, 85, 92, 135n.79, 139n.21; traditional interpretation of, 83–4
meaning, 140n.37
Merton, R. K., 3, 120n.7
Miller, D. L., 72
mind, content/capacity distinction, 72, 80, 83, 101, 105, 108, 113–14, 141n.39; nature of, 28, 34, 61, 113; social basis of, 28, 58ff, 87, 100

Natanson, M., 130n.25
naturalism, *see* positivism
Nisbet, R. A., 119n.2, n.4

objectification, 90
objectivity, 5, 77, 91
Ollman, B., 23
O'Neill, J., 124n.59
oversocialized conception of man, 55, 65, 79, 82

passage, 76–7, 88; *see also* change
perception, 74–5
perspectives, 7; objective reality of, 75, 77, 81; reflexive reconstruction of, 77, 80, 90, 101, 148n.22
Petrovic, G., 23
Plamenatz, J., 12
positivism, 13, 19, 74, 76, 123n.53; and the distortion of praxis, 114; and individualism, 15, 16, 19, 20, 110, 126n.81; and the sociology of knowledge, 46, 50, 111
power and alienation, 149n.25, 151n.40
praxis, 24–31, 39, 42, 45, 48, 52, 87, 92, 94, 113, 129n.22; as absolute or criteria, 29, 117; and sociality, 27–8; and self-consciousness, 28–9, 32, 34, 50–1; relationship to alienation and reification, 48–53, 99ff, 103, 115
prediction, 77–8

rationality, irrationality, 112–13
rationalization, 9, 132n.54
reality as 'reality-for-man', 24ff, 74–7, 81
reification, 43, 45, 47, 50, 96–8, 100, 102ff; and socialization, 100ff
relationism, 7
relativism, 4–6, 22–3, 91, 110, 116–17
Remmling, G., 126n.1

Scheler, M., 10
Schroyer, T., 128n.8
science as social process, 75–6
self, the nature of, 61, 64, 142n.49; the social basis of, 61ff, 87, 100; and alienation, 100ff
significant symbols, 58–60, 140n.38
sociality, assumption of, 27–8, 31, 56–64, 78–83, 87, 130n.28
socialization, 59ff, 83, 87, 100, 147n.3; as paradoxical, 100ff
social science, 84
society, 31, 63, 87–9, 113
sociology of knowledge; basic insight, 1, 110; and contradiction, 18–21; as critical analysis, 44–7, 83–5, 114, 116; critique of, 3–10, 131n.37; in Marx, 22, 32–7, 44–7; in Mead, 83–5; rationale for, 45, 83, 115, 146n, 142; and relativism, 4–6
symbolic interactionism, 55

Taylor, S., 15–20, 124n.61, 125n.75, n.78, 126n.81
thought, 61, 66, 74, 87, 89–91
truth, *see* knowledge, positivism, correspondence theory

unintended consequences, 105
universality, 78
utilitarianism, 16

Watson, J. B., 57, 138n.14
Weber, M., 39, 132n.54

Routledge Social Science Series

Routledge & Kegan Paul London, Henley and Boston

39 Store Street, London WC1E 7DD
Broadway House, Newtown Road,
Henley-on-Thames, Oxon RG9 1EN
9 Park Street, Boston, Mass. 02108

Contents

International Library of Sociology 3
General Sociology 3
Foreign Classics of Sociology 4
Social Structure 4
Sociology and Politics 5
Criminology 5
Social Psychology 6
Sociology of the Family 6
Social Services 7
Sociology of Eaucation 8
Sociology of Culture 8
Sociology of Religion 9
Sociology of Art and Literature 9
Sociology of Knowledge 9
Urban Sociology 10
Rural Sociology 10
Sociology of Industry and Distribution 10
Anthropology 11
Sociology and Philosophy 12
International Library of Anthropology 12
International Library of Social Policy 13
International Library of Welfare and Philosophy 13
Primary Socialization, Language and Education 14
Reports of the Institute of Community Studies 14
Reports of the Institute for Social Studies in Medical Care 15
Medicine, Illness and Society 15
Monographs in Social Theory 15
Routledge Social Science Journals 16
Social and Psychological Aspects of Medical Practice 16

Authors wishing to submit manuscripts for any series in this catalogue should send them to the Social Science Editor, Routledge & Kegan Paul Ltd, 39 Store Street, London WC1E 7DD

●*Books so marked are available in paperback*
All books are in Metric Demy 8vo format (216 × 138mm approx.)

International Library of Sociology

General Editor John Rex

GENERAL SOCIOLOGY

Barnsley, J. H. The Social Reality of Ethics. *464 pp.*
Brown, Robert. Explanation in Social Science. *208 pp.*
● Rules and Laws in Sociology. *192 pp.*
Bruford, W. H. Chekhov and His Russia. *A Sociological Study. 244 pp.*
Burton, F. and **Carlen, P.** Official Discourse. *On Discourse Analysis, Government Publications, Ideology. About 140 pp.*
Cain, Maureen E. Society and the Policeman's Role. *326 pp.*
●**Fletcher, Colin.** Beneath the Surface. *An Account of Three Styles of Sociological Research. 221 pp.*
Gibson, Quentin. The Logic of Social Enquiry. *240 pp.*
Glucksmann, M. Structuralist Analysis in Contemporary Social Thought. *212 pp.*
Gurvitch, Georges. Sociology of Law. *Foreword by Roscoe Pound. 264 pp.*
Hinkle, R. Founding Theory of American Sociology 1883-1915. *About 350 pp.*
Homans, George C. Sentiments and Activities. *336 pp.*
Johnson, Harry M. Sociology: *a Systematic Introduction. Foreword by Robert K. Merton. 710 pp.*
●**Keat, Russell** and **Urry, John.** Social Theory as Science. *278 pp.*
Mannheim, Karl. Essays on Sociology and Social Psychology. *Edited by Paul Keckskemeti. With Editorial Note by Adolph Lowe. 344 pp.*
Martindale, Don. The Nature and Types of Sociological Theory. *292 pp.*
●**Maus, Heinz.** A Short History of Sociology. *234 pp.*
Myrdal, Gunnar. Value in Social Theory: *A Collection of Essays on Methodology. Edited by Paul Streeten. 332 pp.*
Ogburn, William F. and **Nimkoff, Meyer F.** A Handbook of Sociology. *Preface by Karl Mannheim. 656 pp. 46 figures. 35 tables.*
Parsons, Talcott, and **Smelser, Neil J.** Economy and Society: *A Study in the Integration of Economic and Social Theory. 362 pp.*
Podgórecki, Adam. Practical Social Sciences. *About 200 pp.*
Raffel, S. Matters of Fact. *A Sociological Inquiry. 152 pp.*
●**Rex, John.** (Ed.) Approaches to Sociology. *Contributions by Peter Abell,*
Sociology and the Demystification of the Modern World. *282 pp.*
●**Rex, John** (Ed.) Approaches to Sociology. *Contributions by Peter Abell, Frank Bechhofer, Basil Bernstein, Ronald Fletcher, David Frisby, Miriam Glucksmann, Peter Lassman, Herminio Martins, John Rex, Roland Robertson, John Westergaard and Jock Young. 302 pp.*
Rigby, A. Alternative Realities. *352 pp.*
Roche, M. Phenomenology, Language and the Social Sciences. *374 pp.*
Sahay, A. Sociological Analysis. *220 pp.*

Strasser, Hermann. The Normative Structure of Sociology. *Conservative and Emancipatory Themes in Social Thought. About 340 pp.*
Strong, P. Ceremonial Order of the Clinic. *About 250 pp.*
Urry, John. Reference Groups and the Theory of Revolution. *244 pp.*
Weinberg, E. Development of Sociology in the Soviet Union. *173 pp.*

FOREIGN CLASSICS OF SOCIOLOGY

● **Gerth, H. H.** and **Mills, C. Wright.** From Max Weber: *Essays in Sociology. 502 pp.*
● **Tönnies, Ferdinand.** Community and Association. *(Gemeinschaft and Gesellschaft.) Translated and Supplemented by Charles P. Loomis. Foreword by Pitirim A. Sorokin. 334 pp.*

SOCIAL STRUCTURE

Andreski, Stanislav. Military Organization and Society. *Foreword by Professor A. R. Radcliffe-Brown. 226 pp. 1 folder.*
Carlton, Eric. Ideology and Social Order. *Foreword by Professor Philip Abrahams. About 320 pp.*
Coontz, Sydney H. Population Theories and the Economic Interpretation. *202 pp.*
Coser, Lewis. The Functions of Social Conflict. *204 pp.*
Dickie-Clark, H. F. Marginal Situation: *A Sociological Study of a Coloured Group. 240 pp. 11 tables.*
Giner, S. and **Archer, M. S.** (Eds.). Contemporary Europe. *Social Structures and Cultural Patterns. 336 pp.*
● **Glaser, Barney** and **Strauss, Anselm L.** Status Passage. *A Formal Theory. 212 pp.*
Glass, D. V. (Ed.) Social Mobility in Britain. *Contributions by J. Berent, T. Bottomore, R. C. Chambers, J. Floud, D. V. Glass, J. R. Hall, H. T. Himmelweit, R. K. Kelsall, F. M. Martin, C. A. Moser, R. Mukherjee, and W. Ziegel. 420 pp.*
Kelsall, R. K. Higher Civil Servants in Britain: *From 1870 to the Present Day. 268 pp. 31 tables.*
● **Lawton, Denis.** Social Class, Language and Education. *192 pp.*
McLeish, John. The Theory of Social Change: *Four Views Considered. 128 pp.*
● **Marsh, David C.** The Changing Social Structure of England and Wales, 1871-1961. *Revised edition. 288 pp.*
Menzies, Ken. Talcott Parsons and the Social Image of Man. *About 208 pp.*
● **Mouzelis, Nicos.** Organization and Bureaucracy. *An Analysis of Modern Theories. 240 pp.*
Ossowski, Stanislaw. Class Structure in the Social Consciousness. *210 pp.*
● **Podgórecki, Adam.** Law and Society. *302 pp.*
Renner, Karl. Institutions of Private Law and Their Social Functions. *Edited, with an Introduction and Notes, by O. Kahn-Freud. Translated by Agnes Schwarzschild. 316 pp.*

Rex, J. and **Tomlinson, S.** Colonial Immigrants in a British City. *A Class Analysis. 368 pp.*

Smooha, S. Israel: Pluralism and Conflict. *472 pp.*

Wesolowski, W. Class, Strata and Power. *Trans. and with Introduction by G. Kolankiewicz. 160 pp.*

Zureik, E. Palestinians in Israel. *A Study in Internal Colonialism. 264 pp.*

SOCIOLOGY AND POLITICS

Acton, T. A. Gypsy Politics and Social Change. *316 pp.*

Burton, F. Politics of Legitimacy. *Struggles in a Belfast Community. 250 pp.*

Etzioni-Halevy, E. Political Manipulation and Administrative Power. *A Comparative Study. About 200 pp.*

● **Hechter, Michael.** Internal Colonialism. *The Celtic Fringe in British National Development, 1536–1966. 380 pp.*

Kornhauser, William. The Politics of Mass Society. *272 pp. 20 tables.*

Korpi, W. The Working Class in Welfare Capitalism. *Work, Unions and Politics in Sweden. 472 pp.*

Kroes, R. Soldiers and Students. *A Study of Right- and Left-wing Students. 174 pp.*

Martin, Roderick. Sociology of Power. *About 272 pp.*

Myrdal, Gunnar. The Political Element in the Development of Economic Theory. *Translated from the German by Paul Streeten. 282 pp.*

Wong, S.-L. Sociology and Socialism in Contemporary China. *160 pp.*

Wootton, Graham. Workers, Unions and the State. *188 pp.*

CRIMINOLOGY

Ancel, Marc. Social Defence: *A Modern Approach to Criminal Problems. Foreword by Leon Radzinowicz. 240 pp.*

Athens, L. Violent Criminal Acts and Actors. *About 150 pp.*

Cain, Maureen E. Society and the Policeman's Role. *326 pp.*

Cloward, Richard A. and **Ohlin, Lloyd E.** Delinquency and Opportunity: *A Theory of Delinquent Gangs. 248 pp.*

Downes, David M. The Delinquent Solution. *A Study in Subcultural Theory. 296 pp.*

Friedlander, Kate. The Psycho-Analytical Approach to Juvenile Delinquency: *Theory, Case Studies, Treatment. 320 pp.*

Gleuck, Sheldon and **Eleanor.** Family Environment and Delinquency. *With the statistical assistance of Rose W. Kneznek. 340 pp.*

Lopez-Rey, Manuel. Crime. *An Analytical Appraisal. 288 pp.*

Mannheim, Hermann. Comparative Criminology: *a Text Book. Two volumes. 442 pp. and 380 pp.*

Morris, Terence. The Criminal Area: *A Study in Social Ecology. Foreword by Hermann Mannheim. 232 pp. 25 tables. 4 maps.*

Podgorecki, A. and **Łos, M.** *Multidimensional Sociology. About 380 pp.*

Rock, Paul. Making People Pay. *338 pp.*

● **Taylor, Ian, Walton, Paul,** and **Young, Jock.** The New Criminology. *For a Social Theory of Deviance. 325 pp.*

● **Taylor, Ian, Walton, Paul** and **Young, Jock.** (Eds) Critical Criminology. *268 pp.*

SOCIAL PSYCHOLOGY

Bagley, Christopher. The Social Psychology of the Epileptic Child. *320 pp.*

Brittan, Arthur. Meanings and Situations. *224 pp.*

Carroll, J. Break-Out from the Crystal Palace. *200 pp.*

● **Fleming, C. M.** Adolescence: Its Social Psychology. *With an Introduction to recent findings from the fields of Anthropology, Physiology, Medicine, Psychometrics and Sociometry. 288 pp.*

● The Social Psychology of Education: *An Introduction and Guide to Its Study. 136 pp.*

Linton, Ralph. The Cultural Background of Personality. *132 pp.*

● **Mayo, Elton.** The Social Problems of an Industrial Civilization. *With an Appendix on the Political Problem. 180 pp.*

Ottaway, A. K. C. Learning Through Group Experience. *176 pp.*

Plummer, Ken. Sexual Stigma. *An Interactionist Account. 254 pp.*

● **Rose, Arnold M.** (Ed.) Human Behaviour and Social Processes: *an Interactionist Approach. Contributions by Arnold M. Rose, Ralph H. Turner, Anselm Strauss, Everett C. Hughes, E. Franklin Frazier, Howard S. Becker et al. 696 pp.*

Smelser, Neil J. Theory of Collective Behaviour. *448 pp.*

Stephenson, Geoffrey M. The Development of Conscience. *128 pp.*

Young, Kimball. Handbook of Social Psychology. *658 pp. 16 figures. 10 tables.*

SOCIOLOGY OF THE FAMILY

Bell, Colin R. Middle Class Families: *Social and Geographical Mobility. 224 pp.*

Burton, Lindy. Vulnerable Children. *272 pp.*

Gavron, Hannah. The Captive Wife: *Conflicts of Household Mothers. 190 pp.*

George, Victor and **Wilding, Paul.** Motherless Families. *248 pp.*

Klein, Josephine. Samples from English Cultures.

1. Three Preliminary Studies and Aspects of Adult Life in England. *447 pp.*
2. Child-Rearing Practices and Index. *247 pp.*

Klein, Viola. The Feminine Character. *History of an Ideology. 244 pp.*

McWhinnie, Alexina M. Adopted Children. *How They Grow Up. 304 pp.*

● **Morgan, D. H. J.** Social Theory and the Family. *About 320 pp.*

● **Myrdal, Alva** and **Klein, Viola.** Women's Two Roles: *Home and Work. 238 pp. 27 tables.*

Parsons, Talcott and **Bales, Robert F.** Family: Socialization and Interaction Process. *In collaboration with James Olds, Morris Zelditch and Philip E. Slater. 456 pp. 50 figures and tables.*

SOCIAL SERVICES

Bastide, Roger. The Sociology of Mental Disorder. *Translated from the French by Jean McNeil. 260 pp.*

Carlebach, Julius. Caring For Children in Trouble. *266 pp.*

George, Victor. Foster Care. *Theory and Practice. 234 pp.*

Social Security: *Beveridge and After. 258 pp.*

George, V. and **Wilding, P.** Motherless Families. *248 pp.*

● **Goetschius, George W.** Working with Community Groups. *256 pp.*

Goetschius, George W. and **Tash, Joan.** Working with Unattached Youth. *416 pp.*

Heywood, Jean S. Children in Care. *The Development of the Service for the Deprived Child. Third revised edition. 284 pp.*

King, Roy D., Ranes, Norma V. and **Tizard, Jack.** Patterns of Residential Care. *356 pp.*

Leigh, John. Young People and Leisure. *256 pp.*

● **Mays, John.** (Ed.) Penelope Hall's Social Services of England and Wales. *About 324 pp.*

Morris, Mary. Voluntary Work and the Welfare State. *300 pp.*

Nokes, P. L. The Professional Task in Welfare Practice. *152 pp.*

Timms, Noel. Psychiatric Social Work in Great Britain (1939-1962). *280 pp.*

● Social Casework: *Principles and Practice. 256 pp.*

SOCIOLOGY OF EDUCATION

Banks, Olive. Parity and Prestige in English Secondary Education: a Study in Educational Sociology. *272 pp.*

● **Blyth, W. A. L.** English Primary Education. *A Sociological Description.* 2. Background. *168 pp.*

Collier, K. G. The Social Purposes of Education: *Personal and Social Values in Education. 268 pp.*

Evans, K. M. Sociometry and Education. *158 pp.*

● **Ford, Julienne.** Social Class and the Comprehensive School. *192 pp.*

Foster, P. J. Education and Social Change in Ghana. *336 pp. 3 maps.*

Fraser, W. R. Education and Society in Modern France. *150 pp.*

Grace, Gerald R. Role Conflict and the Teacher. *150 pp.*

Hans, Nicholas. New Trends in Education in the Eighteenth Century. *278 pp. 19 tables.*

● Comparative Education: *A Study of Educational Factors and Traditions. 360 pp.*

● **Hargreaves, David.** Interpersonal Relations and Education. *432 pp.*

● Social Relations in a Secondary School. *240 pp.*

School Organization and Pupil Involvement. *A Study of Secondary Schools.*

- ● **Mannheim, Karl** and **Stewart, W.A.C.** An Introduction to the Sociology of Education. *206 pp.*
- ● **Musgrove, F.** Youth and the Social Order. *176 pp.*
- ● **Ottaway, A. K. C.** Education and Society: An Introduction to the Sociology of Education. *With an Introduction by W. O. Lester Smith. 212 pp.*
- **Peers, Robert.** Adult Education: *A Comparative Study. Revised edition. 398 pp.*
- **Stratta, Erica.** The Education of Borstal Boys. *A Study of their Educational Experiences prior to, and during, Borstal Training. 256 pp.*
- ● **Taylor, P. H., Reid, W. A.** and **Holley, B. J.** The English Sixth Form. *A Case Study in Curriculum Research. 198 pp.*

SOCIOLOGY OF CULTURE

- **Eppel, E. M.** and **M.** Adolescents and Morality: *A Study of some Moral Values and Dilemmas of Working Adolescents in the Context of a changing Climate of Opinion. Foreword by W. J. H. Sprott. 268 pp. 39 tables.*
- ● **Fromm, Erich.** The Fear of Freedom. *286 pp.*
- ● The Sane Society. *400 pp.*
- **Johnson, L.** The Cultural Critics. *From Matthew Arnold to Raymond Williams. 233 pp.*
- **Mannheim, Karl.** Essays on the Sociology of Culture. *Edited by Ernst Mannheim in co-operation with Paul Kecskemeti. Editorial Note by Adolph Lowe. 280 pp.*
- **Zijderfeld, A. C.** On Clichés. *The Supersedure of Meaning by Function in Modernity. About 132 pp.*

SOCIOLOGY OF RELIGION

- **Argyle, Michael** and **Beit-Hallahmi, Benjamin.** The Social Psychology of Religion. *About 256 pp.*
- **Glasner, Peter E.** The Sociology of Secularisation. *A Critique of a Concept. About 180 pp.*
- **Hall, J. R.** The Ways Out. *Utopian Communal Groups in an Age of Babylon. 280 pp.*
- **Ranson, S., Hinings, B.** and **Bryman, A.** Clergy, Ministers and Priests. *216 pp.*
- **Stark, Werner.** The Sociology of Religion. *A Study of Christendom.*
  - Volume II. *Sectarian Religion. 368 pp.*
  - Volume III. *The Universal Church. 464 pp.*
  - Volume IV. *Types of Religious Man. 352 pp.*
  - Volume V. *Types of Religious Culture. 464 pp.*
- **Turner, B. S.** Weber and Islam. *216 pp.*
- **Watt, W. Montgomery.** Islam and the Integration of Society. *320 pp.*

SOCIOLOGY OF ART AND LITERATURE

Jarvie, Ian C. Towards a Sociology of the Cinema. *A Comparative Essay on the Structure and Functioning of a Major Entertainment Industry. 405 pp.*

Rust, Frances S. Dance in Society. *An Analysis of the Relationships between the Social Dance and Society in England from the Middle Ages to the Present Day. 256 pp. 8 pp. of plates.*

Schücking, L. L. The Sociology of Literary Taste. *112 pp.*

Wolff, Janet. Hermeneutic Philosophy and the Sociology of Art. *150 pp.*

SOCIOLOGY OF KNOWLEDGE

Diesing, P. Patterns of Discovery in the Social Sciences. *262 pp.*

● **Douglas, J. D.** (Ed.) Understanding Everyday Life. *370 pp.*

Glasner, B. Essential Interactionism. *About 220 pp.*

● **Hamilton, P.** Knowledge and Social Structure. *174 pp.*

Jarvie, I. C. Concepts and Society. *232 pp.*

Mannheim, Karl. Essays on the Sociology of Knowledge. *Edited by Paul Kecskemeti. Editorial Note by Adolph Lowe. 353 pp.*

Remmling, Gunter W. The Sociology of Karl Mannheim. *With a Bibliographical Guide to the Sociology of Knowledge, Ideological Analysis, and Social Planning. 255 pp.*

Remmling, Gunter W. (Ed.) Towards the Sociology of Knowledge. *Origin and Development of a Sociological Thought Style. 463 pp.*

URBAN SOCIOLOGY

Aldridge, M. The British New Towns. *A Programme Without a Policy. About 250 pp.*

Ashworth, William. The Genesis of Modern British Town Planning: *A Study in Economic and Social History of the Nineteenth and Twentieth Centuries. 288 pp.*

Brittan, A. The Privatised World. *196 pp.*

Cullingworth, J. B. Housing Needs and Planning Policy: *A Restatement of the Problems of Housing Need and 'Overspill' in England and Wales. 232 pp. 44 tables. 8 maps.*

Dickinson, Robert E. City and Region: *A Geographical Interpretation. 608 pp. 125 figures.*

The West European City: *A Geographical Interpretation. 600 pp. 129 maps. 29 plates.*

Humphreys, Alexander J. New Dubliners: *Urbanization and the Irish Family. Foreword by George C. Homans. 304 pp.*

Jackson, Brian. Working Class Community: *Some General Notions raised by a Series of Studies in Northern England. 192 pp.*

● **Mann, P. H.** An Approach to Urban Sociology. *240 pp.*

Mellor, J. R. Urban Sociology in an Urbanized Society. *326 pp.*

Morris, R. N. and **Mogey, J.** The Sociology of Housing. *Studies at Berinsfield. 232 pp. 4 pp. plates.*

Rosser, C. and **Harris, C.** The Family and Social Change. *A Study of Family and Kinship in a South Wales Town. 352 pp. 8 maps.*

● **Stacey, Margaret, Batsone, Eric, Bell, Colin** and **Thurcott, Anne.** Power, Persistence and Change. *A Second Study of Banbury. 196 pp.*

RURAL SOCIOLOGY

Mayer, Adrian C. Peasants in the Pacific. *A Study of Fiji Indian Rural Society. 248 pp. 20 plates.*

Williams, W. M. The Sociology of an English Village: *Gosforth. 272 pp. 12 figures. 13 tables.*

SOCIOLOGY OF INDUSTRY AND DISTRIBUTION

Dunkerley, David. The Foreman. *Aspects of Task and Structure. 192 pp.*

Eldridge, J. E. T. Industrial Disputes. *Essays in the Sociology of Industrial Relations. 288 pp.*

Hollowell, Peter G. The Lorry Driver. *272 pp.*

● **Oxaal, I., Barnett, T.** and **Booth, D.** (Eds) Beyond the Sociology of Development. *Economy and Society in Latin America and Africa. 295 pp.*

Smelser, Neil J. Social Change in the Industrial Revolution: *An Application of Theory to the Lancashire Cotton Industry, 1770–1840. 468 pp. 12 figures. 14 tables.*

Watson, T. J. The Personnel Managers. *A Study in the Sociology of Work and Employment. 262 pp.*

ANTHROPOLOGY

Brandel-Syrier, Mia. Reeftown Elite. *A Study of Social Mobility in a Modern African Community on the Reef. 376 pp.*

Dickie-Clark, H. F. The Marginal Situation. *A Sociological Study of a Coloured Group. 236 pp.*

Dube, S. C. Indian Village. *Foreword by Morris Edward Opler. 276 pp. 4 plates.*

India's Changing Villages: *Human Factors in Community Development. 260 pp. 8 plates. 1 map.*

Firth, Raymond. Malay Fishermen. *Their Peasant Economy. 420 pp. 17 pp. plates.*

Gulliver, P. H. Social Control in an African Society: a Study of the Arusha, Agricultural Masai of Northern Tanganyika. *320 pp. 8 plates. 10 figures.*

Family Herds. *288 pp.*

Jarvie, Ian C. The Revolution in Anthropology. *268 pp.*

Little, Kenneth L. Mende of Sierra Leone. *308 pp. and folder.*

Negroes in Britain. *With a New Introduction and Contemporary Study by Leonard Bloom. 320 pp.*

Madan, G. R. Western Sociologists on Indian Society. *Marx, Spencer, Weber, Durkheim, Pareto. 384 pp.*

Mayer, A. C. Peasants in the Pacific. *A Study of Fiji Indian Rural Society. 248 pp.*

Meer, Fatima. Race and Suicide in South Africa. *325 pp.*

Smith, Raymond T. The Negro Family in British Guiana: *Family Structure and Social Status in the Villages. With a Foreword by Meyer Fortes. 314 pp. 8 plates. 1 figure. 4 maps.*

SOCIOLOGY AND PHILOSOPHY

Barnsley, John H. The Social Reality of Ethics. *A Comparative Analysis of Moral Codes. 448 pp.*

Diesing, Paul. Patterns of Discovery in the Social Sciences. *362 pp.*

● **Douglas, Jack D.** (Ed.) Understanding Everyday Life. *Toward the Reconstruction of Sociological Knowledge. Contributions by Alan F. Blum, Aaron W. Cicourel, Norman K. Denzin, Jack D. Douglas, John Heeren, Peter McHugh, Peter K. Manning, Melvin Power, Matthew Speier, Roy Turner, D. Lawrence Wieder, Thomas P. Wilson and Don H. Zimmerman. 370 pp.*

Gorman, Robert A. The Dual Vision. *Alfred Schutz and the Myth of Phenomenological Social Science. About 300 pp.*

Jarvie, Ian C. Concepts and Society. *216 pp.*

Kilminster, R. Praxis and Method. *A Sociological Dialogue with Lukács, Gramsci and the early Frankfurt School. About 304 pp.*

● **Pelz, Werner.** The Scope of Understanding in Sociology. *Towards a More Radical Reorientation in the Social Humanistic Sciences. 283 pp.*

Roche, Maurice. Phenomenology, Language and the Social Sciences. *371 pp.*

Sahay, Arun. Sociological Analysis. *212 pp.*

Slater, P. Origin and Significance of the Frankfurt School. *A Marxist Perspective. About 192 pp.*

Spurling, L. Phenomenology and the Social World. *The Philosophy of Merleau-Ponty and its Relation to the Social Sciences. 222 pp.*

Wilson, H. T. The American Ideology. *Science, Technology and Organization as Modes of Rationality. 368 pp.*

International Library of Anthropology

General Editor Adam Kuper

Ahmed, A. S. Millenium and Charisma Among Pathans. *A Critical Essay in Social Anthropology. 192 pp.*

Pukhtun Economy and Society. *About 360 pp.*

Brown, Paula. The Chimbu. *A Study of Change in the New Guinea Highlands. 151 pp.*

Foner, N. Jamaica Farewell. *200 pp.*

Gudeman, Stephen. Relationships, Residence and the Individual. *A Rural Panamanian Community. 288 pp. 11 plates, 5 figures, 2 maps, 10 tables.*

The Demise of a Rural Economy. *From Subsistence to Capitalism in a Latin American Village. 160 pp.*

Hamnett, Ian. Chieftainship and Legitimacy. *An Anthropological Study of Executive Law in Lesotho. 163 pp.*

Hanson, F. Allan. Meaning in Culture. *127 pp.*

Humphreys, S. C. Anthropology and the Greeks. *288 pp.*

Karp, I. Fields of Change Among the Iteso of Kenya. *140 pp.*

Lloyd, P. C. Power and Independence. *Urban Africans' Perception of Social Inequality. 264 pp.*

Parry, J. P. Caste and Kinship in Kangra. *352 pp. Illustrated.*

Pettigrew, Joyce. Robber Noblemen. *A Study of the Political System of the Sikh Jats. 284 pp.*

Street, Brian V. The Savage in Literature. *Representations of 'Primitive' Society in English Fiction, 1858–1920. 207 pp.*

Van Den Berghe, Pierre L. Power and Privilege at an African University. *278 pp.*

International Library of Social Policy

General Editor Kathleen Jones

Bayley, M. Mental Handicap and Community Care. *426 pp.*

Bottoms, A. E. and **McClean, J. D.** Defendants in the Criminal Process. *284 pp.*

Butler, J. R. Family Doctors and Public Policy. *208 pp.*

Davies, Martin. Prisoners of Society. *Attitudes and Aftercare. 204 pp.*

Gittus, Elizabeth. Flats, Families and the Under-Fives. *285 pp.*

Holman, Robert. Trading in Children. *A Study of Private Fostering. 355 pp.*

Jeffs, A. Young People and the Youth Service. *About 180 pp.*

Jones, Howard, and **Cornes, Paul.** Open Prisons. *288 pp.*

Jones, Kathleen. History of the Mental Health Service. *428 pp.*

Jones, Kathleen, with **Brown, John, Cunningham, W. J., Roberts, Julian** and **Williams, Peter.** Opening the Door. *A Study of New Policies for the Mentally Handicapped. 278 pp.*

Karn, Valerie. Retiring to the Seaside. *About 280 pp. 2 maps. Numerous tables.*

King, R. D. and **Elliot, K. W.** Albany: Birth of a Prison—End of an Era. *394 pp.*

Thomas, J. E. The English Prison Officer since 1850: *A Study in Conflict. 258 pp.*

Walton, R. G. Women in Social Work. *303 pp.*

● **Woodward, J.** To Do the Sick No Harm. *A Study of the British Voluntary Hospital System to 1875. 234 pp.*

International Library of Welfare and Philosophy

General Editors Noel Timms and David Watson

● **McDermott, F. E.** (Ed.) Self-Determination in Social Work. *A Collection of Essays on Self-determination and Related Concepts by Philosophers and Social Work Theorists. Contributors: F. B. Biestek, S. Bernstein, A. Keith-Lucas, D. Sayer, H. H. Perelman, C. Whittington, R. F. Stalley, F. E. McDermott, I. Berlin, H. J. McCloskey, H. L. A. Hart, J. Wilson, A. I. Melden, S. I. Benn. 254 pp.*

● **Plant, Raymond.** Community and Ideology. *104 pp.*

Ragg, Nicholas M. People Not Cases. *A Philosophical Approach to Social Work. About 250 pp.*

● **Timms, Noel** and **Watson, David.** (Eds) Talking About Welfare. *Readings in Philosophy and Social Policy. Contributors: T. H. Marshall, R. B. Brandt, G. H. von Wright, K. Nielsen, M. Cranston, R. M. Titmuss, R. S. Downie, E. Telfer, D. Donnison, J. Benson, P. Leonard, A. Keith-Lucas, D. Walsh, I. T. Ramsey. 320 pp.*

● (Eds). Philosophy in Social Work. *250 pp.*

● **Weale, A.** Equality and Social Policy. *164 pp.*

Primary Socialization, Language and Education

General Editor Basil Bernstein

Adlam, Diana S., *with the assistance of Geoffrey Turner and Lesley Lineker.* Code in Context. *About 272 pp.*

Bernstein, Basil. Class, Codes and Control. *3 volumes.*

● 1. *Theoretical Studies Towards a Sociology of Language. 254 pp.*

2. *Applied Studies Towards a Sociology of Language. 377 pp.*

● 3. *Towards a Theory of Educational Transmission. 167 pp.*

Brandis, W. and **Bernstein, B.** Selection and Control. *176 pp.*

Brandis, Walter and **Henderson, Dorothy.** Social Class, Language and Communication. *288 pp.*

Cook-Gumperz, Jenny. Social Control and Socialization. *A Study of Class Differences in the Language of Maternal Control. 290 pp.*

● **Gahagan, D. M** and **G. A.** Talk Reform. *Exploration in Language for Infant School Children. 160 pp.*

Hawkins, P. R. Social Class, the Nominal Group and Verbal Strategies. *About 220 pp.*

Robinson, W. P. and **Rackstraw, Susan D. A.** A Question of Answers. *2 volumes. 192 pp. and 180 pp.*

Turner, Geoffrey J. and **Mohan, Bernard A.** A Linguistic Description and Computer Programme for Children's Speech. *208 pp.*

Reports of the Institute of Community Studies

Baker, J. The Neighbourhood Advice Centre. A Community Project in Camden. *320 pp.*

● **Cartwright, Ann.** Patients and their Doctors. *A Study of General Practice. 304 pp.*

Dench, Geoff. Maltese in London.*A Case-study in the Erosion of Ethnic Consciousness. 302 pp.*

Jackson, Brian and **Marsden, Dennis.** Education and the Working Class: *Some General Themes raised by a Study of 88 Working-class Children in a Northern Industrial City. 268 pp. 2 folders.*

Marris, Peter. The Experience of Higher Education. *232 pp. 27 tables.*

● Loss and Change. *192 pp.*

Marris, Peter and **Rein, Martin.** Dilemmas of Social Reform. *Poverty and Community Action in the United States. 256 pp.*

Marris, Peter and **Somerset, Anthony.** African Businessmen. *A Study of Entrepreneurship and Development in Keyna. 256 pp.*

Mills, Richard. Young Outsiders: *a Study in Alternative Communities. 216 pp.*

Runciman, W. G. Relative Deprivation and Social Justice. *A Study of Attitudes to Social Inequality in Twentieth-Century England. 352 pp.*

Willmott, Peter. Adolescent Boys in East London. *230 pp.*

Willmott, Peter and **Young, Michael.** Family and Class in a London Suburb. *202 pp. 47 tables.*

Young, Michael and **McGeeney, Patrick.** Learning Begins at Home. *A Study of a Junior School and its Parents. 128 pp.*

Young, Michael and **Willmott, Peter.** Family and Kinship in East London. *Foreword by Richard M. Titmuss. 252 pp. 39 tables.*

The Symmetrical Family. *410 pp.*

Reports of the Institute for Social Studies in Medical Care

Cartwright, Ann, Hockey, Lisbeth and **Anderson, John J.** Life Before Death. *310 pp.*

Dunnell, Karen and **Cartwright, Ann.** Medicine Takers, Prescribers and Hoarders. *190 pp.*

Farrell, C. My Mother Said. . . . *A Study of the Way Young People Learned About Sex and Birth Control. 200 pp.*

Medicine, Illness and Society

General Editor W. M. Williams

Hall, David J. Social Relations & Innovation. *Changing the State of Play in Hospitals. 232 pp.*

Hall, David J., and **Stacey, M.** (Eds) Beyond Separation. *234 pp.*

Robinson, David. The Process of Becoming Ill. *142 pp.*

Stacey, Margaret *et al.* Hospitals, Children and Their Families. *The Report of a Pilot Study. 202 pp.*

Stimson G. V. and **Webb, B.** Going to See the Doctor. *The Consultation Process in General Practice. 155 pp.*

Monographs in Social Theory

General Editor Arthur Brittan

● **Barnes, B.** Scientific Knowledge and Sociological Theory. *192 pp.*

Bauman, Zygmunt. Culture as Praxis. *204 pp.*

● **Dixon, Keith.** Sociological Theory. *Pretence and Possibility. 142 pp.*

Meltzer, B. N., Petras, J. W. and **Reynolds, L. T.** Symbolic Interactionism. *Genesis, Varieties and Criticisms. 144 pp.*

● **Smith, Anthony D.** The Concept of Social Change. *A Critique of the Functionalist Theory of Social Change. 208 pp.*

Routledge Social Science Journals

The British Journal of Sociology. *Editor – Angus Stewart; Associate Editor – Leslie Sklair. Vol. 1, No. 1 – March 1950 and Quarterly. Roy. 8vo. All back issues available. An international journal publishing original papers in the field of sociology and related areas.*

Community Work. *Edited by David Jones and Marjorie Mayo. 1973. Published annually.*

Economy and Society. *Vol. 1, No. 1. February 1972 and Quarterly. Metric Roy. 8vo. A journal for all social scientists covering sociology, philosophy, anthropology, economics and history. All back numbers available.*

Ethnic and Racial Studies. *Editor – John Stone. Vol. 1 – 1978. Published quarterly.*

Religion. Journal of Religion and Religions. *Chairman of Editorial Board, Ninian Smart. Vol. 1, No. 1, Spring 1971. A journal with an inter-disciplinary approach to the study of the phenomena of religion. All back numbers available.*

Sociology of Health and Illness. *A Journal of Medical Sociology. Editor – Alan Davies; Associate Editor – Ray Jobling. Vol. 1, Spring 1979. Published 3 times per annum.*

Year Book of Social Policy in Britain, The. *Edited by Kathleen Jones. 1971. Published annually.*

Social and Psychological Aspects of Medical Practice

Editor Trevor Silverstone

Lader, Malcolm. Psychophysiology of Mental Illness. *280 pp.*

● **Silverstone, Trevor** and **Turner, Paul.** Drug Treatment in Psychiatry. *Revised edition. 256 pp.*

Whiteley, J. S. and **Gordon, J.** Group Approaches in Psychiatry. *256 pp.*

Printed in Great Britain by
Lowe & Brydone Printers Limited, Thetford, Norfolk